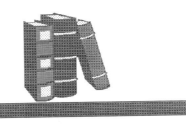

Rodale's Visual Encyclopedia of Needlecrafts

Unique Look-and-Stitch Lessons and Projects

Carolyn Christmas

Rodale Press, Inc.
Emmaus, Pennsylvania

For Our Children

Taryn, Courtney, Whitney,
Austin,
Erin, and Candice

If you have any questions or comments concerning this book, please write to:
  Rodale Press, Inc.
  Book Readers' Service
  33 East Minor Street
  Emmaus, PA 18098

Library of Congress
Cataloging-in-Publication Data

Christmas, Carolyn
  Rodale's visual encyclopedia of needlecrafts / by Carolyn Christmas.
    p. cm.
  ISBN 0–87596–718–3 (hardcover: alk. paper)
  1. Needlework. 2. Fancy work. I. Rodale Press. II. Title.
TT750.C47 1996
746.4—dc20   95–29999

RODALE PRESS STAFF
Vice President and Editorial Director,
  Home and Garden Books: Margaret Lydic Balitas
Senior Editor, Craft Books: Cheryl Winters Tetreau
Editors: Marya Kissinger Amig and Susan Huxley
Associate Art Director: Mary Ellen Fanelli
Designer: Marta Strait
Front Cover Photographer: John Hamel
Front Cover Photo Stylist: Marianne Grape Laubach
Copy Editor: Carolyn Mandarano
Manufacturing Coordinator: Melinda B. Rizzo

CAROLYN CHRISTMAS DESIGN GROUP STAFF
President, Designer, and Editorial Director:
  Carolyn Brooks Christmas
Vice President, Photo Stylist, Book Designer, and
  Illustrator: Greg Smith
Vice President, Book Designer, Illustrator, and
  Photographer: Rusty Lingle
Production Coordinator, Production Manager,
  and Illustrator: Minette Collins Smith

The author and editors who compiled this book have tried to make all of the contents as accurate and as correct as possible. Illustrations, photographs, and text have all been carefully checked and cross-checked. However, due to the variability of materials, personal skill, and so on, neither the author nor Rodale Press assumes any responsibility for any damages or other losses incurred that result from the material presented herein. All instructions and diagrams should be carefully studied and clearly understood before beginning any project.

Distributed in the book trade by St. Martin's Press

2 4 6 8 10 9 7 5 3   hardcover

OUR MISSION

We publish books that empower people's lives.

RODALE BOOKS

Contents

//

Acknowledgments

I would like to thank the following companies and individuals who generously contributed their skills, talents, locations, props, products, or other support for this book.

Products

Bernina of America—*sewing machine and accessories*

Charles Craft, Inc.—*cross-stitch fabrics*

Darice—*plastic canvas, plastic canvas yarns and cording*

The DMC Corporation—*embroidery threads, sewing threads, quilting threads, machine embroidery threads, crochet threads*

Fairfield Processing—*pillow forms, stuffing, quilt batting*

Fiskars—*scissors, rotary cutter*

J.&P. Coats—*embroidery threads, sewing threads, quilting threads, crochet threads, knitting and crochet yarns*

Kreinik Mfg. Co., Inc.—*metallic braids and threads*

Land's End catalog—*sweaters for duplicate stitch*

Lion Brand Yarns—*knitting and crochet yarns*

Rainbow Gallery—*plastic canvas fibers*

Spinrite—*knitting and crochet yarns, plastic canvas yarn*

Therm O Web—*Heat n Bond fusible web*

Uniek Crafts—*plastic canvas, plastic canvas yarns and cording*

Zweigart Fabrics and Canvas—*cross-stitch fabrics*

Projects

Dorris Brooks—*Popcorn Filet Afghan, stitching Teatime Trivet and Coasters and Gilded Poinsettias*

Janice Kellenberger—*stitching Christmas Carousel Horse*

Rusty Lingle—*original artwork for Christmas Carousel Horse*

John Sauls Antiques, Tyler, TX—*lending Pretty Pansies and New York Beauty quilts*

Minette Collins Smith—*stitching Elegant Bookmark and Bronze Roses Vest*

Locations

Murphy's Furniture, Tyler, TX—page 60

John Sauls Antiques, Tyler, TX—pages 8 and 170

Ellis Stewart Printing, Big Sandy, TX—page 144

Props

B & B Bygones, Gladewater, TX—page 138

Country Girl Collection, Gladewater, TX—pages 28, 208, and 232

Bearly Worn, Gladewater, TX—pages 64 and 202

Main Street Treasures, Gladewater, TX—page 235

The Needlepoint Studio, Emmaus, PA—front cover

Stitches & Stuff, Longview, TX—pages 36 and 112

Also, heartfelt thanks to the Rodale Press staff, Sydney and Dorris Brooks, Ann Lingle, Mary Lingle, Helen Snyder, Maurice and Juanita Collins, Mike Clark, James Christmas, Glenda Chamberlain, Scott Campbell, Debbie Davie, Sam and Brenda Collins, Bennie and Betty Cornutt, Diana Taylor, John Struen, Stephen McNeely, Steven Manley, Karen Rasco, Heidi Harlan, Elaine Williams, Erin Lingle, and Kimberly McCullough.

Introduction

In writing this book, I tried to see everything from a beginner's point of view and yet include lots and lots of appealing information for the more experienced stitcher. The book does not require reading from start to finish—you will not miss crucial information if you decide to begin with a middle chapter.

In each chapter, you'll find an "Equipment" section, which reviews all of the supplies you'll need to start a particular form of needlework. The "Getting Started" section in each chapter features large photographs showing hands in the correct positions for beginning. These are especially helpful if you're the type of person who enjoys being shown how to do something new, rather than learning it by reading instructions.

In each chapter, you'll find one easy, one intermediate, and one challenging project. None are extremely difficult; however, the challenging projects generally require a larger investment of time than the easier ones. Occasionally, projects in one chapter may refer to page numbers for instructions in another chapter for preparing patterns or finishing techniques. I prepared the book in this way to prevent repeating the same information.

The handy colored tabs at the right-hand margins will help you find what you're looking for in a hurry as you flip through the book. Each chapter begins with its own table of contents, so you don't have to return to the main table of contents at the front of the book to find what you're looking for.

Along with many of the projects, I've included boxes called "Something Different." These boxes use an item from the project or feature part of the pattern in a different way. These "miniprojects" are quick and easy to make and require very few extra instructions. I hope they'll get your imagination racing, so that when you see a needlework pattern, you'll also see many possibilities other than the one shown.

This book is a terrific guide for learning about the eight techniques included. It is not meant to be an end-all guide to the absolutely right and wrong ways of needlework. There are things you can do to make your stitching time easier and more fun, and I've shared these with you. I always try to remember that somewhere, at some time, one lone stitcher discovered or created each and every one of these techniques, and that as time goes by, we all contribute what we've learned to the growing pool of information.

This book is both a culmination and a new beginning for me. It is the crowning touch on my years as a needlework designer, editor, and writer. At the same time, it is the first work of a new, yet familiar, career since I have come full circle, out of the world of editing other designers' and authors' work and back home to designing and writing.

I hope that you enjoy owning and using this book and that it not only adds to your stitching skills but also contributes to your enjoyment of needlework.

Warm regards,

Carolyn

Carolyn Christmas

Appliqué

Appliqué, the application of one fabric to another, has been a popular technique for centuries. In the days before printed fabrics were available, appliqué was first used to embellish plain fabric with ecclesiastical designs.

Appliqué reached its peak in the United States between 1750 and 1850, when traditional motifs were combined with careful quilting for a family's most treasured quilts. Today's appliqué artist enjoys a palette of exciting options for creating quilts and decorating clothing and accessories.

Equipment

To create beautiful appliqué designs, you'll need only a few essentials—thread, needles, scissors, and fabric. Other supplies such as a rotary cutter, cutting mat, see-through ruler, and template materials may be helpful depending on the type of appliqué project.

Fabric

Any light- to medium-weight fabric may be used for appliqué. However, if an item is to be laundered, be sure to select washable fabrics. Light- to medium-weight cottons and cotton blends work best.

Firmly woven fabrics are effective for appliqué—any fabric that frays easily will be difficult to work with. Felt may be used for certain types of appliqué. Some designs can be enhanced and embellished further with lace, ribbons, and leather.

Background fabric for quilts, pillows, and other items should generally be of the same weight and fiber content as the appliqué pieces. However, many other types of background fabrics can be used. Sweatshirt knit, denim, and suede are just a few examples of fabrics that are often used for appliqué backgrounds.

Rotary Cutter, See-Through Ruler, and Cutting Mat

A rotary cutter, rigid see-through ruler marked with 45° angle lines, and self-healing cutting mat make the task of cutting bias strips easy and accurate.

Fusible Web

With brand names like Heat n Bond and Pellon's Wonder-Under, paper-backed fusible web products make machine appliqué easier by securing the appliqué pieces firmly to the background fabric before sewing.

Freezer Paper

Available in grocery stores, ordinary plastic-coated freezer paper is ironed directly onto fabric and peeled away when no longer needed.

Straight Pins

The best pins to use for appliqué are long (1½") with glass or plastic heads. Rusty or burred pins can snag or leave marks on fabric.

Needles and Needle Threader

For hand appliqué, choose sharps made specially for hand sewing and appliqué. Experiment with different needle sizes to see which are the most comfortable. Size 10 or 12 sharps are generally best for hand appliqué. Use a needle threader for threading the smallest needles. For buttonhole stitch appliqué, use larger-eye crewel needles.

Thread

For hand appliqué, use high-quality cotton or cotton-covered polyester thread. For machine appliqué, rayon threads manufactured specially for this purpose create a beautiful, lustrous satin stitch. Six-strand embroidery floss, pearl cotton, or other decorative threads may be used for buttonhole stitch appliqué.

Scissors

For cutting large pieces of fabric, use good-quality dressmaking shears. For trimming seams and clipping threads, use a small, very sharp pair of embroidery scissors. Reserve a sharp, inexpensive pair of scissors for cutting template materials.

Template Material

Templates are firm patterns used to mark patterns on fabric. Template plastic, available at quilt, fabric, and craft shops, is ideal. Thin cardboard, heavy watercolor paper, or a manila file folder may also be used.

Pencils and Pens

Use a sharp graphite pencil for tracing appliqué patterns onto fabric. For tracing patterns onto template material, use a fine-line permanent marker.

Needle Pointer

//////////////////////

Appliqué designs can often make use of even the smallest bits of fabrics, and using a variety of fabrics can help your appliqué creations be their most beautiful. Keep an appliqué scrap bag handy while you cut out other sewing, craft, and quilting projects, and you will soon have a beautiful selection of scraps just perfect for appliqué.

Getting Started

Preparing to hand appliqué involves learning the slip stitch, selecting fabrics, making templates, and transferring designs onto fabric. The tiny slip stitch is almost invisible when made correctly.

Slip Stitch

1 To make a slip stitch, begin by bringing the needle up through the background fabric and the edge of the fold of the appliqué piece.

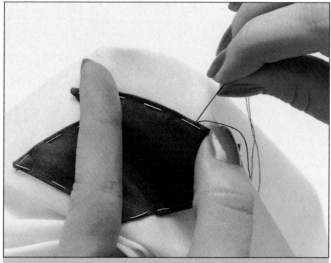

2 Insert the needle back into the background fabric just under the fold of the appliqué piece, close to the point where the thread comes out of the background fabric.

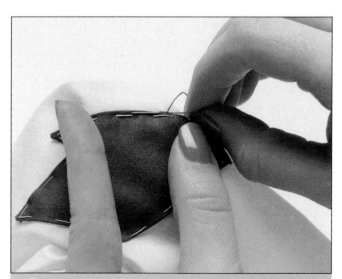

3 Bring the needle back up through the background fabric about ⅛" to the left (closer if desired), catching just the edge of the fold of the appliqué piece.

4 Pull the thread through, pulling the stitch firmly and flattening the appliqué with your thumb. Continue stitching in this manner.

Selecting Colors

When planning an appliqué project, one of the first steps is to select fabric colors. A palette of reds, greens, golds, blues, purples, and browns gives a very traditional look to appliqué. Pinks, lavenders, yellows, and other pastels are lovely with appliqué designs featuring florals, ribbons, and bows.

Whatever color palette you choose, make sure each color is balanced with the others. For example, it's best not to add only one very light color to a project that has medium or dark tones.

You may choose to work with a balance of prints to solids, all solids, or all prints. If you select prints, small-scale types work best for most appliqué. However, a single panel of large-scale print fabric may offer many colors and patterns. Careful placement and cutting of appliqués from large-scale prints can result in a beautiful, color-coordinated project.

Needle Pointer

////////////////////

Background fabric is as important to appliqué as pattern fabric. Depending on the effect you'd like to create, light-colored background fabric is usually best. However, dark backgrounds can be combined with brightly colored pattern fabrics for striking results. Instead of choosing solid-colored background fabric, try choosing subtle prints in your color choice. Fabrics manufactured especially for quilting are good choices because there are many selections available that feature small prints in simple gradations of a single color. These types of background fabrics add visual texture and interest to appliqué without taking away from the pattern design.

Enlarging Patterns

Appliqué patterns can be enlarged using a copy machine or by this grid method.

1. Trace the design using gridded paper. Or use plain paper, a ruler, and a pencil to draw a grid over the design as shown below (left).

2. On a larger piece of paper, draw a larger grid, using the same number of lines as the smaller grid. If you are using a pattern that states the grid size needed, such as "1 square = 1 inch," draw a grid of 1" or the required-size squares.

3. Assign corresponding numbers to the horizontal lines and letters to the vertical lines on both grids. Place a dot on the large grid wherever the pattern line intersects a grid line on the reduced pattern as shown below (right). Add more dots and connect to draw the design, referring to the smaller grid.

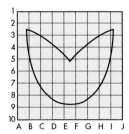

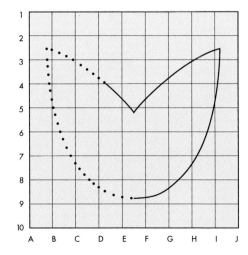

Making Templates

Templates for appliqué can be made from any thin, sturdy material that will hold a firm edge and can be cut easily with scissors.

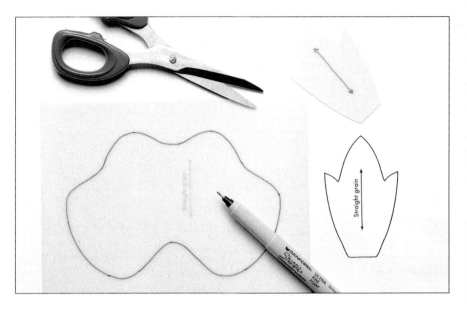

Making Templates from Plastic

1. Lay a piece of clear or semi-opaque template plastic over the desired appliqué pattern.

2. Using a fine-line permanent marker, trace the pattern onto the plastic. Use a ruler to help draw accurate straight lines.

3. Carefully cut out the template, cutting just inside the line, using scissors for curved lines and a rotary cutting tools if desired, for straight lines.

4. Using the marker, write the pattern name and direction of the grain line on the template. Other information such as the template number may be added.

Making Templates from Cardboard

1. Using white paper and a sharp pencil or fine-line marker, trace the pattern, adding a grain line and other information as desired.

2. Cut the shape out carefully just inside the lines, and glue the paper pattern onto a piece of thin cardboard, heavy watercolor paper, or a manila file folder.

3. Allow the template to dry, then cut it out.

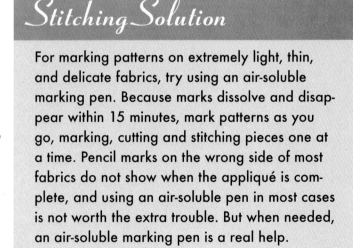

Stitching Solution

For marking patterns on extremely light, thin, and delicate fabrics, try using an air-soluble marking pen. Because marks dissolve and disappear within 15 minutes, mark patterns as you go, marking, cutting and stitching pieces one at a time. Pencil marks on the wrong side of most fabrics do not show when the appliqué is complete, and using an air-soluble pen in most cases is not worth the extra trouble. But when needed, an air-soluble marking pen is a real help.

Transferring Designs

Sharpen your pencil often while transferring designs for the cleanest, thinnest lines.

Marking Appliqué Pieces

1. Press the appliqué fabrics.

2. To mark the fabric, position the templates on the wrong side of the fabric, making sure to leave at least ½" between the pattern pieces and ¼" from the fabric edges. If grain lines are shown on the templates, align them with the fabric grain line.

3. Use a silver graphite pencil for marking appliqué patterns on most fabrics. If the silver graphite lines do not show clearly enough on your fabric, use a white, light blue, or regular graphite pencil. Holding the template in place firmly, trace carefully around each template as shown.

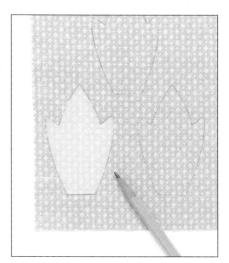

Marking Background Fabric

1. Cut the fabric to the desired size, being sure to add seam allowances if needed. Press.

2. Fold the fabric in half, then in half again to locate the center. Mark the center with a pin or an air-soluble marking pen. Mark the centers on the outside edges.

3. Trace the pattern placement onto plain paper with a fine-line permanent marker.

4. Place the fabric over the paper right side up, centering the design; pin in place. If the markings are not easy to see through the fabric, use a light box. Or try taping the fabric and pattern over a window or using a glass-topped table with a lamp underneath.

5. Lightly trace the design onto the right side of the fabric with a sharp pencil, tracing just slightly inside the lines on the paper as shown. It's very important to trace lightly, because some pencil lines may remain after the appliqué is complete. These can be removed with a fabric eraser if the graphite has not penetrated the fibers.

Needle Pointer

Ordinary household items can sometimes be used for appliqué templates. Trace perfect circles onto the template material or directly onto the fabric using lids from various items such as jars, bottles, and plastic tubs. Since the 1700s, coins have been a traditional favorite for tracing circles for grapes and flower centers in appliqué.

Cutting Out Pieces

When cutting out appliqué designs, use a scant ¼" seam allowance for basted appliqué and a generous ⅛" seam allowance for needle-turn appliqué. There is no seam allowance for satin stitch machine appliqué.

To make curves and corners easier to handle, clipping and trimming are necessary. This may be done while stitching or basting.

For inner curves, clip almost to the marked line along a curve, spacing clips farther apart for gentle curves and closer together for deeper curves (a).

For outer curves on large appliqué pieces, some notching may be needed to prevent bulky pleats from forming under appliqué pieces. Avoid notching except when absolutely necessary because it causes the appliqué to become more fragile. To notch, clip a V-shaped section out of the fabric (b). An alterna-

tive to notching is clipping and overlapping sections of the seam allowance.

For outside corners, trim away the points to reduce bulk (c).

For inside corners, make one clip to the point of the corner (d).

Always use gentle handling for appliqué pieces that have been notched or clipped.

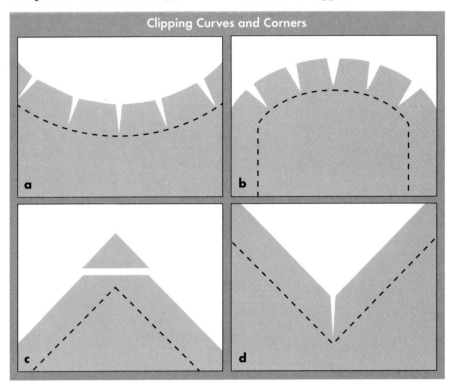
Clipping Curves and Corners

Techniques

Various methods and tools may be used for preparing appliqué pieces and stitching them to background fabric. Experiment with several methods to see which you prefer.

Using Spray Starch

Appropriate for use with either hand or machine appliqué, the spray starch method works well for appliqué shapes with curved edges, such as hearts, circles, and leaves. Any household spray starch may be used.

1. Using a template and fine-line permanent marker, trace the pattern pieces onto heavy water-color paper, a manila file folder, or other thin cardboard. See "Making Templates from Cardboard" on page 14.

2. Cut out the patterns, cutting just inside the traced line.

3. With the fabric wrong side up, place the pattern on the fabric. Using a sharp pencil or fine-line permanent marker and *adding* ¼" seam allowance to all

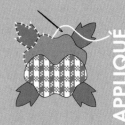

the edges, mark around the motif.

4. Cut out the motif just inside the marked line.

5. If the shape is a circle, baste around the edge using small running stitches.

6. With the wrong side up, place the appliqué piece on a pressing surface. Center the pattern on the appliqué piece. If the shape is a circle, pull up the basting stitches and distribute the gathers evenly.

7. Press the seam allowances over the pattern as shown, applying spray starch as you go. Clip the curves and points as necessary. Press all seam allowances toward the center. Turn the piece over and press it firmly from the right side.

8. Allow the appliqué piece to cool completely, then remove the pattern.

9. Press the motif again from the right side if needed.

10. Pin and appliqué the motif onto the background fabric using your preferred method.

Needle Pointer

If you find it difficult to concentrate a stream of spray starch onto the small seam allowance area, try spraying a small amount of starch into a plastic bowl or tub first. Apply the starch to the seam allowance with a cotton swab.

Basted Appliqué

When basting appliqué pieces, the ¼" seam allowances of each appliqué piece are turned under and basted before they are sewn onto the background fabric.

1. To baste each shape, turn under the seam allowances along the lines, clipping the curves and points as necessary. Finger press and baste with contrasting thread close to the fold. Do not turn under or baste the edges that will be covered by another appliqué piece.

2. Press the pieces, then pin them in place, right side up, on the background fabric. Baste if

desired, and stitch down using a slip stitch. Appliqué any underneath pieces first. Remove the basting threads when the stitching is complete, and press the piece from the back.

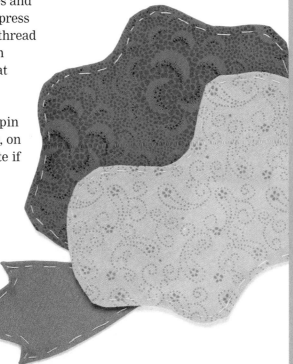

Needle-Turn Appliqué

For needle-turn appliqué, shapes are pinned onto the background fabric first, then the seam allowances are turned under as they're stitched. The tip and shank of the needle are used to coax the seam allowances under.

Pieces without Points

1. Pin the appliqué pieces in place on the background fabric.

2. Using the tip and shank of the needle, turn under ⅛" at a time, pressing flat with your thumb. Stitch using a slip stitch as shown below (left). Clip the curves as needed.

Pieces with Points

1. Pin the appliqué pieces in place on the background fabric.

2. Using the tip and shank of the needle and working up one side of the appliqué to the point, turn under ⅛" of the seam allowance a bit at a time, pressing the seam allowance flat with your thumb. Stitch down using a slip stitch, turning under only the seam allowance for this side as you near the point as shown below (center). Clip the curves and inner points as needed.

3. Take an extra stitch at the point to secure it as shown below (right), then turn the seam allowance under on the other side of the point and press it flat with your thumb. Use the tip and shank of your needle to smooth the seam allowance under the point. Stitch the second side using a slip stitch.

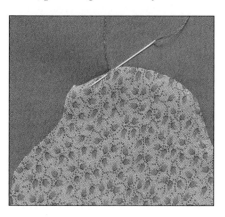

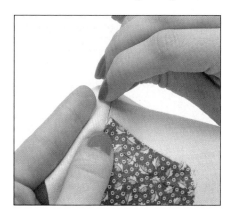

Paper Patch Appliqué

Paper patch appliqué is one of the most accurate methods for preparing appliqué pieces.

1. Using a template, trace each appliqué piece onto plain paper. For asymmetrical pieces, mark the patterns to indicate the right side.

2. Cut out the paper patterns just inside the traced lines.

3. Pin the appliqué patterns to the wrong side of the fabric, with ½" between pattern pieces.

4. Cut out each shape, adding ¼" seam allowances to all edges.

5. Turn the seams under and baste them to the paper. Clip inside curves. On outside curves, take small running stitches through the fabric only to ease in the fullness, taking an occasional stitch through the paper to hold it in place as shown. Do not turn under edges of the shape that will be covered by other pieces.

6. Press all of the appliqué pieces from the right side.

7. Pin, then baste the appliqué pieces to the background fabric.

8. Appliqué the pieces to the background fabric.

9. To remove the paper, cut a small slit in the background fabric behind each piece. Insert the point of your scissors and cut the background fabric to within ¼" of the stitching line. If you prefer not to cut the background, stop appliquéing ½" from the starting point. Remove the paper, then finish stitching the appliqué piece to the background fabric.

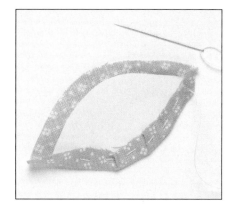

Bias Strips

For vines, stems, and other twining and curved strips in hand appliqué, bias-cut fabric strips are used. Bias-cut fabric has the stretch necessary to make curving strips easier.

Bias Strip Basics

1. To cut perfect bias strips, use a rotary cutter, a cutting mat, and a see-through ruler marked with 45° angle lines. Place the fabric on the cutting mat with the grain line or selvage along a horizontal line on the mat. Use the ruler and cutter to cut the left edge of the fabric straight and perpendicular to the grain line.

2. Align the 45° angle line on the ruler with the bottom edge of the fabric. Cut along the ruler's edge to remove the corner, then cut bias strips the width needed.

3. For finished bias strips that are ¾" to 1" wide, cut strips three times the width needed. For finished bias strips that are narrower than ¾", cut strips twice the width needed.

Wide Strips

1. Place the fabric strip wrong side up on an ironing board, then fold up and press one-third of the strip lengthwise with the tip of the iron. Fold the remaining third of the strip over the first and press as shown, then turn the strip over and press from the right side.

2. To appliqué, baste the strip into position onto the background fabric and stitch into place using a slip stitch. For curved strips, appliqué the inner curves first, then the outer curves.

Narrow Strips

1. Fold the strip in half lengthwise with wrong sides together, and press. Fold in half lengthwise again and press to create a stitch guideline.

2. On the background fabric, mark a single strip placement line where the center of the strip will go.

3. Pin the folded strip along the center placement line, with the center stitch guideline just to the left of the marked line. With a small running stitch, stitch through all thicknesses along the stitch guideline as shown.

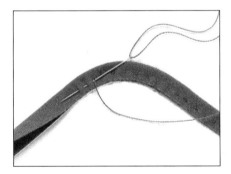

4. Fold the strip to the right and slip stitch down as shown, trimming the raw edges underneath as needed.

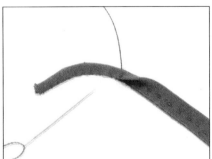

Needle Pointer

For appliqué pieces that are to be quilted, bulk can be reduced by trimming excess background fabric behind the appliqués. If you have used a paper-basting method, you may have completed this step. Cut a small slit in the background fabric behind the appliqué. Insert the point of your embroidery scissors in the slit, then trim away the fabric, leaving a ¼" seam allowance from all stitching lines. If the fabric tends to fray, apply a liquid seam sealer to the raw edges.

Freezer Paper Appliqué

Plastic-coated freezer paper, which is available at your grocery store, is an inexpensive, handy tool for appliqué. There are several ways to use this product.

With the needle-turn method, freezer paper is ironed to the right side of the fabric and acts as a guideline for turning under the edges.

With the freezer paper basting method, freezer paper is used as a tool for "basting" the seam allowances down first. Then it is used for holding appliqué pieces while they are stitched in place.

The freezer paper patch method involves using the freezer paper in a similar manner to the ordinary paper basting technique.

Needle-Turn Appliqué with Freezer Paper

1. With the coated side up, lay the freezer paper over your patterns and trace using a fine-line permanent marker. Use a ruler for the straight edges. Trace one freezer paper pattern for each appliqué piece needed.

2. Cut out the shapes, cutting just inside the traced line.

3. Place the fabric right side up on a pressing surface, and with the freezer paper coated side down, arrange the pattern pieces on the fabric with ¼" between the pieces.

4. Press the freezer paper pieces to the fabric, pressing firmly with an up-and-down motion to avoid ripples.

5. Cut out the appliqué pieces, adding a generous ⅛" seam allowance to all edges.

6. With the freezer paper facing up, position and pin the appliqué pieces onto the background fabric. Hand baste in place if desired,

keeping the basting stitches at least ¼" from the edge of the freezer paper.

7. Clipping the curves and inside points and trimming the outside points as you go, stitch the pieces down following the instructions in "Needle-Turn Appliqué" on page 18. Use the edge of the freezer paper as a guide for turning the seam allowances under as you stitch as shown.

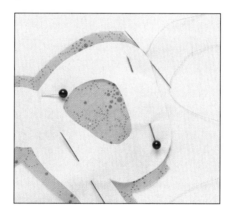

8. Remove the basting stitches and pins; peel away and discard the freezer paper.

Freezer Paper Basting

1. With the coated side of the freezer paper *down*, trace and cut out one freezer paper pattern for each appliqué piece, following Steps 1 and 2 in "Needle-Turn Appliqué with Freezer Paper."

2. Using a plastic or cardboard template and sharp pencil and *adding* ¼" seam allowances to all edges, mark the appliqué shapes on the wrong side of the fabric.

3. Cut out the fabric shapes just inside the traced line.

4. Place the fabric appliqué shapes wrong side up on a pressing surface. Center a freezer paper piece on its matching appliqué shape, with the coated side up.

5. With the tip of the iron, carefully press the seam allowances over the edge of the freezer paper toward the center of the shapes as shown.

6. After all seam allowances are pressed down, place the background fabric right side up on the pressing surface. Position the appliqué shapes on the background fabric and press into place. The exposed freezer paper in the center of each piece will adhere to the background fabric.

7. Appliqué using a slip stitch.

8. To remove the paper, cut a small slit in the background fabric behind each piece. Insert the point of your scissors and cut the background fabric to within ¼" of the stitching line. Remove the paper. If you prefer not to cut the background fabric, stop appliquéing ½" from the starting point, remove the paper, and finish stitching the piece to the background fabric.

Freezer Paper Patch Appliqué

1. Using a template and a fine-line permanent marker and with the coated side of the freezer paper up, trace each appliqué shape onto the freezer paper.

2. Cut out the paper patterns, cutting just inside the traced line.

3. Place the fabric wrong side up on a pressing surface and position the paper patterns, coated side down, on the fabric with ½" between pieces.

4. Press the pieces to fabric, pressing firmly with an up-and-down motion to avoid ripples.

5. Cut out the shapes, adding ¼" seam allowances to all edges.

6. With your fingers, turn the seam allowances under and baste through the freezer paper as shown. Clip the inside curves as necessary. On the outside curves, take small running stitches through the fabric only, and pull slightly to ease in the fullness. Do not turn under edges that will be covered by other appliqué pieces.

7. Press all appliqué pieces from the right side.

8. Pin all of the appliqué pieces to the background fabric.

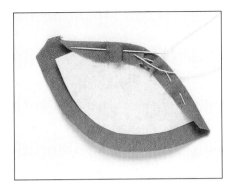

Baste them in place if desired.

9. Appliqué the pieces using your preferred method.

10. To remove the paper, cut a small slit in the background fabric behind each piece. Insert the point of your scissors and cut the background fabric to within ¼" of the stitching line. Remove the paper. If you prefer not to cut the background fabric, stop stitching ½" from the ending point; remove the paper.

Needle Pointer

If you have trouble spacing buttonhole stitches evenly, mark evenly spaced lines on thin masking tape. Position the tape alongside the seam line as you stitch. Match stitches to lines as you work.

Buttonhole Stitch Appliqué

Best suited to appliqué designs with large, simple pieces, buttonhole stitch appliqué is perfect for use with felt. It can also be used for pieces with turned-under edges by applying the basted or spray starch method.

1. Prepare appliqué pieces with one of the following methods: For felt, cut out pieces with no added seam allowances. For appliqué with turned-under edges, prepare pieces using the basted or spray starch method; see pages 16 and 17.

2. Pin the appliqué pieces in place; baste if desired.

3. Choose embroidery floss colors to coordinate or contrast with the pieces. Using a crewel needle and two or three strands of floss, work the buttonhole stitch (a) evenly around each piece (b).

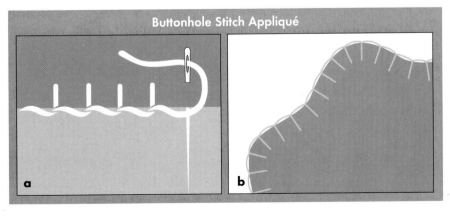

Buttonhole Stitch Appliqué

a

b

Shadow Appliqué

One of the most elegant forms of appliqué, shadow appliqué is also very easy. Shapes are applied to the background fabric using a tiny amount of glue, then topped with a layer of sheer fabric. The layers are then secured with small running stitches.

Since the sheer layer mutes colors, choose very bright colors for appliqué pieces. The top layer may be any sheer fabric.

1. Trace the pattern onto the background fabric following the instructions in "Marking Background Fabric" on page 15.

2. Make templates according to the instructions in "Making Templates" on page 14. Using the templates, trace and cut out the appliqué pieces.

3. Using a glue stick sparingly, stick the appliqué pieces in place on the background fabric (a).

4. Place the sheer fabric on top of the background fabric and smooth it carefully. Pin, then baste along the outside edges and around the appliqué pieces.

5. Using sewing thread or one or two strands of embroidery floss, make small running stitches next to the edge of each appliqué piece (b). Remove the basting stitches. If desired, add running stitch details.

Shadow Appliqué

Cut-and-Sew Appliqué

If all appliqué pieces are from a single-color fabric, cut-and-sew appliqué is a quick and easy method to use.

1. Transfer the pattern onto the right side of the appliqué fabric following the instructions in "Marking Background Fabric" on page 15.

2. Baste the appliqué fabric in its proper position on top of the background fabric with the grain lines of both fabrics running in the same direction.

3. Starting at the point where you wish to begin slip stitching, cut away about 2" of excess fabric from around the marked design, leaving a scant ¼" seam allowance outside the marked line (a).

4. Using matching thread, slip stitch the appliqué to the background fabric, turning the seam allowance under and pressing with your thumb as you go (b).

5. Continue stitching, cutting fabric away from the appliqué design and clipping curves as needed (c).

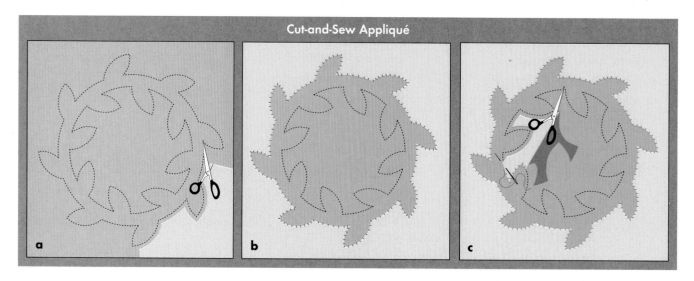

Cut-and-Sew Appliqué

Reverse Appliqué

In reverse appliqué, layers of fabric are stacked, then sections are cut away to reveal the colors underneath. Edges of cutout sections are turned under and stitched down.

Reverse appliqué often has a look that recalls its ethnic history. One form of reverse appliqué, San Blas appliqué, is practiced by the Cuna Indians, who live on islands off the coast of Panama. This type of work features colorful people, animals, and plants.

Another type of reverse appliqué is practiced by the Hmong people of Vietnam. The Pa 'ndau technique features traditional swirls and lines that symbolize flowers, snails, and turtles.

1. Cut three pieces of fabric to the size and shape of the area the appliqué will cover.

2. Stack and baste the first and second layers of fabric together.

3. Draw a design on the top layer using a template or freehand sketching.

4. Pin the layers of fabric together inside and outside the drawn design.

5. Cut along the marked line, being careful to cut only through the top layer (a).

6. Turn under ⅛" and slip stitch the cut edges of the center piece and the outside piece, leaving a channel of the bottom fabric showing through (b). Remove the pins.

7. To add another layer, stack the third color of fabric on top of the previous work and baste it in place along the edges.

8. With a sharp pencil, feel and trace around the edges of the shape underneath. Trace along both sides of the channel.

9. Pin all fabric layers together inside and outside the marked lines.

10. Cut along the inner and outer marked lines; turn under the cut edges and stitch down as before (c).

Needle Pointer

To add extra interest to a reverse appliqué project, make small slits in the top layer. Fold under the edges and stitch down, exposing a strip of the layer below. If desired, insert a strip of another fabric behind the slit. Appliqué in place, making sure slip stitches secure the middle and top fabrics to the layer below.

Reverse Appliqué

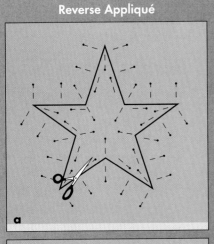

a

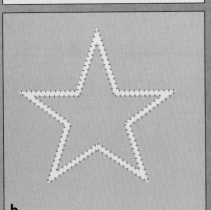

b

c

Machine Appliqué

Machine appliqué can be done on any sewing machine that has a zigzag stitch setting. Select an open-toe machine appliqué foot or a foot that has a channel or groove underneath so that the ridge of stitching will feed evenly through the foot. Use a size 70 universal needle for machine appliqué, and match the top thread to the appliqué pieces.

Before working any type of machine appliqué, stabilize the background fabric to prevent it from puckering, stretching, or becoming distorted as you stitch.

Stabilizing Background Fabric

1. To use a commercial stabilizer, cut a piece of the stabilizer that is slightly larger than the appliqué area. Hold, fuse, or pin the stabilizer to the wrong side of the background fabric underneath the stitching area.

2. To use freezer paper as a stabilizer, iron the coated side of a piece of freezer paper to the wrong side of the background fabric. Make sure the freezer paper piece is slightly larger than the appliqué area.

3. For small areas, plain paper can be used. Hold the paper under the fabric while stitching through both layers.

Satin Stitch Appliqué

1. Thread the bobbin with a fine, machine embroidery–weight cotton thread in a neutral color. This way, you can change top thread colors to match the appliqué without having to change bobbin thread. For the top, use machine embroidery thread or regular sewing thread.

2. Set the machine to a very short stitch length (about 80 stitches per inch) and a medium-width zigzag stitch.

3. Practice on a scrap of fabric. The stitches should be ⅛" to ³⁄₁₆" wide and form an even band of color. To ensure that no bobbin thread will show on the right side, loosen the top tension slightly.

4. Satin stitch around the edges of the appliqué pieces, covering all raw edges. Stitch around the underneath pieces first as shown below (top), then around the overlapping pieces as shown below (bottom).

As you stitch toward an inner or outer point, decrease the stitch width gradually, making an extremely narrow stitch at the point. With the needle in the point, lift the presser foot and turn the appliqué. Lower the presser foot and gradually increase the stitch width as you stitch.

Buttonhole Stitch Machine Appliqué

1. Prepare the appliqué pieces using the spray starch or basted method; see the instructions on pages 16 and 17.

2. Baste in place right side up on the background fabric.

3. To work buttonhole stitch machine appliqué, set your machine to the buttonhole stitch and experiment to find the suitable stitch length and width.

4. Position the stitching just along the outside of the fused pieces, catching the edges in the stitching. If your sewing machine does not have a buttonhole embroidery stitch, a blind hem stitch will work almost as well. The buttonhole stitch makes a straight embroidery stitch as shown below (top), while the blind hemmer makes a tiny V-shape as shown below (bottom).

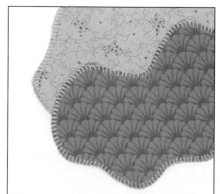

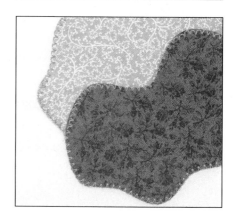

Invisible Machine Appliqué

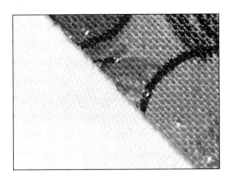

1. To prepare appliqué pieces for invisible machine stitching, use the spray starch or basted method; see the instructions on pages 16 and 17.

2. Pin and baste the appliqué pieces on the background fabric.

3. Use clear monofilament thread as the top thread in your sewing machine. Thread the bobbin with machine embroidery or sewing thread to match the background fabric, and loosen the top tension slightly.

4. Set your machine to the blind hem stitch with a small stitch width. Experiment on scrap fabric before stitching the appliqué to find the best stitch length and width. Stitch carefully, catching just the edge of the appliqué piece with each stitch.

Fusing

To use paper-backed fusible web products with machine appliqué, follow the package instructions carefully on the product you choose. Some products require longer pressing time to properly fuse fabrics together, while others can tolerate only a few seconds of pressing.

1. Trace the appliqué shape (or the reverse if the shape is asymmetrical) onto the paper side of the fusible web. Roughly cut the shape out, leaving about ½" around all of the shape's edges.

2. Following the package instructions for the iron temperature and fusing time, iron the web onto the wrong side of the fabric.

3. Allow to cool, then cut out the paper and fabric along the pattern line. Peel the paper away.

4. Position the appliqué pieces on the background fabric, placing and fusing underneath pieces first as shown. Then add the overlapping pieces and fuse into place.

Needle Pointer

Pressing is the final, finishing touch that highlights the designs and shows off your work to its best advantage, no matter which appliqué method you have chosen. Proper appliqué pressing does not completely flatten the pieces—to do so would show every seam allowance. A terry towel can be used as a cushion between the finished appliqué and the ironing board's hard surface.

To press, place the appliquéd piece facedown on a terry towel, and using light steam, press the wrong side of the background fabric.

Fresh Strawberries

*Bright red strawberries on black-and-white gingham create
a kitchen ensemble that's as fresh as a morning in May.*

Skill Level

Easy

Size

Valance: 15¼" (including 1½" ruffle above the rod pocket) x 70½"

Pot Holder: 8" x 8"

Towel Trim: 6½" x 17½"

Materials

1⅜ yards of black-and-white gingham check cotton

¼ yard of red calico

Scraps of green calico

¼ yard of fusible web

8" x 8" piece of fleece

16" x 27" black-and-white windowpane check kitchen towel

4 yards of red jumbo rickrack

White sewing thread; red and green machine appliqué thread

¼ yard of tear-away stabilizer or piece of plain paper for each strawberry

Instructions

1. From the gingham, cut two 19" x 36" pieces for the valance, two 8" x 8" pieces for the pot holder, and one 7" x 18" piece for the towel. From the red calico, cut 3" wide bias strips to equal 38" in length for the pot holder bias binding, piecing as needed.

2. For the valance, stitch the short ends of the gingham strips together using a ¼" seam allowance. Press. Fold under one long edge ¼"; press. Fold under ¼" again; press. Stitch along the turned-under edge to form a narrow hem. Narrow hem the short edges in the same manner. Cut one 2-yard length of rickrack. With the right side of the rickrack facing the wrong side of the fabric on the hemmed long side, stitch along the edge of the fabric and through the center of the

rickrack. Fold the remaining long edge of the fabric under ¼"; press. Fold under 3"; press and pin in place. Stitch 1½" from the top of the fold to form the header, then stitch near the turned-under edge to form the rod pocket.

3. For the pot holder, hold the fabric pieces together and fold in half lengthwise, then crosswise. Holding all the corners together and cutting through all the thicknesses at once, round off the corners. Cut four 8" lengths of rickrack. Stitching through the center of the rickrack, sew one piece of rickrack 1" from each edge of the right side of one piece.

4. For the towel trim, fold all the edges of the gingham piece under ¼"; press. Cut two 18" lengths of rickrack. Holding one piece of rickrack under each folded-under long edge, stitch from the right side along the edge of the fabric through the center of the rickrack. Stitch again ¼" from the fabric edge.

5. Using the Strawberry and Leaf patterns below, trace 10 strawberries and 10 leaves onto the fusible web. Following the instructions in "Fusing" on page 25, fuse the strawberry patterns to the red calico and the leaf patterns to the green calico. Cut

them out. Working with the strawberries first and then the leaves, fuse eight strawberries evenly spaced about 2½" from the bottom of the valance. Fuse one strawberry diagonally centered on the rickrack-trimmed pot holder piece and one strawberry in the center of the towel trim piece.

Following the instructions in "Stabilizing Background Fabric" and "Satin Stitch Appliqué" on page 24, stabilize and machine appliqué each strawberry.

6. Place the towel-trim strip on the towel as desired; pin in place. Stitch along the long edges, stitching over the previous stitching. Turn the excess fabric under at the sides; stitch along the side edges.

7. Stack the pot holder fabrics as follows: the plain gingham right side down, the fleece square, and the appliqué piece right side up. For the bias binding, fold the long edges of the binding strips to meet in the center. Fold in half lengthwise; press. Pin and slip stitch the binding around both sides of the edges of the pot holder. Turn under one short end and trim to ¼"; slip stitch in place. For the loop, cut 4" of binding. Folding the ends under ¼", slip stitch the ends to the back of the pot holder at one corner.

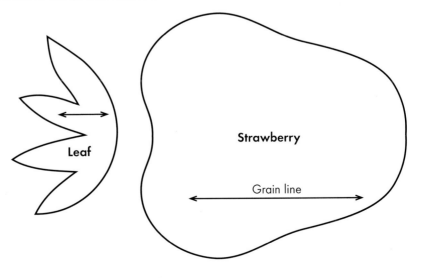

Leaf

Strawberry

Grain line

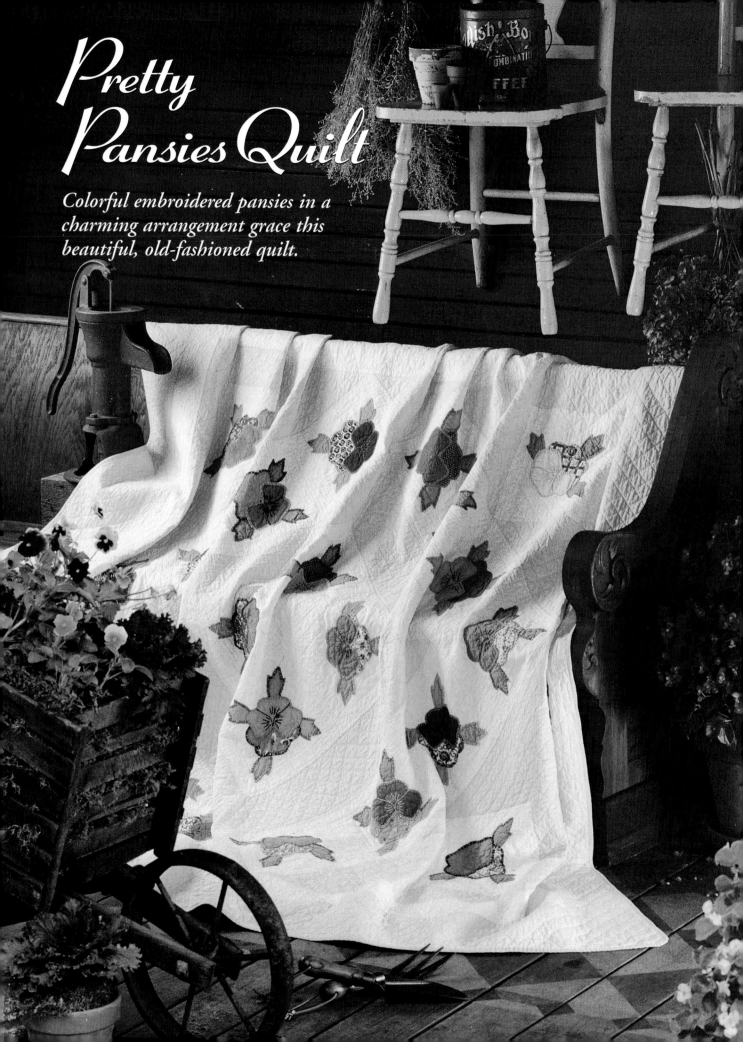

Pretty Pansies Quilt

*Colorful embroidered pansies in a
charming arrangement grace this
beautiful, old-fashioned quilt.*

Skill Level

Intermediate

Size

74" x 88"

Materials

5 yards of white cotton

5 yards of light green cotton

Scraps of calicos, prints and solid cotton fabrics for the pansies

½ yard of medium green cotton for the leaves

6 yards of lining

1 yard of light green cotton for binding

Plain paper

Fine-line permanent marker

Six-strand embroidery floss to match and contrast with the pansies and leaves

Instructions

Note: All seam allowances for the quilt are ¼".

1. From the white, cut 22 blocks, each 10½" square. Also from the white, cut two 3½" x 40" strips and two 3½" x 62" strips, piecing if needed. From the light green, cut four 5¾" x 30" strips, two 6½" x 88" strips, and two 6½" x 74" strips. From the green, also cut two 29¾" squares and one 10½" square; carefully cut the green squares exactly in half diagonally. From the binding fabric, cut a 2¼" wide bias binding strip to equal 334" in length.

2. Prepare templates from the Pansy and Leaf patterns on page 30, according to the instructions in "Making Templates" on page 14. From the prints and solids, cut 44 pansy pieces, coordinating two fabrics for each of 22 pansies. Overlapping the pansy pieces as shown in the Embroidery Diagram on page 30, transfer the markings for embroidery onto each pair of pansy pieces, tracing or using a hot-iron transfer pencil. From the medium green, cut 84 leaves.

3. Using two strands of floss and following the instructions in "Buttonhole Stitch Appliqué" on page 21, arrange and appliqué the pansies and leaves to the white blocks, sewing only three leaves to each of four blocks as shown in Diagram A on page 31. Sew four leaves to each of the remaining blocks as shown. Using two strands of matching floss and a stem stitch (see "Stitches" on page 122), embroider details on each pansy.

4. Set aside the four blocks that have only three leaves each. For the center of the quilt, sew together four pansy blocks so that the large sections of pansies face the center as shown in Diagram B on page 31.

5. Sew the narrow green strips to the center section, mitering the corners according to the instructions on page 193.

6. Sew seven pansy blocks together as shown in Diagram C on page 31. Repeat. Sew these sections to the center section, and sew the small green triangles to the center of the sides as shown in Diagram A.

7. Sew the large green triangles to the center section, forming a rectangle.

8. Mitering the corners, sew the white strips, then the wide green strips to the rectangle. Appliqué the remaining pansy blocks in place on the large triangles as shown in Diagram A, with the large sections of the pansies facing the center of the quilt.

9. Follow the instructions on pages 194 through 201 for finishing the quilt.

Stitching Solution

Here's a tip for keeping a large number of cut appliqué pieces together for a big project like a quilt. Stack pieces, either all of one shape or enough for one block. Thread a needle with sewing thread, and knot the end. Run the needle through all of the shapes, and cut the thread, leaving a 6" tail. The thread tail is long enough to keep pieces from coming off, and as you appliqué, you can easily remove pieces one at a time.

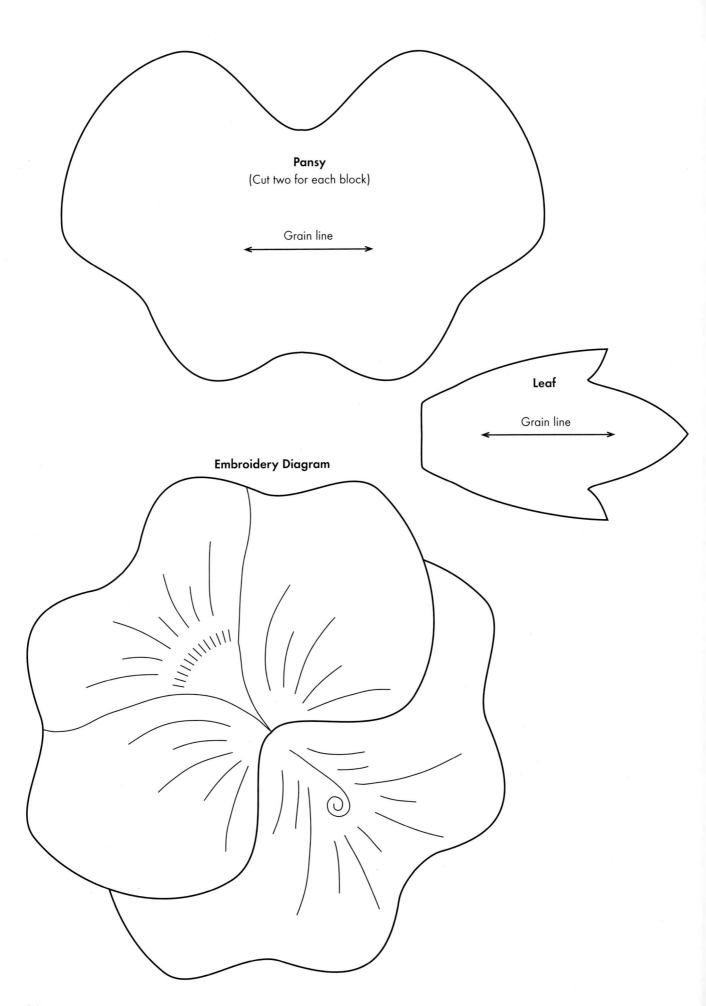

Pansy
(Cut two for each block)

Grain line

Leaf

Grain line

Embroidery Diagram

Diagram A

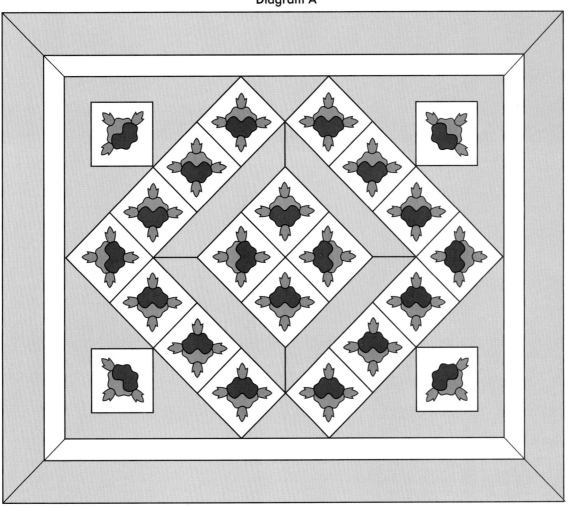

Diagram B   **Diagram C**

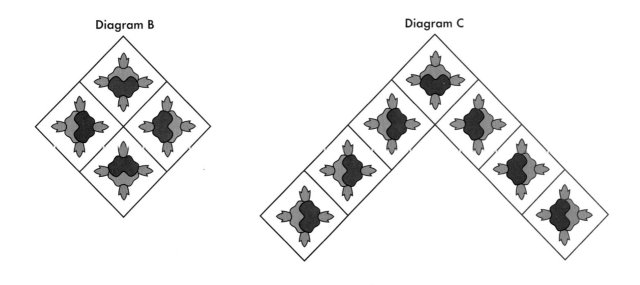

Folk Art Pillow

Traditional tulips, circles, leaves, and stems create a ruffled country-style pillow with a whimsical, folk art flair.

Skill Level

Challenging

Size

14" x 14"

Materials

12½" x 12½" piece of off-white cotton

⅛ yard of red pindot cotton

⅝ yard of green calico

Scraps of dark blue, light blue, dark gold, medium gold, light gold, and red calicos

2 yards of ¼" off-white cord

Matching sewing threads

14" pillow form

Dressmaker's straight pins

Instructions

1. From the green calico, cut one 15" square and 6" wide strips to equal 116", piecing as necessary to make the ruffle. From the red pindot, cut four 2¾" x 15" strips.

2. Prepare the templates for patterns A through I on page 34 according to the instructions in "Making Templates" on page 14. Mark and cut the appliqué pieces according to the instructions on pages 14 through 16. Cut five 1" wide bias strips from the green calico. Using a nickel for the pattern, mark and cut 12 circles from the assorted fabrics.

3. Fold a piece of plain paper in half lengthwise. Open the paper and place it on top of the Placement Pattern on page 35 so that the lengthwise crease in the paper is aligned with the center front line. Trace the Placement Pattern onto the left half of the paper. Again fold the paper in half lengthwise. Trace the Placement Pattern from the left side of the paper onto the right side. Trace the Placement Pattern from the paper onto the background fabric according to the instructions in "Marking Background Fabric" on page 15.

4. Using your preferred hand appliqué method, appliqué the pieces to the background fabric in this order: vase (A), stems, heart (B), bow (C), circles, large flower (D, E, then F), small leaves (G) and large leaves (H, then I). Press from the wrong side.

5. Using ¼" seam allowances, sew the red pindot strips to the edges of the off-white square, mitering or squaring the corners according to the instructions on page 193. Press.

6. With right sides together, stitch the short ends of the 116" green calico strip together to form a ring. Fold in half length-wise with the wrong sides together and the raw edges even; press. Sew two rows of gathering stitches ⅝" and ⅜" from the raw edges. Divide the ring into quarters and mark with four straight pins at the raw edges. Place the ring on the right side of the pillow front with all raw edges even and the pins positioned at the corners. Draw up the gathering stitches until the ruffle fits the sides of the pillow front. Adjust the ruffles so there is slightly more full-ness at the corners. Baste. Pin the pillow front and back together with all raw edges even.

7. Using a ½" seam allowance, stitch, leaving an opening to insert the pillow form. Turn right side out; press. Insert the pillow form; slip stitch the opening closed. Hand tack the cord to the front of the pillow at the base of the ruffle.

Something Different

Fuse a few motifs from this design onto a plain white sweat-shirt. Outline the motifs with button-hole machine embroidery in sparkly metallic gold or silver for a beautiful casual look.

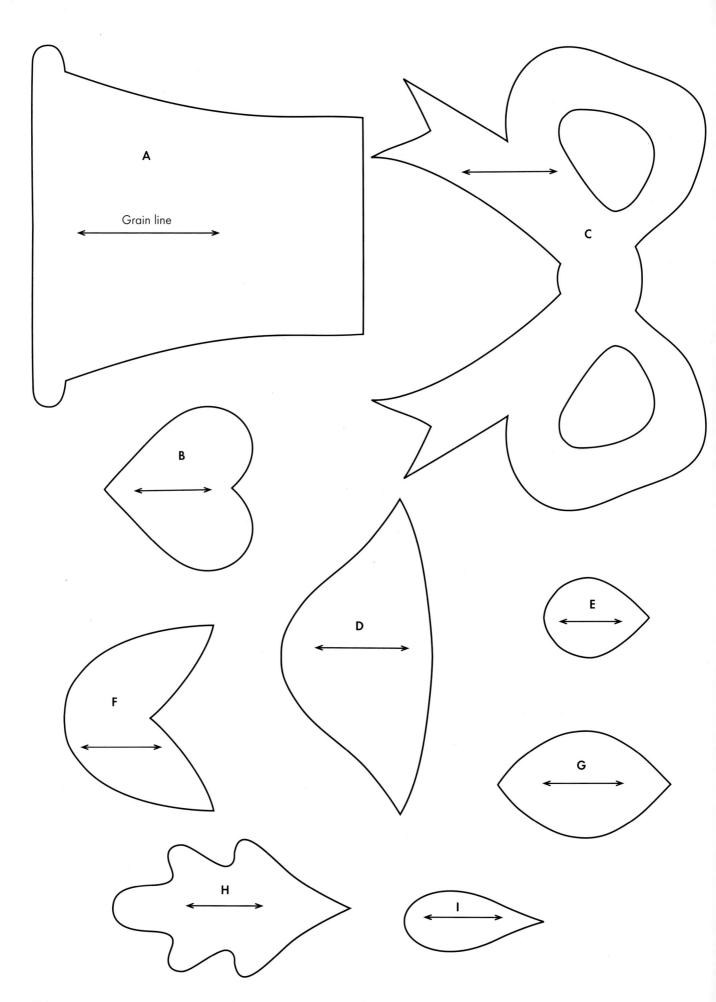

A

Grain line

C

B

D

E

F

G

H

I

Placement Pattern

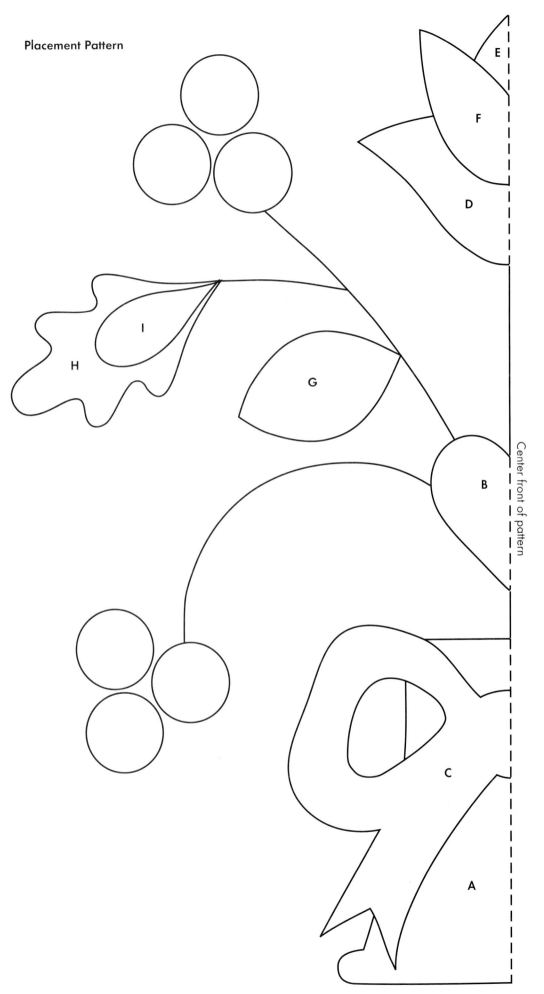

E

F

D

Center front of pattern

B

I

H

G

C

A

Crochet

*I*t's hard to imagine that a delicately beautiful Irish rose doily is made using a technique that has origins that trace back centuries to the crude knotting and looping of fishnets! But it's true—the art of crochet is almost as old as mankind itself.

During American colonial days, ladies crocheted "Afghanistan blankets" from scraps of yarn left over from knitting. In the mid-1800s, making and selling fine crocheted lace saved many Irish families from certain starvation when potato crops failed.

Based on pulling one loop through another, crochet is a timeless art that continues to be a popular and versatile technique.

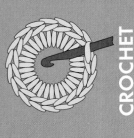

CROCHET

Equipment

With a hook and a ball of yarn or thread, you're all set to create beautiful crocheted projects. Small hooks and fine threads are essential for making delicate crocheted lace, while larger hooks and fluffy yarns are great for making afghans, sweaters, and more.

Threads

Crochet threads are numbered by weight. The higher the number, the finer the thread. Crochet thread is available in sizes 100, 80, 70, 50, 30, 20, 10, 8, 5, and 3. Sizes 20, 10, and 8 are the most popular sizes for making doilies.

Yarns

Yarns are primarily divided into four weights—baby weight, sport weight, worsted weight, and bulky. Baby weight yarn is generally used for making socks, bonnets, booties, afghans, and other baby items.

Sport weight yarn is a good choice for making crocheted sweaters and other garments, and worsted weight is the ever-popular 4-ply yarn that is the favorite for making afghans. Bulky yarn can be used for afghans also, as well as for a variety of other items for wearing and decorating. For ordinary afghans, sweaters, and home-decor items, it's usually best to select machine-washable and machine-dryable yarns. Care instructions are given on most yarn labels.

THREADS

Size 20

Size 12

Size 10

Size 8

Size 5

Size 3

YARNS

Baby weight

Sport weight

Worsted weight

Bulky

Jumbo Hooks

Available in sizes P, Q, and S and most often made of plastic, these oversized hooks are used for crocheting with rug yarn, fabric strips, or multiple strands of yarn.

Afghan Hooks

Available in sizes E to K (3.50 mm to 6.50 mm), afghan hooks are used for working afghan crochet (sometimes called Tunisian crochet) with yarn.

Broomstick Lace Needles

These hefty needles come in sizes 17, 19, 35, and 50 and are used in addition to a crochet hook when making broomstick or jiffy lace.

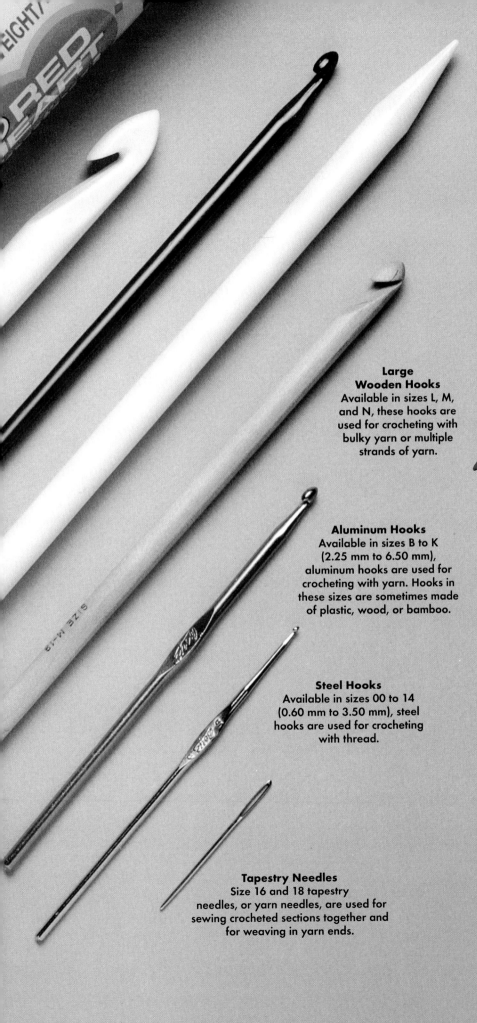

Large Wooden Hooks
Available in sizes L, M, and N, these hooks are used for crocheting with bulky yarn or multiple strands of yarn.

Aluminum Hooks
Available in sizes B to K (2.25 mm to 6.50 mm), aluminum hooks are used for crocheting with yarn. Hooks in these sizes are sometimes made of plastic, wood, or bamboo.

Steel Hooks
Available in sizes 00 to 14 (0.60 mm to 3.50 mm), steel hooks are used for crocheting with thread.

Tapestry Needles
Size 16 and 18 tapestry needles, or yarn needles, are used for sewing crocheted sections together and for weaving in yarn ends.

Needle Pointer

Experiment with different brands of hooks to find the type you prefer. Notice differences in hook shape, weight, and other factors. Most crocheters, when given the choice, establish a preference for one brand of hook over others.

Getting Started

A slip knot forms the basis for the first chain stitch, and the yarn is held by the fingers of the left hand. As you crochet, the hook is held like a pencil is and used to draw yarn loops through the loop on the hook.

Slip Knot

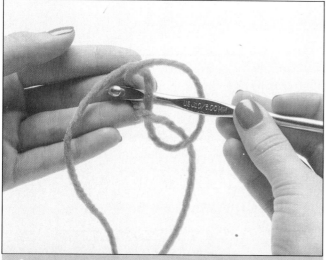

1 To make a slip knot, make a loose knot at least 5" from the end of the yarn. With your right hand, put the end of the hook through the loop as shown. Hook the yarn and draw it through the loop.

2 To make the loop come close to the hook, pull the yarn ends in opposite directions. Do not pull tightly.

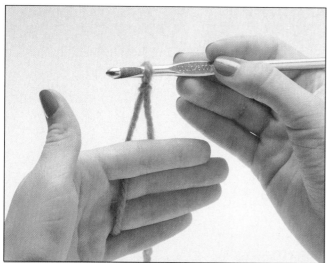

3 About 4" down from the hook, thread the yarn through your fingers as shown. Then bring the hook down in front and to the right of your left hand as shown in Step 4.

4 To support the loop as you start to make a stitch, hold your index finger up and pinch the bottom of the loop on the hook between your thumb and your middle finger.

Chain Stitch

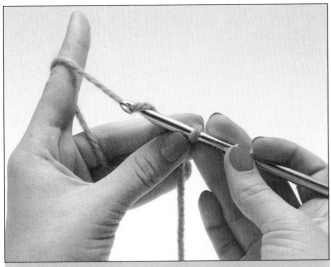

1 To make a yarn over, turn the hook downward and take the hook under the yarn. Catch the yarn with the hook.

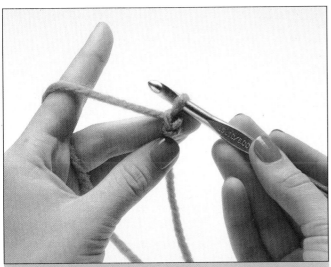

2 To make a chain, yarn over and draw the yarn through the loop on the hook.

Needle Pointer

As you crochet, your left-hand index finger keeps the yarn tension even while your little finger and ring finger keep the yarn from moving through too quickly. With a little practice, you will find the correct working tension.

Stitching Solution

If you have trouble pulling the hook through the stitches or if you often split the yarn with the hook as you crochet, you're probably working too tightly. Most beginning crocheters tend to hold the yarn and hook too tightly. Practice loosening up with your very first stitch. Consciously relax your left hand to allow the yarn to flow through your fingers more freely.

Reading Instructions

Even experienced crocheters can be intimidated by written crochet patterns. Instructions for crochet are written in a stylized form created to use the smallest amount of printed space possible. As a result, they often seem to be written in a mysterious code full of strange words and symbols.

Crochet instructions are actually extremely logical. Abbreviations are easy to learn, and the same abbreviations are generally used by all publishers.

Punctuation marks such as asterisks, parentheses, and brackets are used to set off sequences of stitches that are to be repeated or worked in a certain spot.

Crochet Punctuation Marks

( ) Parentheses enclose a sequence of instructions, and following the parentheses will be an indication of how many times this sequence is to be repeated or where the sequence is to be worked. For example, "(2 dc in next sc) 4 times" means to follow the instructions enclosed in the parentheses a total of four times. "(2 dc, ch 1, 2 dc) in next dc" means to work all of the stitches enclosed in the parentheses in the next double crochet.

* Asterisks may appear alone or in pairs and are often used in combination with parentheses. When used in pairs, asterisks serve essentially the same function as parentheses, with one exception. The instructions of what to do with the crochet sequence enclosed between asterisks may appear directly after the last asterisk or later in the crochet pattern. For example, "*Sc in next 5 sc, (3 sc in next sc) twice*, sc in next 4 sc; repeat between ** 4 times" means to work through to the instructions for repeating, then repeat only the instructions between the asterisks four times. If a single asterisk is used, it is often followed by a sequence of instructions followed by something like "repeat from * across."

[ ] Brackets are used to further clarify sequences of instructions, usually in combination with parentheses and asterisks. For example, "Ch 1, sc in same st, *ch 5, sk next 2 sts, sc in next st, ch 3, sc in next st, ch 3*, [sc in next st, repeat between **]; repeat between [ ] around, join with sl st in first sc" employs all three common forms of crochet punctuation.

International Crochet Symbols

Some crochet patterns include diagrams featuring international crochet symbols. International crochet symbol diagrams look very much like the completed crochet piece, and they are often used for doily patterns and other items made with thread. The chart below lists the more common symbols.

Abbreviations

beg	beginning
ch	chain
cl	cluster
cr-st	cross-stitch
dc	double crochet
dec	decrease
dtr	double treble
hdc	half double crochet
inc	increase
lp(s)	loop(s)
MC	main color
pc	popcorn
rnd(s)	round(s)
sc	single crochet
sk	skip
sl	slip
sl st	slip stitch
sp	space
st(s)	stitch(es)
tog	together
tr	treble crochet
tr tr	triple treble crochet
yo	yarn over

International Crochet Symbols

◯	chain
<	slip stitch
+	single crochet
T	half double crochet
T̄	double crochet
T̄	treble crochet
T̄	double treble crochet
⌇	front post double crochet
⌇	back post double crochet
▽	3-chain picot
⊞	4-chain picot
V	V stitch
W	3-dc shell
⊕	popcorn

Selecting Hooks

Hooks are numbered according to size. Hooks for crocheting with thread are sized from 14, the smallest, to 00, the largest.

Hooks for crocheting with yarn are sized from B to K.

Hooks for crocheting with extra-bulky materials, such as strips of cloth and multiple strands of yarn, come in sizes L, M, N, P, Q, and S.

Equivalences between metric, U.K, and U.S. hooks may be shown slightly different in many published charts. The conversions in this chart are commonly used.

Hook Sizes

U.S.	Metric	U.K.	U.S.	Metric	U.K.
	STEEL HOOKS		0	3.25 mm	
14		7	00	3.50 mm	
13		6½			
12	0.60 mm	6		ALUMINUM HOOKS	
11		5½			
10	0.75 mm	5	B/1	2.25 mm	12
9	1.00 mm	4	C/2	2.75 mm	11
8	1.25 mm	3	D/3	3.25 mm	10
7	1.50 mm	2½	E/4	3.50 mm	9
6	1.75 mm	2	F/5	4.00 mm	8
5		1½	G/6	4.25 mm	7
4	2.00 mm	1	H/8	5.00 mm	6
3		1/0	I/9	5.50 mm	5
2	2.50 mm	2/0	J/10	6.00 mm	4
1	3.00 mm	3/0	K/10½	6.50 mm	2

Needle Pointer

To keep your ball of crochet cotton from rolling away as you work, place it in the bottom section from a clean 2-liter plastic soda bottle. Thread the end through the small opening in the top of the bottle, then replace the bottle bottom.

Checking Gauge

A gauge notation is included with most crochet patterns. This tells you how large or small your stitches should be. The key to making stitches larger or smaller is hook size. Achieving the correct gauge is more important than using the hook size specified.

Gauge is especially important when making wearable items. A tiny gauge difference can add up to several inches across the length or width of a garment.

1. Make a sample piece at least 4" square or one motif using the hook size indicated.

2. Without stretching the crocheted swatch, lay it out flat and measure the stitches and row. If your swatch has more or fewer rows or stitches per inch than stated in the gauge, make the swatch again with a smaller or larger hook.

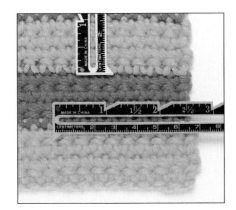

Stitches

Crochet stitches are primarily made up of variations of looping the yarn over the hook and pulling the loops through other loops. Almost every crochet project uses at least one of the basic stitches. Afghan crochet uses special hooks, while combinations of basic stitches add interesting texture to crochet.

Basic Stitches

Slip Stitch (sl st)

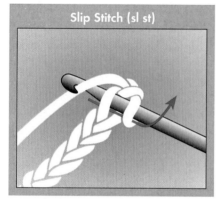

Insert the hook in the indicated stitch, yarn over. With one motion, draw the yarn through the stitch and through the loop on the hook.

Single Crochet (sc)

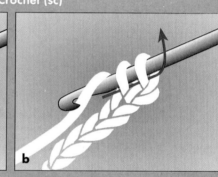

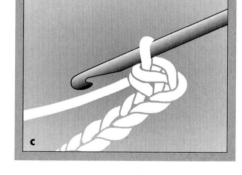

Insert the hook from the front into the indicated stitch or loop (a), yarn over, draw the yarn through the stitch. Yarn over, draw the yarn through the 2 loops on the hook (b). This illustration shows working 1 single crochet in the second loop from the hook (c), which is the proper way to begin a row of single crochet on a chain. To continue the row, single crochet in each chain across the row.

Half Double Crochet (hdc)

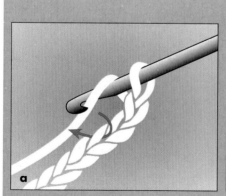

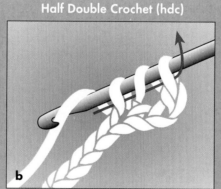

Yarn over, insert the hook from the front into the indicated stitch or loop (a), draw the yarn through the stitch. Yarn over, draw the yarn through all 3 loops at once (b). This illustration shows working 1 half double crochet in the third chain from the hook (c), which is the proper way to begin a row of half double crochet on a chain. To continue the row, half double crochet in each chain across the row.

Double Crochet (dc)

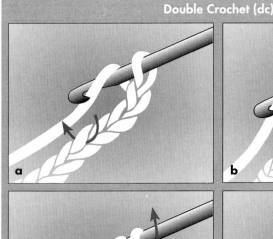

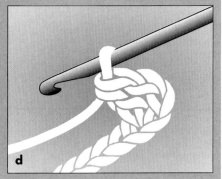

Yarn over, insert the hook from the front into the indicated stitch or loop (a), draw the yarn through the stitch, creating 3 loops on the hook. Yarn over, draw through 2 of the loops on the hook (b); yarn over, draw through the remaining 2 loops on the hook (c). This illustration shows working 1 double crochet in the fourth chain from the hook (d), which is the proper way to begin a row of double crochet on a chain. To continue the row, double crochet in each chain across the row.

Needle Pointer

When you are making any new stitch, always insert the hook under the top two loops of the existing stitch unless the pattern instructs you to do otherwise. The pattern may direct you to "work in front loop only," or "work in back loop only." If the pattern says to "work stitches in ring (or over loop)," this means to insert the hook under the chain stitch, yarn over, and complete the stitch as usual. In this case, the chain ring or loop is encased in stitches.

Stitching Solution

Instructions for motifs often give the gauge measurements for the entire motif, not for a number of stitches. Make a sample motif using the hook size suggested in the pattern, then adjust the hook size as necessary to obtain the correct size motif. One or two hook sizes can make a big difference in the motif size. What to do with extra motifs? Save them and stitch together a "crazy-quilt" afghan when you have enough.

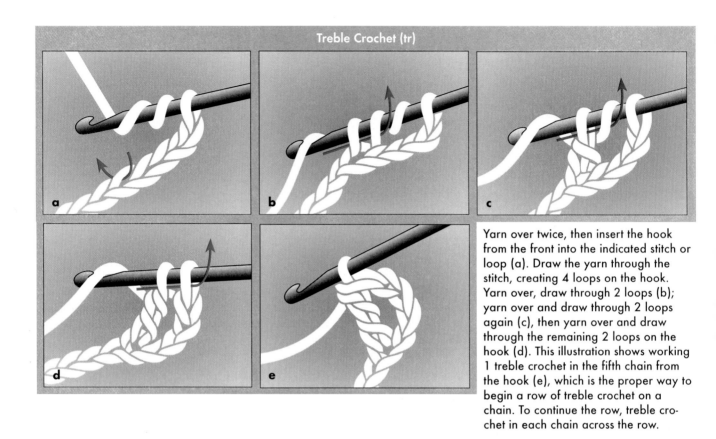

Treble Crochet (tr)

Yarn over twice, then insert the hook from the front into the indicated stitch or loop (a). Draw the yarn through the stitch, creating 4 loops on the hook. Yarn over, draw through 2 loops (b); yarn over and draw through 2 loops again (c), then yarn over and draw through the remaining 2 loops on the hook (d). This illustration shows working 1 treble crochet in the fifth chain from the hook (e), which is the proper way to begin a row of treble crochet on a chain. To continue the row, treble crochet in each chain across the row.

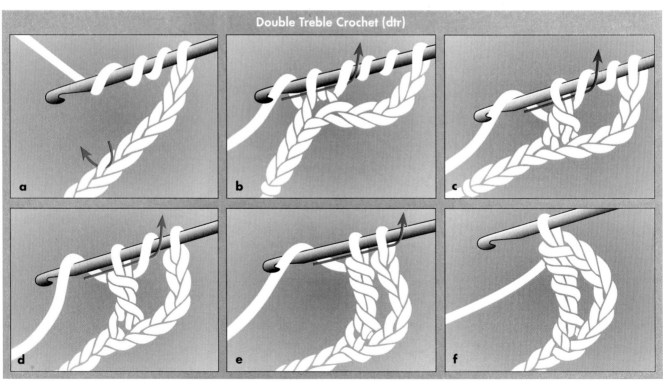

Double Treble Crochet (dtr)

Yarn over 3 times, then insert the hook from the front into the indicated stitch or loop (a). Draw the yarn through the stitch, creating 5 loops on the hook.

(Yarn over, draw through 2 loops) 4 times (b, c, d, and e). This illustration shows working 1 double treble crochet in the sixth chain from the hook (f),

which is the proper way to begin a row of double treble crochet on a chain. To continue the row, double treble crochet in each chain across the row.

Fancy Stitches

Picot

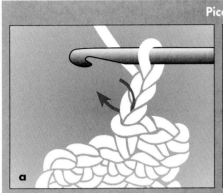

Chain 3 or more, slip stitch into the 3rd or indicated chain from the hook (a). A picot can be made with 3 or more

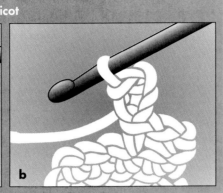

chains. This illustration shows a picot made with 3 chains (b).

Back Loop/Front Loop (back lp/front lp)

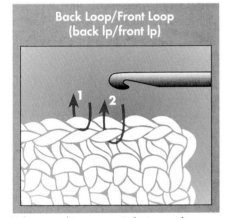

When working any stitch, insert the hook from the front into the back loop (1) or front loop (2) only of the indicated stitch.

Shell

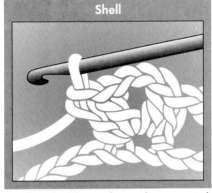

Work 2 double crochet in the next stitch or chain loop, chain 1 or more, then work 2 double crochet in the same stitch or chain loop. A shell can be made with 2 or more double crochets on each side of the center chain or chains.

Front Post Double Crochet (fpdc)

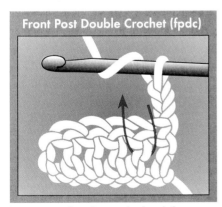

Yarn over, then insert the hook from front to back to front around the next stitch. Yarn over and complete a double crochet as usual.

Back Post Double Crochet (bpdc)

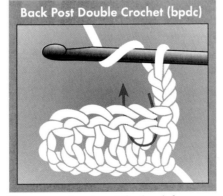

Yarn over, then insert the hook from back to front to back around the next stitch. Yarn over and complete a double crochet as usual.

Needle Pointer

When counting the number of chains you have completed, do not count the chain loop on the hook. To see how this works, chain 3. There are 3 chain stitches plus the loop on the hook.

Reverse Single Crochet (Reverse sc)

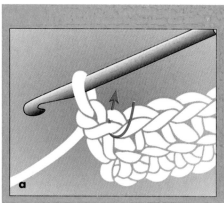

a

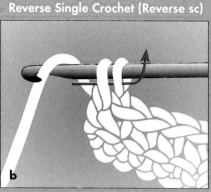

b

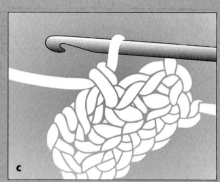

c

This stitch is used to create a distinctive edging. Holding the crochet hook as usual but working from the left to the right, insert the hook in the next stitch to the right (a), yarn over, draw the yarn through the stitch (b). To complete the row, continue working from the left to the right (c).

Cross-Stitch (cr-st)

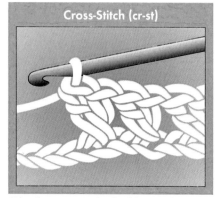

Skip the next stitch, double crochet in the indicated stitch or loop. Working over the double crochet you just made, double crochet in the skipped stitch.

V Stitch (V st)

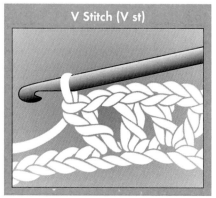

Double crochet in the indicated stitch or loop, chain 1, and double crochet in the same stitch or loop.

Popcorn (pc)

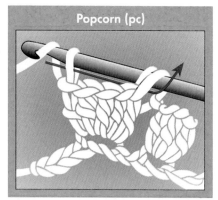

Work 5 double crochets in the indicated stitch or loop. Remove the hook from the loop; insert the hook in the 1st double crochet of the 5 double crochet you just made, then insert the hook in the dropped loop. Yarn over, draw the yarn through the loops on the hook, and chain 1 to secure the popcorn. Push the popcorns to the right or wrong side of your work as needed.

Puff Stitch (puff st)

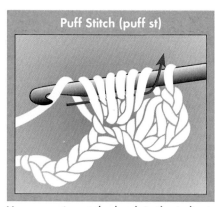

Yarn over, insert the hook in the indicated stitch or loop, and pull up a loop (size will often be indicated in the pattern, or pull up a loop about the height of a double crochet). Yarn over and insert the hook in the same stitch for each loop, drawing up the number of loops indicated in the pattern (usually 2 or 3). Yarn over and draw yarn through all of the loops on the hook.

Star Stitch (star st)

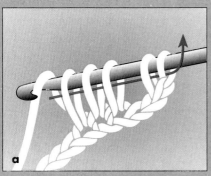

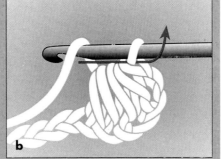

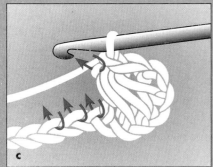

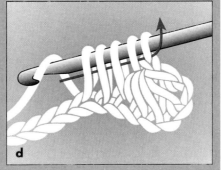

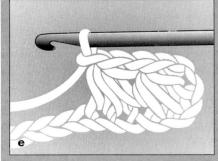

1st Star: Insert the hook into the 2nd chain from the hook, yarn over, and pull up a loop. Insert the hook into the 4th chain from the hook, yarn over, and pull up a loop. Insert the hook into the 5th chain from the hook, yarn over, and pull up a loop. Insert the hook into the 6th chain from the hook, yarn over, and pull up a loop. Yarn over, draw the yarn through all 5 loops on the hook (a), and chain 1 firmly to secure the star (b).

2nd and Remaining Stars: Insert the hook into the loop that closed the last star, yarn over, and pull up a loop. Insert the hook into the same stitch as the last loop of the last star, yarn over, and pull up a loop. Insert the hook and pull up a loop in each of the next 2 stitches (c). Yarn over, draw the yarn through all 5 loops on the hook (d), and chain 1 firmly to secure the star (e).

CROCHET

Needle Pointer

When you are crocheting with cotton thread on hot, sticky days, sprinkle a little baby powder on your hands. Your work will flow more smoothly, and the powder adds a nice scent to the finished project.

Bullion Stitch (bullion st)

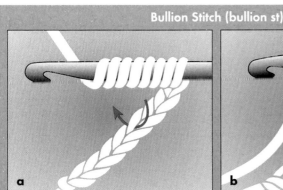

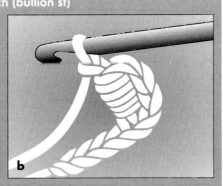

Yarn over as many times as specified in the pattern (usually 7 to 10 times). Insert the hook from the front into the indicated stitch or space (a), yarn over and pull up a loop, then yarn over and draw yarn carefully through all of the loops on the hook. Chain 1 to secure the bullion stitch (b).

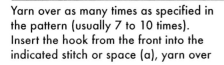

Afghan Crochet Stitches

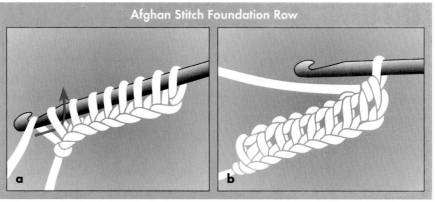

Afghan Stitch Foundation Row

Afghan crochet, sometimes called Tunisian crochet, is worked using an afghan hook, which is a long crochet hook with an end similar to that of a knitting needle.

Each row is worked in two parts, first drawing up the loops and then working them off the hook.

Row 1: Using an afghan hook, chain the number indicated in your pattern. Insert the hook in the 2nd chain from the hook, yarn over, draw up a loop. Keeping all loops on the hook, draw up a loop in each chain across. Do not turn.

To work the loops off the hook, yarn over and draw through 1 loop (a), (yarn over and draw through 2 loops) until only 1 loop remains on the hook (b). The last loop on the hook is the 1st loop of the next row. Do not turn. This row forms Row 1 of most Afghan stitch variations.

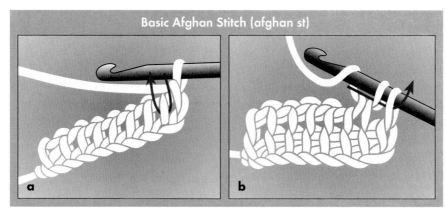

Basic Afghan Stitch (afghan st)

Row 1: Work an Afghan Stitch Foundation Row.
Row 2: Skip the first vertical bar; insert the hook under the next vertical bar (a), draw up a loop. Keeping all loops on the hook, draw up a loop in each vertical bar across to the last vertical bar. For the last afghan stitch, insert the hook under the last bar and the stitch directly behind it, yarn over, and draw up a loop. Work the loops off the hook as in the Afghan Stitch Foundation Row (b).

Repeat Row 2.

To make an increase, draw up 2 loops in one vertical bar.

To make a decrease, insert the hook under the next 2 vertical bars, yarn over, draw the yarn under both bars; draw up a ¼" loop.

Afghan Knit Stitch (afghan k st)

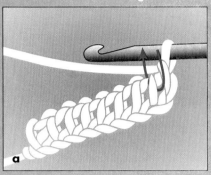
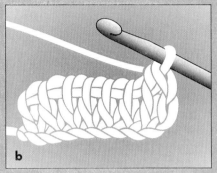

Row 1: Work an Afghan Stitch Foundation Row.

Row 2: Skip the first vertical bar; insert the hook from front to back in the next vertical bars and under the horizontal bar of the next stitch (a). Draw up a loop. Keeping all loops on the hook, draw up a loop between each pair of vertical bars in the same manner across. For the last stitch, insert the hook under the last bar and under the stitch directly behind it, yarn over, draw up a loop. Work the loops off the hook as in the Afghan Stitch Foundation Row (b).

To make an increase, draw up 2 loops between the front and back vertical bars.

To make a decrease, when working off the loops, yarn over and draw the yarn through 2 loops at once.

Afghan Purl Stitch (afghan p st)

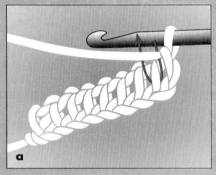
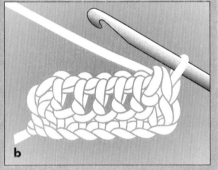

Row 1: Work an Afghan Stitch Foundation Row.

Row 2: Skip the first vertical bar; holding the yarn in front of your work as for working the purl stitch in knitting, insert the hook from right to left under the next vertical bar (a). Draw up a loop. Keeping all loops on the hook, draw up a loop under each vertical bar in the same manner across. For the last stitch, insert the hook under the last bar and under the stitch directly behind it, yarn over, draw up a loop. Work the loops off the hook as in the Afghan Stitch Foundation Row (b).

To make an increase, draw up 2 loops under 1 vertical bar.

To make a decrease, insert the hook under the next 2 vertical bars, yarn over, draw the yarn under both bars; draw up a loop.

Needle Pointer

Afghan crochet is similar to knitting in that all loops in a row are held on the hook at once. The stitches in Afghan crochet are more like knitting than regular crochet stitches, except Afghan crochet fabric is firmer and thicker than knitted fabric.

Stitching Solution

To preserve your treasured cotton thread crochet projects for future generations, wrap and store them in acid-free tissue paper, with extra tissue paper between the folds. Acid-free storage materials are available at framing shops and some needlework and quilting shops.

Techniques

Learning the ins and outs of turning your work, changing colors, and weaving in all the loose ends can make your crochet projects look and feel smoother and prettier. Increasing and decreasing help create shape and dimension. Special effects like filet crochet and Irish crochet are fun to explore. And when your project is finished, it will be ready for a gentle shaping, pressing, and perhaps even trimming with fringe to make it look its best.

Turning Work

When working in rows, chain stitches are used to help turn the crochet fabric. Because stitches vary in height, the number of chain stitches required depends upon the stitch being used. Here are the number of chains required to turn each type of stitch:

Single crochet	ch 1
Half double crochet	ch 2
Double crochet	ch 3
Treble crochet	ch 4
Double treble crochet	ch 5
Triple treble crochet	ch 6

Turning Chains

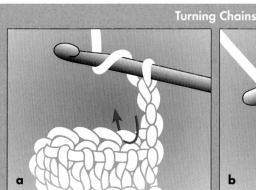
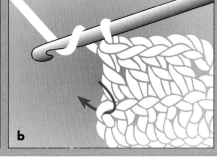

The turning chain often counts as the first stitch of the new row, as specified in the pattern. In this case, for a double crochet, skip the first stitch of the row and work into the next stitch (a). At the end of the row, work the last stitch in the top of the turning chain (b).

Stitching Solution

If your turning chain seems to make a little loop at the beginning of the row, it's probably a tiny bit taller than the other stitches. To correct this, tighten your chain stitches a bit or make your turning chain one chain stitch fewer than specified. For example, try chaining two to turn double crochet.

Changing Colors

To change colors at the end of a row, simply tie a new color around the first and slide the knot up next to the crochet fabric. If you don't want a knot, yarn over with the new color and make the turning chain; turn. To change colors within a row, work off the last loops of the first-color stitch with the second color.

Chain Color Change

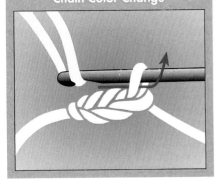

Yarn over with the 2nd color, draw the yarn through the last loop on the hook. Leave a few inches of yarn hanging on the back of the fabric to be woven in later. (See page 55.)

Single Crochet Color Change

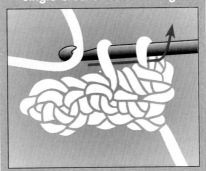

Work single crochet to the point where there are 2 loops on the hook. Drop the first color, yarn over with the 2nd color, and draw the yarn through the last 2 loops of the single crochet.

Half Double Crochet Color Change

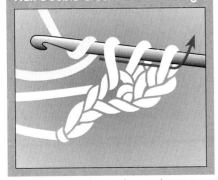

Work half double crochet to the point where there are 3 loops on the hook. Drop the first color, yarn over with the 2nd color, and draw the yarn through all 3 loops on the hook.

Double Crochet Color Change

Work double crochet to the point where there are 2 loops remaining on the hook. Drop the first color, yarn over with the 2nd color, and draw the yarn through the last 2 loops on the hook. Make a treble crochet and double treble crochet color change in the same manner as a double crochet color change.

Needle Pointer

If you have holes or gaps between your stitches at color-change points, make a few stitches beyond a color change. Stop and gently tug on the loose ends of both the first and second colors.

Decreasing

Decreases may be placed anywhere in a row according to the pattern. To decrease, two or more stitches are crocheted together, creating a single stitch.

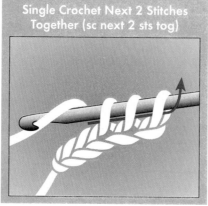

Single Crochet Next 2 Stitches Together (sc next 2 sts tog)

Draw up a loop in each of the next 2 stitches, yarn over, draw the yarn through all 3 loops on the hook.

Half Double Crochet Next 2 Stitches Together (hdc next 2 sts tog)

Yarn over, insert the hook in the next stitch, yarn over, draw the yarn through the stitch. Repeat. Yarn over, draw the yarn through all 5 loops on the hook.

Double Crochet Next 2 Stitches Together (dc next 2 sts tog)

a

b

c

d

e

Yarn over, insert the hook in the indicated stitch or loop (a), yarn over, draw the yarn through the stitch. Yarn over, draw the yarn through 2 lps on the hook (b). Yarn over, insert the hook in the next stitch (c), yarn over, draw the yarn through the stitch. Yarn over, draw the yarn through 2 loops on the hook (d). Yarn over, draw the yarn through the remaining 3 loops on the hook (e). To decrease treble crochet and double treble crochet, work the first stitch of each to the point where there are two loops remaining on the hook. Work the next stitch to the same point, which will leave a total of 3 loops remaining on the hook. Yarn over, draw the yarn through the remaining 3 loops on the hook.

Increasing

To increase, work an extra stitch or stitches wherever indicated in a pattern.

Depending on the project, an increase can be introduced anywhere along a row.

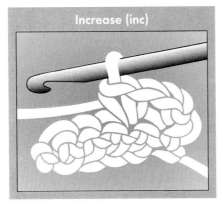

Increase (inc)

Two single crochet in next single crochet (increase).

Joining

When a pattern says "join," always use a slip stitch. This illustration shows joining to form a ring.

To join at the end of a round of half-double crochet or double crochet, slip stitch in the top of the chain-2 or chain-3 that forms the first stitch of the round.

Join with Slip Stitch (sl st)

Insert the hook in the indicated stitch, yarn over. With one motion, draw the yarn through the stitch and through the loop on the hook.

Needle Pointer

To give a more even appearance to increases or decreases along the edge of your work, place the increases or decreases one stitch in from the edge each time.

Weaving in Loose Ends

This technique prevents the yarn ends from working loose any time the crocheted piece is stretched.

1. Thread one loose end into a size 16 or 18 tapestry needle. Weave the end through the back of the stitches for several inches, then turn and weave back in the other direction. Do not pull tightly. Clip the yarn end and stretch the area slightly. The yarn end will disappear into the stitches.

2. To work in loose ends when crocheting with thread, use the same technique, but use a smaller tapestry needle. If you anticipate your thread crochet item will not be used actively or stretched in any way, it is only necessary to weave the ends in one direction. Weave carefully on lacy crochet, making sure the woven-in strand does not show from the front of the item.

Jacquard Crochet

Jacquard crochet is named after the Jacquard loom, created by Joseph Jacquard in the early 1800s. Although no form of crochet can be duplicated by machine, Jacquard crochet is similar to fabric created by the Jacquard loom in that each stitch may be a different color. This form of crochet evolved as crocheters, inspired by the new fabrics of the last century, began to experiment to create flat, multicolored fabric in crochet.

Designed using graphs in combination with written instructions, Jacquard crochet is almost always made with all single, half double, or double crochet. The changes in color form the design rather than the texture of the stitches.

Jacquard crochet is worked with a strand of yarn for each color used. A separate ball of yarn for each color section is used, or the unused yarn is held to the back of work and worked over or carried loosely.

Regardless of the stitch used, color changes in Jacquard crochet are all made in the same fashion—by working off the last loops of the last stitch with the new color.

Filet Crochet

Filet crochet is among the easiest of crochet lace techniques to master, and it produces some of the most beautiful results. Filet is generally worked with fine crochet thread rather than with yarn, and it is used to make doilies, runners, and other delicate, lacy items.

Filet crochet is composed of a square mesh pattern, with some of the spaces open and others filled. Only two or three stitches are used, most commonly chain and double crochet. Filled spaces are created with double crochet, and open spaces are created with chain stitches, following a grid-like diagram. The pattern is worked back and forth in rows, and the diagram is read from right to left on odd-numbered (right side) rows and left to right on even-numbered (wrong side) rows.

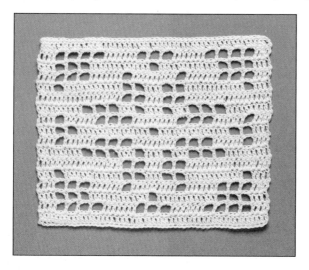

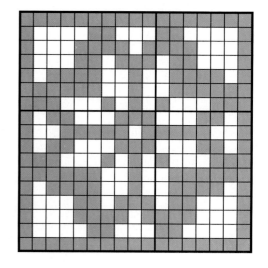

Irish Crochet

Inspired by expensive Venetian lace, Irish crochet was developed in the convents of Ireland in the mid-nineteenth century. Irish crochet motifs traditionally consist of florals, leaves, shamrocks, and cordings, and these motifs are most stunning worked in fine cotton thread. Motifs are worked separately and then joined together on a mesh background. Fine examples of Irish crochet include doilies, runners, bedspreads, and other household decorations, as well as collars, lace edgings, and clothing.

Broomstick Lace

Broomstick lace loops are formed over a broomstick or a large knitting needle with a diameter between ½" and 1".

1. Chain a foundation chain equal to the length desired, with the total number of stitches divisible by five.

2. Transfer the last chain to a broomstick or large knitting needle and draw up a loop in the next chain (a). Transfer the loop to the knitting needle. Draw up a loop in each chain across, and transfer each loop in the same manner.

3. To work the loops off, insert the hook from the right to the left through 5 loops on the knitting needle. Draw the yarn through the 5 loops (b), chain 1. Working in the center of all 5 loops at the same time, work 4 single crochets in the center of the loops (c). Repeat across.

4. To continue, draw up another row of loops and work them off in the same manner.

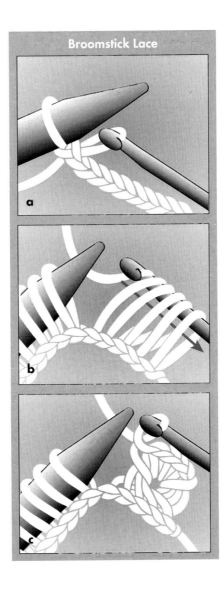

Broomstick Lace

a

b

c

Needle Pointer

To save counting and recounting rows when working filet crochet, try tying a piece of contrasting thread on the side that is toward you when you are working the even-numbered rows.

Finishing

Various methods may be used for joining pieces of crochet. Afghan panels and blocks can be sewn together with matching yarn and needle or crocheted together with a slip stitch or single crochet. Seams for sweaters may be whip-stitched or woven.

Most crochet worked with cotton, washable wool, or synthetic yarn does not need blocking, but a light steaming can smooth slight puckers in the seams and stitches and give the project a professional look.

Items crocheted with thread, such as doilies or ornaments, often require shaping or stiffening. There are several liquid fabric stiffening products available that can be thinned with water to achieve the degree of stiffness you desire. Baskets and bowls should be stiffened with full-strength liquid stiffener. Doilies, collars, and other items requiring a softer look should be prepared with stiffener thinned up to 50 percent with water.

When choosing a stiffening product, be sure to read the instructions on the package before beginning. The most important steps in the stiffening process are saturating the crochet piece thoroughly and removing as much of the excess liquid as possible before drying.

Joining Motifs and Sewing Seams

1. To join crochet pieces with a nearly invisible sewn seam, hold the pieces edge to edge with the right sides together. Using a size 16 or 18 tapestry needle threaded with matching yarn and working in one loop of the stitches only, whipstitch or weave the crochet pieces together as shown above (top left).

2. To crochet two pieces together, hold them edge to edge with the right sides together. Working in one loop of the stitches only, slip stitch or single crochet the pieces together as shown.

Steaming and Blocking

1. To steam a flat piece of finished crochet such as an afghan, smooth it out on the floor, a bed, or a towel-covered table.

2. Set the iron to the permanent press setting with steam, and preheat the iron. Hold the iron just above the crocheted piece as shown above (right), allowing the steam to penetrate the yarn. Move the iron slowly back and forth over all of the areas, smoothing the steamed crochet and flattening seams gently with your hands.

3. To block a piece of crochet to exact measurements, stretch it, then pin it using rustproof pins to towels before steaming. Measure carefully and square up the corners before steaming.

Fringe

1. Cut a piece of cardboard 6" wide and ½" longer than the desired fringe measurement. Most afghans look best with 7" fringe, but yours may require a shorter fringe.

2. Wrap the yarn evenly around the length of cardboard, without stretching the yarn, until the cardboard is filled.

3. Insert one blade of your scissors between the yarn and the cardboard at one end, and cut the strands all the way across.

4. For each fringe, select the number of strands specified in the pattern. Hold the strands together and fold them in half.

5. To attach the fringe, insert the hook through the wrong side of the stitch at the afghan edge, and draw the fold of the strands through, creating a loop as shown on the opposite page (top).

Insert the loose ends of the fringe through the loop and pull them evenly and snugly as shown (center). Repeat for the remaining fringe as shown (bottom), cutting more strands as needed.

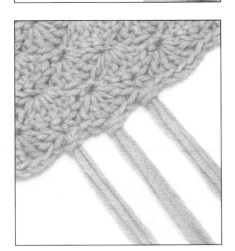

6. After all of the fringe is attached, spread the afghan on a flat surface, smooth the knots and strands, and trim the ends evenly.

Shaping and Stiffening

1. To stiffen doilies and other flat items, use a 24" square of cardboard or foam core board as a base. Using a ruler, mark the board in 1" squares, then draw a series of progressively wider circles from the center using a compass. To stiffen baskets, bowls, and other dimensional items, use plastic or ceramic bowls, Styrofoam balls or egg shapes, or even balloons as base shapes.

2. Cover all base surfaces and shapes with clear plastic wrap, taping at the back to secure.

3. To saturate the crochet with stiffener, place the crochet and stiffener in a reclosable plastic bag. Work the stiffener into the stitches by squeezing and kneading the bag thoroughly, adding more stiffener as needed. Press out the excess air and close the bag. Allow the sealed bag to rest for at least 15 minutes.

4. Remove the crochet from the bag, squeezing out the excess stiffener. Stretch the wet piece and shape it on the board or base shape as shown, fitting the piece to the pattern dimensions and blotting excess stiffener with a soft cloth as you work.

5. Using rustproof straight pins, pin the crochet to the board or base shape. Let it dry completely before removing it.

Needle Pointer

For doilies and other items that need just a little soft shaping, dampen them with spray starch before pinning them to the shaping board.

Popcorn Filet Afghan

Popcorn stitches and filet panels form interesting textures in this rich red throw. Choose washable yarn for lasting beauty.

Skill Level

Easy

Size

43" x 66" plus fringe

Materials

42 oz. of burgundy 4-ply worsted-weight yarn

Size H crochet hook, or size needed to obtain gauge

Gauge

4 sc = 1"

Instructions

Note: To make popcorn stitch (pc), 5 dc in stitch, remove hook from loop, insert hook in 1st dc, draw dropped loop through, ch 1.

Row 1: Ch 146, sc in 2nd ch from hook, sc in each ch across, ch 1, turn.

Row 2: Sc in each st across, ch 3, turn.

Row 3: Dc in next 2 sts, *ch 1, sk next st, pc in next st, sk next st, dc in next 3 sts, **(ch 1, sk next st, dc in next st) 5 times, ch 1, sk next st, dc in next 3 sts, repeat from ** once; repeat from * 3 times, ch 1, sk next st, pc in next st, sk next st, dc in last 3 sts, ch 1, turn.

Row 4: Sc in each st across, ch 3, turn.

Row 5: Dc in next 2 sts, *ch 1, sk next st, pc in next st, sk next st, dc in next 3 sts, **(ch 1, sk next st, dc in next st) 2 times, ch 1, sk next st, pc in next st, sk next st, dc in next st, ch 1, sk next st, dc in next st, ch 1, sk next st, dc in next 3 sts, repeat from ** once; repeat from * 3 times, ch 1, sk next st, pc in next st, sk next st, dc in last 3 sts, ch 1, turn.

Row 6: Sc in each st across, ch 3, turn.

Row 7: Dc in next 2 sts, *ch 1, sk next st, pc in next st, sk next st, dc in next 3 sts, **ch 1, (sk next st, dc in next st, ch 1, sk next st, pc in next st) 2 times, sk next st, dc in next st, ch 1, sk next st, dc in next 3 sts, repeat from ** once; repeat from * 3 times, ch 1, sk next st, pc in next st, sk next st, dc in last 3 sts, ch 1, turn.

Row 8: Sc in each st across, ch 3, turn.

Row 9: Dc in next 2 sts, *(ch 1, sk next st, pc in next st, sk next st, dc in next 3 sts, **ch 1, sk next st, pc in next st, sk next st, dc in next st, (ch 1, sk next st, dc in next st) 2 times, ch 1, sk next st, pc in next st, sk next st, dc in next 3 sts, repeat from ** once; repeat from * 3 times, ch 1, sk next st, pc in next st, sk next st, dc in last 3 sts, ch 1, turn.

Row 10: Sc in each st across, ch 3, turn.

Rows 11 to 156: Repeat rows 3 to 10 consecutively. Fasten off.

Fringe

For each fringe, cut three strands, each 14" long. Follow the instructions on pages 58 and 59 for attaching fringe to the afghan.

Something Different

To make a tassel, wind the yarn around a 6" piece of cardboard 40 times. Cut one end as for fringe, tie a separate piece of yarn around the top to secure, and wind another piece of yarn around the strands about 1" down from the top.

Wild Irish Rose Doily

A single rose motif graces the center of this stunning yet simple doily design.

Skill Level

Intermediate

Size

10" across

Materials

30 yards of size 10 crochet cotton
Size 5 steel crochet hook

Gauge

10 sc = 1"

Instructions

Rnd 1: Ch 10, join with sl st in 1st ch to form ring. Ch 1, 17 sc in ring, join with sl st in 1st sc.

Rnd 2: Ch 6, sk 2 sc, hdc in next sc, (ch 4 [ch-lp made], sk 2 sc, hdc in next sc) 4 times, ch 4, sl st in 2nd ch of ch-4 (6 ch-lps).

Rnd 3: Sl st in ch-lp, ch 1, (sc, hdc, 3 dc, hdc, sc) in each ch-lp around, join with sl st in 1st sc.

Rnd 4: Sl st into back of joining sl st on Rnd 2, *ch 5, keeping thread at back of work, sl st in back of next hdc on Rnd 2, repeat from * 4 times, ch 5, sl st in same st as 1st sl st.

Rnd 5: Sl st in ch-lp, ch 1, (sc, hdc, 5 dc, hdc, sc) in each ch-lp around, join with sl st in 1st sc.

Rnd 6: Sl st into back of sl st on Rnd 4, *ch 6, keeping thread at back of work, sl st in back of next sl st in Rnd 4, repeat from * around.

Rnd 7: Sl st in ch-lp, ch 1, (sc, hdc, 7 dc, hdc, sc) in each ch-lp around, join with sl st in 1st sc.

Rnd 8: Sl st into back of sl st on Rnd 6, *ch 7, keeping thread at back of work, sl st in back of next sl st on Rnd 6, repeat from * around.

Rnd 9: Ch 1, sc in same st, (ch 5, sk 2 ch, sc in next ch, ch 5, sk 1 ch, sc in next ch, ch 5, sk 2 ch, sc in next sl st) around, ch 2, dc in 1st sc (18 ch-lps).

Rnd 10: Ch 1, sc in same lp, (ch 5, sc in next lp) around, ending with ch 2, dc in 1st sc.

Rnds 11 and 12: Ch 1, sc in same lp, (ch 6, sc in next lp) around, ending with ch 3, dc in 1st sc.

Rnds 13 and 14: Ch 1, sc in same lp, (ch 7, sc in next lp) around, ending with ch 3, tr in 1st sc.

Rnd 15: Ch 3, 2 dc in same lp, *ch 3, sc in next sc, ch 3, 3 dc in next lp, repeat from * around, ending with ch 3, sl st in top of ch 3.

Rnd 16: Ch 3, dc in next 2 dc, dc in ch-3 lp, *ch 5, dc in next ch-3 lp, dc in each of next 3 dc, dc in next ch-3 lp, repeat from * around, ending with dc in last ch-3 lp, sl st in top of ch 3.

Rnd 17: Sl st in next 2 dc, ch 1, sc in same dc, *ch 3, 5 dc in next ch-5 lp, ch 3, sk 2 dc, sc in next dc, repeat from * around, ending with dc in 1st sc.

Rnd 18: Ch 8, *dc in next ch-3 lp, dc in each of next 5 dc, dc in next ch-3 lp, ch 5, repeat from * around, ending with sl st in 3rd ch of ch-8.

Rnd 19: Ch 6, *sc in next ch-5 lp, ch 3, dc in each of next 7 dc, ch 3, repeat from * around, ending with sl st in 3rd ch of ch 6.

Rnd 20: Sl st across ch-3 to sc, ch 1, sc in same sc, *ch 5, sk 2 dc, dc in each of next 3 dc, ch 5, sc in next sc, repeat from * around, ending with ch 2, dc in 1st sc.

Rnd 21: Ch 1, sc in same lp, *ch 5, sk 1 dc, sc in next dc, ch 5, sc in next ch-5 lp, repeat from * around, ending with ch 2, dc in 1st sc.

Rnd 22: Ch 1, sc in same lp, (ch 5, sc in next lp) around, ending with ch 2, dc in 1st sc.

Rnds 23 and 24: Ch 1, sc in same lp, (ch 6, sc in next lp) around, ending with ch 3, dc in 1st sc.

Rnd 25: ch 1, sc in same lp, (ch 6, sl st in 3rd ch from hook [picot made], ch 3, sc in next lp) around, ending with sl st in 1st sc. End off.

Something Different

Make an elegant shade pull by crocheting the rose through Rnd 7. Then chain twice the length needed for the shade pull; double the chain and sew the end to the rose. Attach the loop to the shade with small whipstitches.

Angelic Baby Dress

Crocheted with washable cotton yarn, this lacy baby dress is the perfect shower gift. Make button-trimmed booties to match for a beautiful set.

Skill Level

Challenging

Size

Dress: 24" at chest, 11½" long; fits size 3 to 6 months

Materials

7 oz. of white sport weight cotton yarn

Size 0 crochet hook, or size needed to obtain gauge

Five ⅜" white shank buttons

½ yard of ¼" satin ribbon

Gauge

5 sc = 1"; 5 rows = 1"

Instructions

Bodice

Row 1: Ch 60, sc in 2nd ch from hook and in next 9 ch, (ch 1, sc in next 14 ch) 3 times, ch 1, sc in next 7 ch, turn.

Row 2: Ch 1, sc in next 7 sc, *(sc, ch 1, sc) in next ch-1 sp, sc in 14 sc, repeat from * 2 times, (sc, ch 1, sc) in next ch-1 sp, sc in next 10 sc, turn.

Rows 3 to 10: Ch 1, *sc in each sc to next ch-1 sp, (sc, ch 1, sc in ch-1 sp), repeat from * three times, sc in each remaining sc, turn.

Row 11: Ch 1, sc in each sc to next ch-1 sp, (sc, ch 1, sc) in ch-1 sp, sc in each sc to next ch-1 sp, sc in ch-1 sp, ch 8, sc in next ch-1 sp, sc in each sc to next ch-1 sp, ch 8, sl st in 1st ch-1 sp made, end off. Join yarn in ch-1 sp at beginning of last ch-8, sc in ch-1 sp, sc in each remaining sc. End off.

Skirt

Rnd 1: Join in any st, 2 sc in same st, sc in next st, 2 sc in next st, (ch 5, 2 sc in next st, sc in next st, 2 sc in next st) around, ch 5, join with sl st in first sc. (It may be necessary to skip one or two sts at end of rnd to make rnd come out even).

Rnd 2: Sl st in next sc, ch 1, sc in same sc, sc in each of next 2 sc, (ch 3, sc in ch-5 lp, ch 3, sk 1 sc, sc in next 3 sc) around, ch 3, sc in last ch-5 lp, ch 3, join with sl st in 1st sc.

Rnd 3: Sl st in next sc, ch 1, sc in same sc, ch 3, sc in ch-3 lp, sc in next sc, sc in next ch-3 lp, ch 3, (sk 1 sc, sc in next sc, ch 3, sc in next ch-3 lp, sc in next sc, sc in next ch-3 lp, ch 3) around, join with sl st in 1st sc.

Rnd 4: 2 sl st in next ch-3 lp, ch 1, sc in same lp, sc in next 3 sc, sc in next ch-3 lp, (ch 5, sc in next ch-3 lp, sc in next 3 sc, sc in next ch-3 lp) around, join with sl st in 1st sc.

Repeat Rnds 2 to 4 until the dress is about 11" long, ending with Rnd 3. Do not fasten off.

Shell Edging

Rnd 1: Sl st into next sc, ch 3, 4 dc in same st, sc in next ch-3 lp, 5 dc in next sc, sc in next ch-3 lp, (sk 1 sc, 5 dc in next sc, sc in next ch-3 lp, 5 dc in next sc, sc in next ch-3 lp) around, join with sl st in top of ch-3. Fasten off.

Armhole Shell Edging

Lap the short end (front) of the shoulder over the long end (back); sew three overlapping stitches together at armhole edge.

Rnd 1: Join at bottom back of bodice, sk 1 st, 5 dc in next st, (sk 1 st, sc in next st, sk 1 sts, 5 dc in next st) across, fasten off.

Repeat for the remaining armhole edge.

Sew three buttons across the back bodice edge at the shoulder; to button, push the buttons through the stitches.

Tie the ribbon in a bow; sew firmly to the bodice.

Booties

Row 1: Beginning at the instep, ch 7, sc in 2nd ch from hook and in each ch across, turn.

Rows 2 to 7: Ch 1, sc in each sc across, turn.

Rnd 8: Ch 22, sl st in end of same row, ch 1, working in end of rows, sc in each row across, sc in each sc across toe, sc in end of each row along side, sc in each ch around, join with sl st in 1st sc.

Rnds 9 to 11: Ch 1, sc in each sc around, join with sl st in 1st sc.

Rnd 12: For the sole, ch 1, working in back lps only, sc in next 7 sc, sc next 2 sts tog, sc in next 3 sc, sc next 2 sts tog, sc in next 15 sc, sc next 2 sts tog, sc in next 2 sc, sc next 2 sts tog, sc in remaining sc around, join with sl st in 1st sc.

Rnd 13: Ch 1, sc in next 7 sc, sc next 2 sts tog, sc in next sc, sc next 2 sts tog, sc in next 15 sc, sc next 2 sts tog, sc in next sc, sc in remaining sc around, join with sl st in 1st sc.

Rnd 14: Ch 1, sc in next 6 sc, sc next 2 sts tog, sc in next sc, sc next 2 sts tog, sc in next 13 sc, sc next 2 sts tog, sc in next sc, sc next 2 sts tog, sc in remaining sc around, join, end off.

Flatten the sole and sew the center seam.

Bootie Straps

Row 1: With the right side facing and the instep to your right, working in free lps of ch, join with sl st in 4th ch from instep, ch 1, sc in next sc, turn.

Rows 2 to 14: Ch 1, sc in each sc, turn.

Fasten off.

For the other bootie strap, join the yarn at the opposite side of the instep.

Sew one button firmly to each bootie, sewing through the end of both the strap and the bootie.

Cross-Stitch

The simple act of crossing one tiny stitch over the other forms the basis for counted cross-stitch. This stitch, when rendered in delicate shadings of six-strand floss and other fibers, creates works of art that are no less gorgeous, no less subtle, and no less satisfying than grand masterpiece paintings!

The stitches are few and simple to learn, but the possibilities of counted cross-stitch are endless, making it one of the most popular forms of needlework in the world.

A wealth of fabrics, from homespun to luxurious, along with fibers of every hue, are available for counted cross-stitch.

Equipment

Many fabrics, stitching fibers, and accessories are made specially for stitching counted cross-stitch. These quality materials help create beautiful stitched pieces that will last for generations.

Evenweave Fabric

Evenweave fabric has equally spaced horizontal and vertical threads of the same thickness. This allows the cross-stitches to form neat, even squares. To determine a fabric's thread count, count the number of threads per inch.

Linen

Made from fibers of the flax plant, linen is strong and durable. Linen comes in a variety of beautiful colors and stitch counts from 18 to 50. The weave of linen is less even than the weave of Aida cloth, and each cross-stitch is worked over two threads.

Aida

Manufactured specifically for cross-stitch, Aida cloth is available in many colors and stitch counts from 6 to 18. Aida cloth is especially easy to work with because the holes are clearly visible for inserting the needle with each stitch.

Hardanger

Hardanger is a 22-count fabric that is woven with evenly spaced double threads. Designs on this fabric are most often stitched over one double thread, although they can be stitched over two double threads for an 11-count design.

Hoops

Even though cross-stitch can be worked without any type of hoop or frame, most stitchers enjoy the stability a hoop gives. Hoops come in many sizes, in both round and oval.

Waste Canvas

When basted onto a garment or other fabric, waste canvas forms a grid for counted cross-stitch that is removed after all stitching is complete. This loosely woven canvas comes in several thread counts and has a distinctive blue-and-white weave.

Perforated Paper and Plastic

Perforated paper and plastic look almost identical. Both have holes evenly spaced to form a 14-count grid and come in a rainbow of colors. Either is ideal for stitching items that require cutting out because the edges require no finishing.

Needles

Size 24 or 26 blunt tapestry needles are the perfect size for stitching on most cross-stitch fabric or perforated paper. A sharp-pointed crewel needle is required when working with waste canvas.

Frames

Frames are easier on the fabric than hoops and come in many sizes and shapes. Once fabric is mounted in a frame, it doesn't have to be removed until stitching is complete. Scroll frames hold the fabric rolled at the top and bottom.

Seed Beads

Seed beads can be added to any 11- or 14-count cross-stitch design, using one bead per stitch.

Scissors

Small, sharp scissors are essential for cutting floss and removing mistakes. For cutting fabrics, use your best dressmaking shears.

Stitching Fibers

Six-strand floss comes in hundreds of colors and is available in silk, rayon, and cotton. Pearl cotton comes in #3, #5, #8, and #12, with #3 being the thickest. Flower thread has a matte finish and a tight twist. No ply separation is needed. Blending filament is a fine, shiny fiber that can be used alone or combined with other thread. Ribbon thread, a narrow embroidery ribbon, comes in a large number of colors in satin and metallic. Metallic braids come in fine, medium, and heavy and are available in dozens of colors.

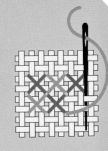

Needle Pointer

The perfect needle for cross-stitch is small enough not to widen the gap between the fabric threads as it passes through. It should glide through quickly and easily, requiring almost no effort from the stitcher. If your finger gets sore from pushing the needle, your needle may be too big.

Getting Started

Aida cloth is the preferred stitching fabric for beginners because the holes are clearly visible. A cross-stitch over one square of Aida cloth is the basis for many beautiful projects. Place the fabric in a hoop or frame before beginning.

Cross-Stitch Basics

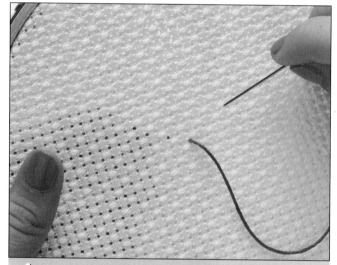

1 To begin stitching, bring the needle up from the underside of the fabric at the starting point, holding about 1" of the thread behind the fabric. Stitch over this end with your first few stitches to secure.

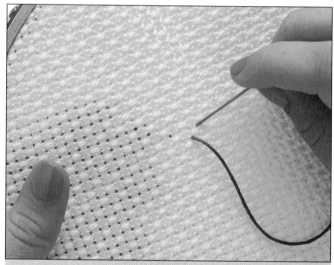

2 To create the bottom half of a cross-stitch, insert the needle in the opposite diagonal point of one square on the fabric; pull the needle through from the bottom, leaving the surface thread taut.

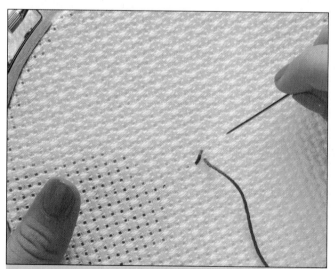

3 To make the top half of a cross-stitch, bring the needle up through the fabric again at the corner point of the same square.

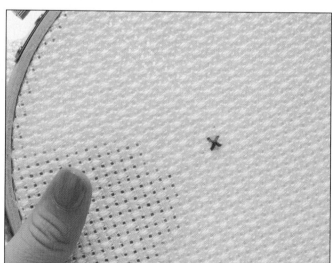

4 To complete a cross-stitch, insert the needle in the remaining corner of the square and pull the needle through to the underside, forming an X.

To avoid embroidery hoop marks, be sure to remove the fabric from the hoop when you're not stitching and smooth out any wrinkles and creases. For maximum protection, mount a piece of muslin or similar fabric on top of the cross-stitch fabric before placing it in the hoop. Carefully cut a circle out of the muslin about 1" smaller than the hoop. Secure the cross-stitch fabric in the hoop with the muslin circle sandwiched in between. This protects the cross-stitch fabric from hoop marks and soil from your hands.

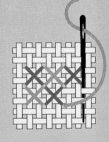

CROSS-STITCH

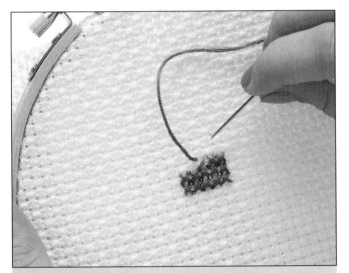

5 In order for a finished cross-stitched piece to have a smooth look, it's important to make all of the top crosses on the stitches face in the same direction.

Needle Pointer

To determine a fabric's thread count, count the number of threads per inch. If you will be stitching over two threads, the stitch count will be half that number. For example, stitching over two threads on 28-count fabric gives the same results as stitching over one thread on 14-count fabric.

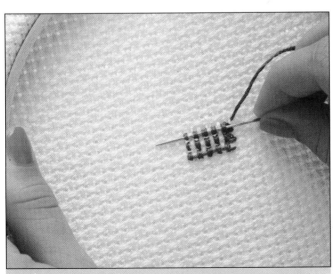

6 To finish a thread, run the needle under the back side of several stitches; carefully pull the needle and thread through without distorting the stitches on the right side. Clip the thread.

Preparing to Stitch

Careful preparation of your fabric will help get your cross-stitch project off to a good start. Press the fabric to remove creases and wrinkles. Before making the first stitch, you must consider how large to cut the fabric. If your design is a pillow or other project that requires a large unstitched area, be sure to leave plenty of fabric around the edges of the design. For a small project, about 3" around all of the edges should be sufficient.

Preparing Fabric

1. Determine the dimensions of a stitched design on any fabric by using this formula: the number of stitches across the design area divided by the number of threads per inch of fabric equals the size of the fabric in inches.

2. After determining the design area size, measure the fabric carefully as shown, then cut evenly along the horizontal and vertical threads.

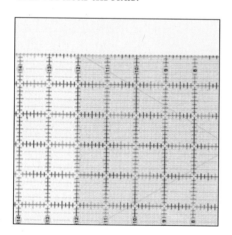

3. To prevent the fabric from raveling as you stitch and to give the cross-stitched piece a finished edge, hand overcast or machine zigzag along all edges as shown above (top center). Edges may also be treated with a fray preventer.

4. Find the center of the fabric by folding it first horizontally and then vertically, and mark the center with a pin or a small stitch as shown. Find the center of the graph by counting the squares or following the arrows. Position your fabric in the hoop or frame, centering the marked center point.

Preparing Floss

1. To prepare six-strand floss for stitching, the strands must be separated and the desired number of plies recombined. Cut the floss in 14" to 18" lengths. Hold all six strands together in one hand and pull one strand straight out with the other hand as shown above (top right). Place the number of strands needed together, with the ends even, and smooth with your fingers.

2. If the floss requires more smoothing after recombining, pull the strands across the surface of a damp sponge as shown.

3. Because red floss tones can bleed, soak the floss in a solution of 1 tablespoon of white vinegar and 1 cup of water as shown. Allow the floss to air dry.

Working from Graphs

Graphs, or charts, are made up of colors and symbols to indicate the exact color, type, and placement of each stitch. Some cross-stitch graphs are black and white with symbols only, while others are color only, and still others are a combination of color and symbols. Each square on the graph represents one cross-stitch over one square on Aida cloth or two or more threads on evenweave.

Each cross-stitch graph has a color key indicating which color floss and what type of stitch corresponds with each color or symbol. Most color keys have abbreviated headings for cross-stitch (x),

Stitching Solution

To make stitching easier, try marking a grid on the fabric with a water-soluble marking pen. Test first to make sure the ink will disappear in water, then mark a grid equal to the bold 10-count lines on the graph. If you would prefer not to mark the fabric or if the fabric is dark, baste along the lines instead. Aida cloth is available with a removable thread grid for easy stitching.

quarter cross-stitch (¼x), half cross-stitch (½x), three-quarter cross-stitch (¾x), French knot (Fr), and backstitch (B'st). Many color keys include floss brands DMC, Anchor (ANC), and J. & P. Coats (JPC). Abbreviations for other stitching fibers or beads may also be included.

Many graphs are too large to fit on one page and must be divided over two or more pages. In this case, an area of the design is shaded on one or both pages. The shading indicates the areas of the pattern that overlap to form the complete design. The shaded areas are to be stitched only once.

Needle Case

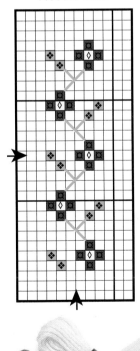

Color Key

X	DMC	ANC	JPC	COLOR
▣	550	102	4107	Darkest Amethyst
❖	367	217	6018	Pistachio Green Dk.
◊	3078	292	2292	Yellow Cream

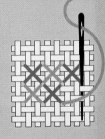

CROSS-STITCH

Needle Pointer

To work a single, isolated cross-stitch, leave a 2" to 3" tail at the beginning and the end of the stitch. Weave the tails through the back of the stitch; tie the tails in a square knot and trim the ends.

Starting and Stopping

Mount your fabric in a hoop or frame as desired. Begin stitching the center of the design in the center of the fabric.

In addition to stitching over the starting thread as shown on page 70, the waste knot and loop stitch methods are often used to secure the starting thread.

Waste Knot

1. Make a knot in the end of the floss. Insert the needle into the fabric from the front several stitches over from where your first cross-stitch will be.

2. Come up at the position of the first stitch and stitch the first few cross-stitches over the floss end as shown.

3. Leave the waste knot in place until the floss end is secure, then cut off the knot.

Loop Stitch

1. If you will be stitching with an even number of plies, cut the floss to twice the desired length. Separate the plies, then take half the number of plies needed and fold them in half.

2. Thread the loose ends through the eye of a needle.

3. Bring the needle up from the back of the fabric at the first stitch, leaving the loop underneath the fabric.

4. Take the needle down through the fabric and through the loop as shown; pull to secure.

Ending a Thread

1. To end a thread, run the needle under several stitches at the back of your work, then clip the floss end.

2. When you finish a section of color and move to a new section of the same color, do not carry the thread across more than ½" of an unstitched area. Instead, end the thread and begin stitching again in the new area.

Neater Stitching

For even stitches, maintain uniform tension as you work. If the floss becomes twisted, turn your work over so the needle hangs down from the work, allowing the twisted floss to unwind.

Your work will be neater if you always try to make each stitch by coming up in an empty, or unoccupied, hole and going down in an occupied hole.

When moving from one section of a color to another section of the same color across a stitched area, run the needle under the back side of the stitches.

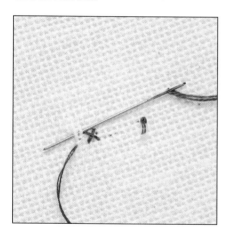

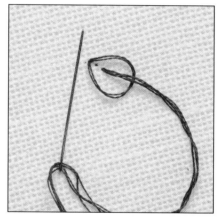

Stitching Solution

To make stitching go faster, try threading several needles at once. Keep the threaded needles handy along with their corresponding skeins of floss, so when one of your needles runs out of thread, you can pick up another and keep right on stitching. Multiple needles can be threaded with the same color for large areas of a single color or with different colors for shaded areas. Be sure to keep track of floss numbers for the extra threaded needles.

Methods of Stitching

With the stab method, the needle and floss are brought completely through the fabric twice with each cross-stitch. With this method, fabric can be pulled tightly in a hoop or a frame, and stitches on Aida are generally more uniform and perfect than with the sewing method.

The sewing method is the preferred method for stitching on linen and some other even-weaves, but it can also be used on Aida. All work is done from the front of the fabric. Stitches on linen are prettiest when worked with the sewing method and no hoop.

Stab Method

1. For the first half of the stitch, bring the needle up from the back of the fabric to the front. Then take the needle down, and reach underneath and pull it completely through to the underside.

2. For the second half of the stitch, bring the needle back up through the fabric at the next point, and take it back down at the next point, reaching underneath and pulling it through as before.

3. If you use a freestanding frame or hoop, try keeping one hand on top of the work and one underneath. See "Getting Started" on page 70 for detailed photographs of this method.

Sewing Method

Begin stitching with the waste knot or loop stitch method. Make cross-stitches as if you were hand sewing, with the needle going from the front to the back to the front of the fabric in one motion with each stitch as shown.

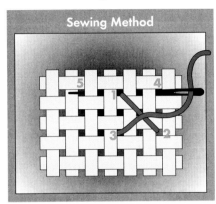

Sewing Method

Each cross-stitch may be completed individually as shown, or the bottom half of several stitches may be completed first.

Do not pull the thread too tightly, or the stitches and the fabric will become distorted. A hoop or a frame may be used with this method, but keep in mind that the fabric cannot be pulled taut.

Working on Evenweave

1. To make the first stitch on linen or other evenweave fabric, bring the needle up where a vertical thread crosses a horizontal thread as shown (1).

2. Take the needle down at the opposite diagonal point, again where a vertical thread crosses a horizontal thread as shown (2).

Each cross-stitch may be completed individually, or the bottom half of several stitches may be worked first.

Working on Evenweave

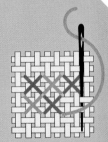

Needle Pointer

Floss comes in hundreds of colors, but even more variations can be created for extra-subtle shading with a technique called "blended needle." This is accomplished by combining of two or more different-color strands of floss in a needle.

Stitches

One reason counted cross-stitch is so popular is because it's easy to learn. There are only a few basic stitches in counted cross-stitch. Cross-stitches are generally used to work a pattern, and embroidery stitches are added to accent and embellish the cross-stitched design.

Cross-Stitches

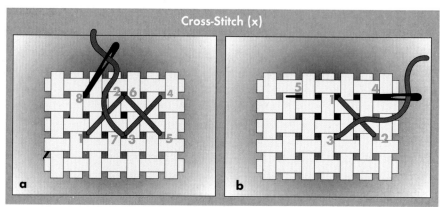

There are two methods for making basic cross-stitches. For the first method, make the bottom half of more than one cross-stitch, then make the top half of each stitch (a). For the second method, complete both the bottom and top halves of each cross-stitch before beginning the next cross-stitch (b).

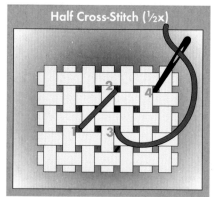

To make half cross-stitches, stitch the bottom half of complete cross-stitches. Half cross-stitches may slant in either direction.

To make quarter cross-stitches on Aida, pierce the center of the Aida squares with the needle to create stitches that are a quarter of complete cross-stitches. Quarter cross-stitches may slant in any direction.

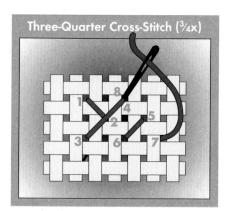

To make three-quarter cross-stitches, combine half cross-stitches with quarter cross-stitches. Three-quarter cross-stitches may slant in any direction.

Stitching Solution

To add extra pizzazz to your cross-stitched design, try adding embroidery in fuzzy, shiny, or metallic fibers. These interesting, luxurious threads are fun to use, and they add beautiful texture to a cross-stitched piece. When working with specialty fibers on clothing or other washable items, be sure to read the cleaning instructions on the fiber packaging.

Embroidery Stitches

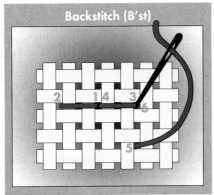

Backstitch (B'st)

Backstitches are generally worked with fewer strands than cross-stitches. Backstitches add outlines and other thin lines, and they are worked after all cross-stitches have been completed.

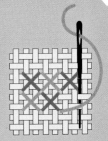

Needle Pointer

To make the needle glide through the fabric more smoothly, push it through a used dryer fabric-softener sheet occasionally as you stitch.

Lazy Daisy

Lazy daisy stitches are embroidery stitches that are often used in cross-stitch to create flower petals and other details.

French Knot (Fr)

French knots, usually the last stitches worked in cross-stitch, add interest and texture.

Techniques

Personalize a cross-stitch design with letters like the ones below, or add pretty beads for a charming touch. When the stitching is complete, careful cleaning and finishing will make your cross-stitched project look its very best.

Personalizing

When planning a personalized design, use uppercase and lower-case letters together, or use letters of only one case as desired. For large, monogram-style letters that are part of the design, choose colors that coordinate with the design's motif. Choose a neutral color for adding your initials and date as a signature.

1. Plan the placement of your letters carefully. Using graph paper, carefully count from the graph to the paper, centering the letters on the paper. Remember that the size of the design is determined by the fabric thread count, not the size of the graph paper.

2. When you are happy with your planned design, stitch it using the same number of strands of floss for cross-stitches as the remainder of the design. Use fewer strands for backstitches, using the same number of strands of floss as the backstitches in the remainder of the design.

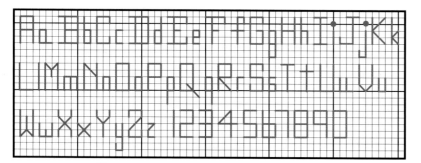

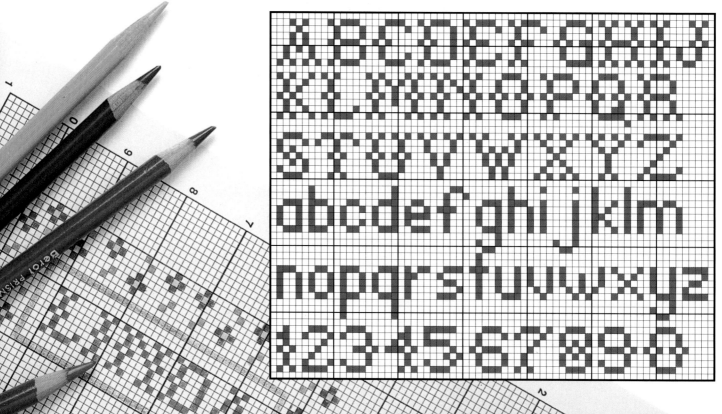

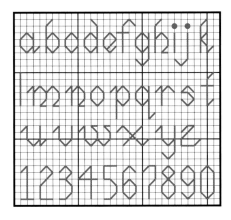

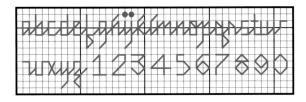

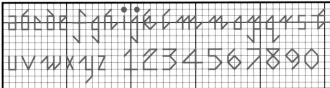

Stitching Solution

Add a pretty border design to a stitched name or verse, and create perfect corners with a little easy planning. Draw or photocopy four copies of the border design, the cut out the border strips. Arrange the strips into a frame shape around the lettering, making it smaller or larger as desired and folding and mitering the corners to create a pleasing pattern. When you are pleased with the design, tape the strips together.

Needle Pointer

To make beads easy to pick up for stitching, wrap a piece of masking tape, sticky side out, around your left index finger. Pick up several beads at a time with your taped finger, and pick the beads off the tape with your needle as needed while stitching.

Seed Beads

A variety of colorful, pearlized and metallic-finish beads are manufactured specially for use with counted cross-stitch. These beads add beautiful dimension and sparkle to a stitched design, and they are fun to use.

1. Use a small needle and thread or floss to match the fabric. Knot the thread at the beginning and end of the beaded section for security, especially if you are adding beads to clothing.

2. Stitching in the same direction as the bottom half of a cross-stitch, bring the needle up at the bottom of the stitch, thread a bead onto the needle, and take the needle down at the top of the stitch as shown.

Seed Beads

Finishing

Before framing or sewing into a pillow or other project, almost every cross-stitched piece benefits from a gentle hand washing to remove surface dirt, hoop marks, and hand oils. If you prefer, cross-stitched pieces may also be dry-cleaned. Never press your work before cleaning, as this will set hoop marks and soils that should be removed.

Cleaning

1. Use a gentle soap such as baby shampoo, mild white laundry soap flakes, or gentle white dishwashing liquid and a large, clean bowl or sink. If you prefer to use a liquid product made for hand washing, make sure the product you choose contains no chlorine bleach. Make a cool sudsy solution in the bowl or sink, and fill another bowl or sink with plain cool water.

2. Soak the stitched piece in the sudsy water for five to ten minutes. Then gently squeeze the suds through the fabric several times as shown without rubbing or twisting it.

3. Rinse the piece several times in fresh cool water until no suds remain. If floss colors run or fade, continue to rinse until the water becomes clear.

4. Remove the fabric from the water and lay it on a soft, white towel as shown.

5. Smooth the fabric on the towel, blot any excess water, and roll the piece in the towel, pressing gently as shown.

Pressing Dry and Blocking

1. Remove the damp piece from the towel and place it face down on a dry, white towel. To prevent color stains, it's important to keep the stitched piece flat, not allowing the stitched areas to touch other areas of the fabric.

2. Smooth the fabric flat with your hands and use a ruler or T-square to help make sure the edges are straight and the corners are square.

3. Cover the back of the stitched piece with a damp press cloth and press with a dry iron as shown. Press until the cross-stitch fabric is completely dry. Allow the stitched piece to lie in this position until it is cool.

Framing

For projects you wish to keep well preserved for future generations, acid-free matting and framing materials are the best choice. Cross-stitched pieces can also be mounted on cardboard, mat board, foam core board, or adhesive mat boards designed specially for mounting needlework. If you prefer a padded look, cut quilt batting to fit a mounting board.

Self-Stick Mounting Boards

1. Center the blocked cross-stitched piece over the mounting board of your choice, with quilt batting between if desired. Leaving 1½" to 3" around all edges, trim any excess fabric.

2. To use a needlework mounting board with a self-stick surface, smooth the cross-stitched piece onto the board until the fabric is taut and the edges are smooth and even. Turn the board right side down and smooth the fabric to the back, mitering the corners and trimming the fabric as needed.

Other Types of Mounting Boards

1. Place the finished cross-stitched piece faceup over the board, centering the design. Turn the fabric and the board face-down, and turn up the corners as shown. Smooth the fabric, check to see if the design is still centered on the front, then secure the edges. Tape or glue the corners in place, then turn in the ends and sides as shown.

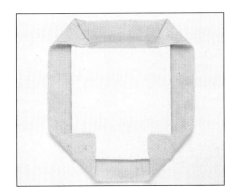

2. To secure the edges at the back of the mat board, hand sew back and forth across the fabric folds on the back or glue or tape the fabric to the board as shown.

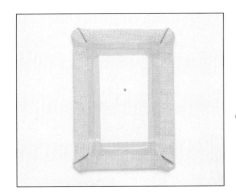

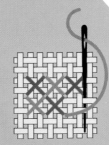

Needle Pointer

When stitching on light-color fabric, it is helpful to place a dark-color cloth on your lap and vice versa.

Sampler Sewing Accessories

The charm of a pretty cross-stitch sampler accents a beautiful and practical set of sewing accessories.

Easy

Size

Sampler is 6" x 8"; pincushion is 3½" x 4½", not including fringe; needle case is 2⅛" x 2⅞", not including fringe.

Materials

11-count natural Aida: 10" x 12" piece for sampler; two 6" x 7" pieces for pincushion; one 3½" x 5" piece for needle case

Six-strand embroidery floss as indicated in color key

2" x 3" piece of white cotton fabric for needle case

Wooden box with 6" x 8" frame lid and mounting piece

Fiberfill

6" x 8" piece of thick quilt batting

Fabric glue

Instructions

1. For the sampler box, center and stitch the Sampler design on page 84 on the large piece of Aida, using three strands of floss for cross-stitches and one strand for backstitches.

2. Place the quilt batting over the mounting piece in the box lid, and mount the stitched piece in the lid according to the manufacturer's instructions.

3. For the pincushion, center and stitch the Pincushion design on page 85 on one 6" x 7" piece of Aida using three strands of floss for cross-stitches and one strand for backstitches. Hold the wrong side of the stitched piece to the wrong side of the matching piece of Aida. Stitching one square outside the design, backstitch with the darkest purple floss through

both pieces around the design, leaving an opening on one side for stuffing. Stuff with fiberfill; stitch the remaining backstitches.

4. Trim both Aida pieces to 1" beyond the backstitching all around. To make fringe, pull out threads along the top, bottom, and sides to within two threads of the backstitching.

5. For the needle case, center and stitch the Needle Case design on page 85 on one short end of the remaining piece of Aida, placing the design ½" from the edge and using three strands of floss for cross-stitches and one strand for backstitches. Stitching one

square outside the design and stitching around a 25 x 40-square area, backstitch around the outside with the darkest purple floss. Fold the stitched piece in half with the stitched area on top; backstitch through both layers one square from the fold, forming the "spine" for the needle case.

6. Trim the needle case to about ⅜" outside the backstitching. To make fringe, pull out threads from all of the edges to within two threads of the backstitching.

7. Run a tiny bead of glue along the inside of the needle case spine. Fold the white fabric in half; press the fold into the glue.

Something Different

Dress up a plain handkerchief with a fancy cross-stitched monogram. Stitch the letter of your choice in the corner of the handkerchief using embroidery floss and waste canvas.

Sampler

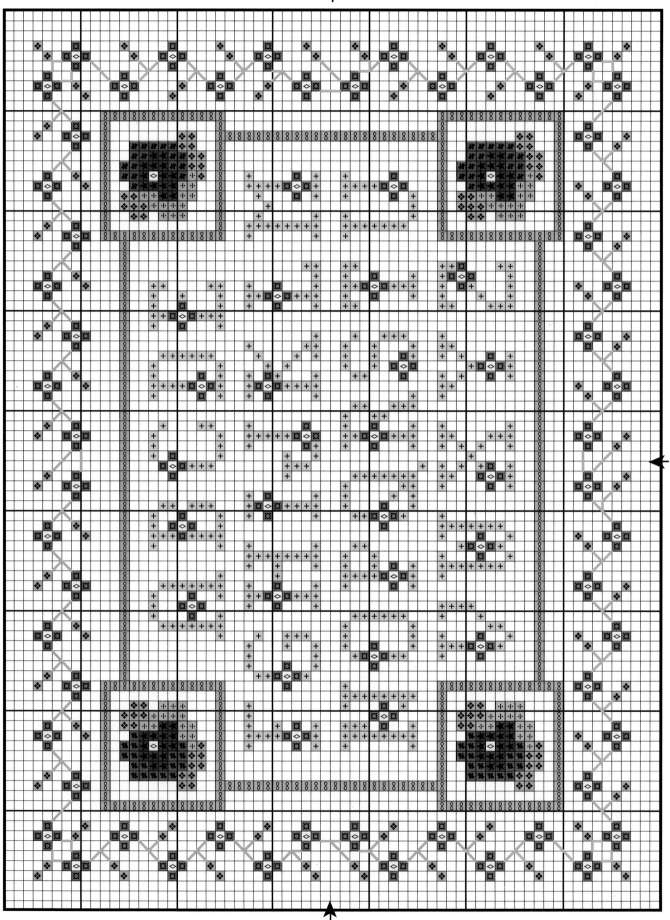

Stitching Solutions

To create a gift in a hurry, combine flowers and sections of borders from this design with letters for a "monogrammed" jar insert, sachet bag, or bookmark.

Needle Case

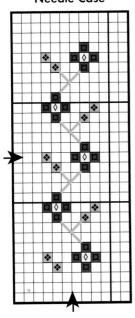

Color Key

X	B'st	DMC	ANC	JPC	COLOR
⬚		550	102	4107	Darkest Amethyst
∞		553	98	4097	Violet Med.
★		221	897	3243	Darkest Victorian Rose
▓		3722	1027	3241	Shell Pink Med.
÷		224	893	32396	Victorian Rose Lt.
❖	╱	367	217	018	Pistachio Green Dk.
+		368	214	6016	Pistachio Green Lt.
◊		3078	292	2292	Yellow Cream

Pincushion

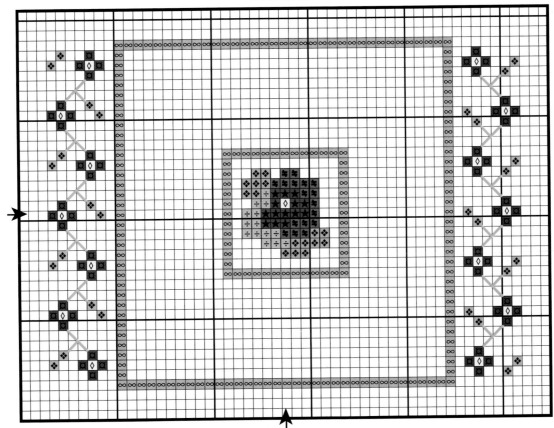

Elegant Bookmark

Stitch a stunning keepsake with a
feminine floral design for
the book lover on your gift list.

Elegant Bookmark

Skill Level

Intermediate

Size

3¾" x 8½"

Materials

3¾" x 8½" prefinished, lace-trimmed 18-count bookmark; or a bookmark made from a 2½" x 7½" piece of white 18-count Aida, a 22" length of ½" white flat lace, a 6" length of ¼" white satin ribbon, and a ½" white lace flower appliqué

Six-strand embroidery floss as indicated in the color key

Instructions

1. If you are using a prefinished bookmark, center and stitch the Elegant Bookmark design using two strands of floss for the cross-stitches and one strand of floss for the backstitches.

2. To make a bookmark, carefully trim the Aida along the lines to 2½" x 7½". Pin the lace around the edges of the Aida, folding it at the corners and lapping the wrong side of the lace slightly over the right side of the Aida. Stitch the lace to the Aida using a narrow zigzag stitch; press. At the corners, topstitch the folded lace so it lies flat. Trim if necessary. Fold the ribbon to form a loop and stitch or glue the ribbon and lace appliqué in place at the center bottom of the bookmark. Cross-stitch the design following Step 1.

Bookmark Design Stitch Count:
25 wide x 81 high

Color Key

X	B'st	DMC	ANC	JPC	COLOR
÷		963	073	3173	Baby Pink
+	╱	36873	068	3088	Mauve Med.
+		685	1028	3089	Darkest Mauve
◊		800	144	7020	Blueberry Pale
∧		799	136	7030	Blueberry Med.
○		798	131	7022	Blueberry Dk.
=		744	301	2293	Tangerine Pale
△		907	255	6001	Parrot Green Lt.
▲		3363	262	6316	Celery Green Med.

Christmas Carousel Horse

This festive carousel horse is a celebration
of the art of cross-stitch! It's a gorgeous
holiday accent for your home.

Skill Level

Challenging

Size

12" x 16" framed

Materials

20" x 24" piece of white 28-count Jobelan

12" x 16" mounting board and frame

Instructions

1. Center and stitch the Christmas Carousel Horse design on pages 90 and 91, stitching over two threads and using two strands of floss for the cross-stitches and one strand of floss for the backstitches, straight stitches, and French knots.

2. Mount the stitched piece on the mounting board and frame as desired. For more information, see "Framing" on page 81.

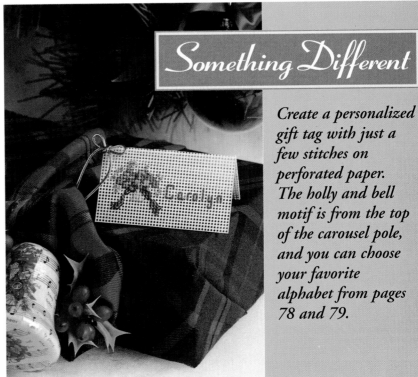

Something Different

Create a personalized gift tag with just a few stitches on perforated paper. The holly and bell motif is from the top of the carousel pole, and you can choose your favorite alphabet from pages 78 and 79.

Stitching Solution

If you would prefer a more subtle, Victorian palette for this carousel horse, choose soft pinks, lavenders, blues, and greens in place of the vivid colors used here. There is no need to change the base, pole, star, and horse colors unless you choose extremely pale colors. To further soften a Victorian color palette, stitch tiny pearl seed beads around the saddle and bridle and on the ornaments.

Christmas Carousel Horse

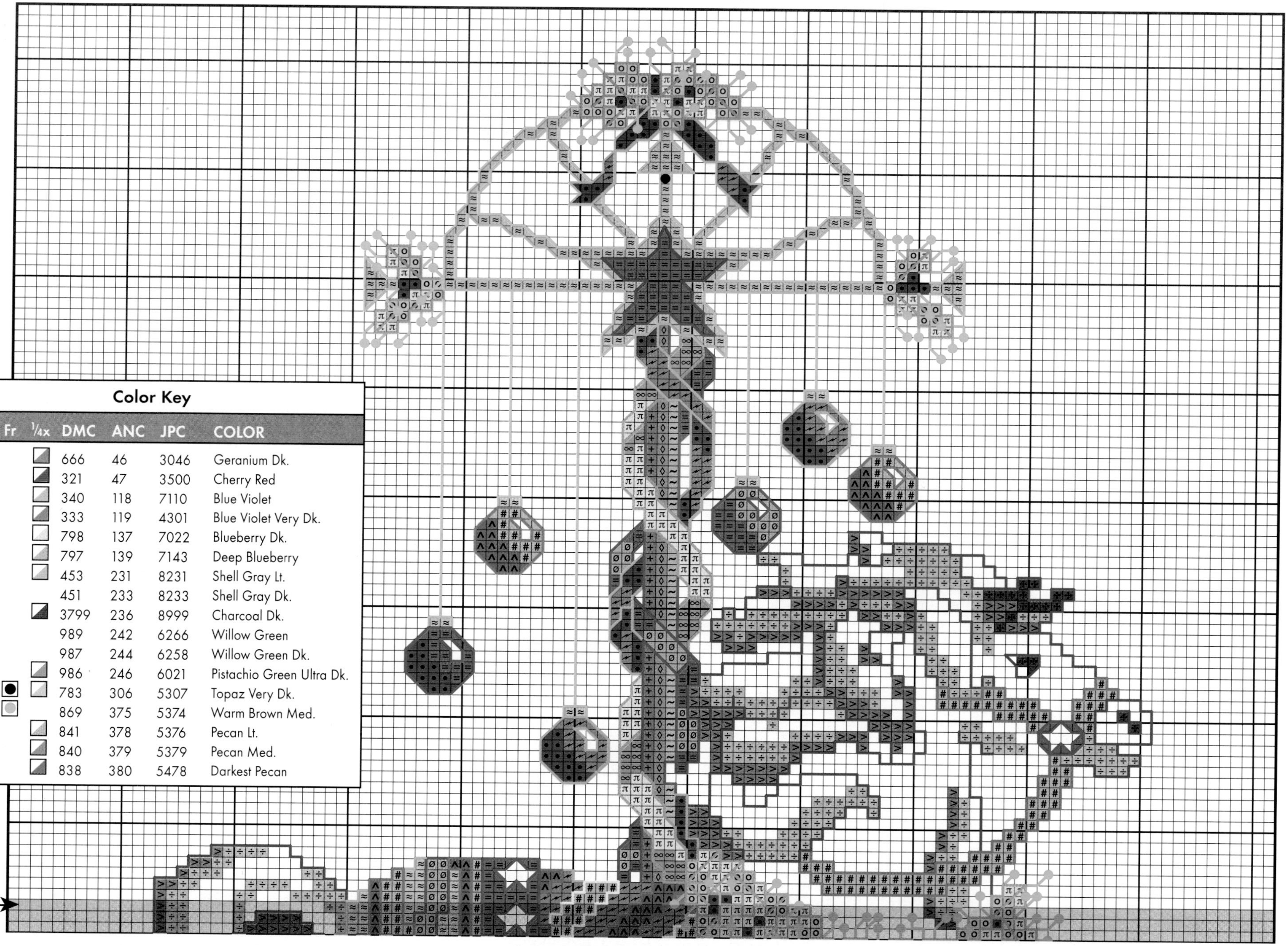

Color Key

X	B'st	Fr	¹/₄x	DMC	ANC	JPC	COLOR
				666	46	3046	Geranium Dk.
				321	47	3500	Cherry Red
				340	118	7110	Blue Violet
				333	119	4301	Blue Violet Very Dk.
				798	137	7022	Blueberry Dk.
				797	139	7143	Deep Blueberry
				453	231	8231	Shell Gray Lt.
				451	233	8233	Shell Gray Dk.
				3799	236	8999	Charcoal Dk.
				989	242	6266	Willow Green
				987	244	6258	Willow Green Dk.
				986	246	6021	Pistachio Green Ultra Dk.
				783	306	5307	Topaz Very Dk.
				869	375	5374	Warm Brown Med.
				841	378	5376	Pecan Lt.
				840	379	5379	Pecan Med.
				838	380	5478	Darkest Pecan

Pattern continues on next page

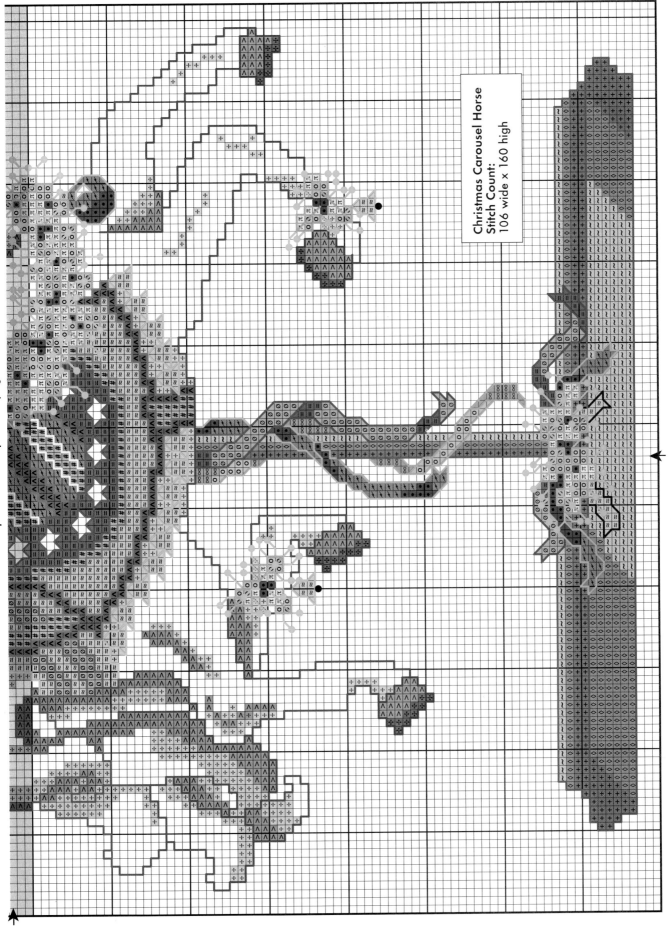

Overlap area is from previous page.

Christmas Carousel Horse
Stitch Count:
106 wide x 160 high

Duplicate Stitch

Duplicate stitch is a quick-to-learn way to add color and design to knitted wearables and other items. The technique is appropriately named because each stitch follows, or duplicates, the path of one knit stitch.

By using a large tapestry needle and colorful six-strand embroidery floss and other fibers, you can achieve the look of expensive knitted-in designs at a fraction of the cost. You don't have to know how to knit to do duplicate stitch—this technique may be worked on hand-knitted or purchased items.

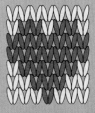

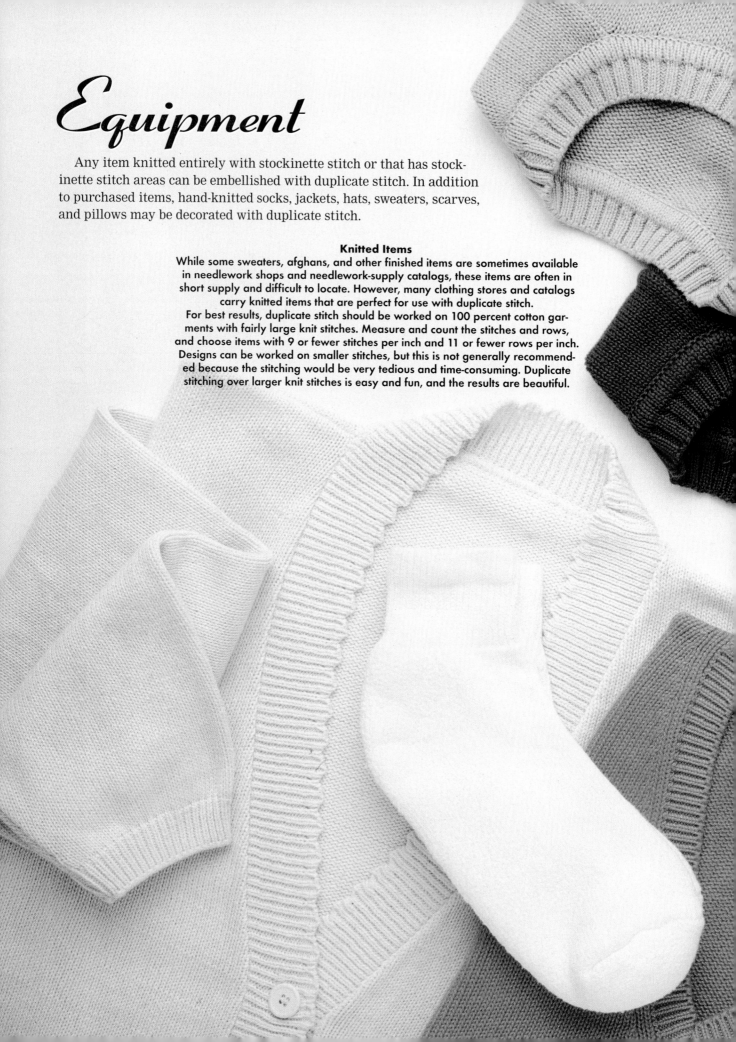

Equipment

Any item knitted entirely with stockinette stitch or that has stockinette stitch areas can be embellished with duplicate stitch. In addition to purchased items, hand-knitted socks, jackets, hats, sweaters, scarves, and pillows may be decorated with duplicate stitch.

Knitted Items

While some sweaters, afghans, and other finished items are sometimes available in needlework shops and needlework-supply catalogs, these items are often in short supply and difficult to locate. However, many clothing stores and catalogs carry knitted items that are perfect for use with duplicate stitch.

For best results, duplicate stitch should be worked on 100 percent cotton garments with fairly large knit stitches. Measure and count the stitches and rows, and choose items with 9 or fewer stitches per inch and 11 or fewer rows per inch. Designs can be worked on smaller stitches, but this is not generally recommended because the stitching would be very tedious and time-consuming. Duplicate stitching over larger knit stitches is easy and fun, and the results are beautiful.

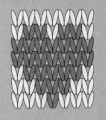

Needle Pointer

If you are planning a duplicate stitch design for a sweater, try on the sweater first. Using a large safety pin, mark the approximate place where you want the center of the design to fall. Then take the sweater off and count the stitches to see where the edges of the design will be. Try on the sweater again to be sure you like the placement of the design.

Stitching Fibers

The most commonly used stitching fiber for duplicate stitch is cotton six-strand embroidery floss. The strands are combined as needed for proper coverage of the knit stitches, with up to 12 strands at a time being used. (See "Preparing Floss" on page 72.) Floss comes in hundreds of colors, and in addition to cotton, it is available in silk and rayon.

Pearl cotton comes in #3, #5, #8, and #12, with #3 being the thickest. The plies of pearl cotton will not separate, and for most duplicate stitching, one strand is used.

Ribbon floss is a narrow ribbon that is made specially for stitching, and it works well for some duplicate stitch. Ribbon floss comes in a large number of colors in satin as well as metallic.

Metallic braids come in fine, medium, and heavy weight and are available in dozens of jewel-tone colors. One strand of medium or heavy braid is most often used for duplicate stitch. Metallic blending filament can be combined with embroidery floss to add subtle luster to the stitches.

Needles

Blunt tapestry needles in sizes 16, 18, and 20 are used for duplicate stitch.

Getting Started

Each duplicate stitch traces the path of one knitted stitch. Each stitch is worked by bringing the needle up at the base of the stitch, sliding it under the top of the stitch, and inserting it into the base.

Duplicate Stitch Basics

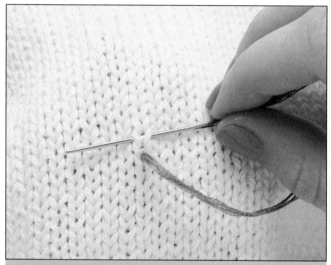

1 Bring the needle up from the back of your work at the base of the "V" of the knit stitch. Insert the needle at the top right point of the "V," slide it under the stitch, and bring it out at the top left point of the "V."

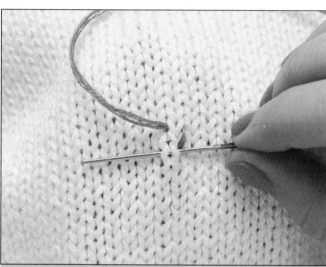

2 To make the next stitch, insert the needle into the base of the "V," slide it under the stitch, and bring it out at the base of the next "V."

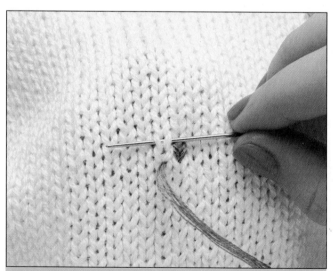

3 To continue working horizontally, insert the needle at the top right point of the "V," then bring it out at the top left point of the "V."

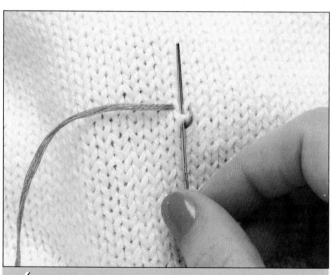

4 To make the second stitch above the first stitch, complete Step 1. Then insert the needle back into the base of the "V," slide it under the stitches, and bring it out at the base of the "V" above the first stitch.

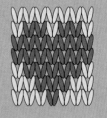
Needle Pointer

As you stitch, be sure to take the point of the needle completely through the knitted fabric to the back each time before bringing it through to the front. Duplicate stitch follows the path of each knit stitch on the back of the work as well as on the front.

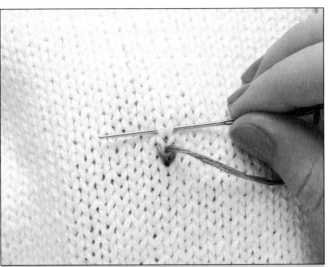

5 Insert the needle at the top right point of the "V," slide it under the stitch, and bring it out at the top left point of the "V." Complete the stitch by inserting the needle at the base of the "V."

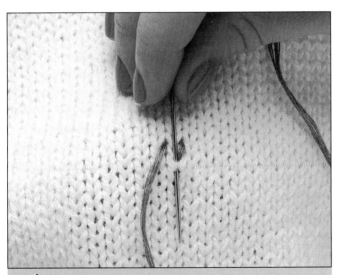

6 To move to the next stitch below the first stitch, complete Step 1. Then insert the needle into the base of the "V," slide it under the stitch, and bring it out at the base of the "V" below the first stitch.

Preparing to Stitch

The gauge of the knitted fabric is very important. The gauge measurement tells you how many knit stitches there are in an inch, measuring both horizontally and vertically. Since the duplicate stitches are the same size as the knit stitches, the gauge measurement helps determine the size of the complete duplicate stitch design.

The gauge measurement of knitted fabric always has more rows per inch than stitches per inch. This is because a knit stitch is not a square—it is wider than it is tall. Each knit stitch looks like the letter "V" as shown.

When a pattern specifies the stitch and row gauge, the stitch gauge is always given first, followed by the row gauge. For example, a 4 x 6 gauge means that a knitted fabric with a gauge of 4 stitches per inch and 6 rows per inch is required. Standard gauges are listed as 4 x 6, 5 x 7, 6 x 8, and 9 x 11.

The number of strands of embroidery floss needed for creating duplicate stitch designs varies according to the gauge of the knitted fabric. The ideal number of strands almost completely covers each knit stitch and does not distort the knit fabric.

Experiment on an inconspicuous area of the knitted fabric, stitching about 2 square inches of duplicate stitches to check coverage as shown. The knit stitches should show through the duplicate stitches occasionally. If too much of the knit stitches are showing, try adding another strand of floss. If the duplicate stitches cause the knitted fabric to become distorted, warped, or buckled, try stitching with fewer strands of floss.

Measuring the Gauge

1. To find the stitch gauge, lay a ruler horizontally along a row of knit stitches, and count the number of V-stitches in an inch as shown.

2. To find the row gauge, lay the ruler vertically along the stitches, and count the number of V-stitches in an inch as shown.

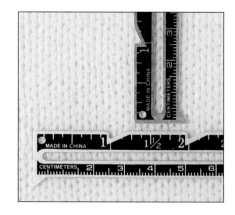

Determining the Design Size and Placement

1. After determining your item's gauge, count the number of stitches in your design, counting both horizontally and vertically.

2. Divide the number of stitches per inch into the number of stitches in the design horizontally.

3. Divide the number of rows per inch into the number of stitches in the design vertically.

4. For example, if your sweater's gauge is 5 x 7 and your design is 50 stitches wide and 35 stitches high, divide 5 into 50 (10) and 7 into 35 (5). Your completed duplicate stitch design will be 10" wide and 5" high.

Preparing the Floss

1. Select the number of strands of embroidery floss for your design following these general rules: Use 15 strands for the 4 x 6 gauge, 12 strands for the 5 x 7 gauge, 9 strands for the 6 x 8 gauge, and 6 strands for the 9 x 11 gauge.

2. Separate the floss strands and recombine the number of strands needed. To separate, cut the floss strand about 20" long; hold it near one end between your thumb and index finger. Pull one strand of floss out at a time.

3. Because red embroidery floss tones sometimes bleed, it's best to make them colorfast before stitching. To do this, soak the floss skein in a solution of 1 tablespoon of white vinegar and 8 ounces of water. Blot the floss and allow it to air dry.

4. If the floss requires smoothing after recombining, pull the cut strands across the surface of a damp sponge before threading your needle.

Working from Graphs

Some duplicate stitch graphs have rectangular blocks instead of square blocks and therefore are different from cross-stitch graphs. In order to be correctly proportional, blocks on a duplicate stitch graph are wider than they are tall, like knit stitches. Some duplicate stitch graphs, like the ones in the patterns on pages 107, 109, and 111, are shown with square blocks. In this case, the design appears elongated on the graph but will appear correct when stitched. The size of your design depends upon the gauge of the knitted piece, not on the size of the graph.

Duplicate stitch graphs are made up of grids of colors and symbols to indicate the color and placement of each stitch. Each block on the grid represents one duplicate stitch over one "V," or knit stitch.

Each duplicate stitch graph is accompanied by a color key indicating which color floss corresponds with each color on the graph. Many color keys include floss brands DMC, Anchor (ANC), and J. & P. Coats (JPC). Abbreviations for other stitching fibers or beads may also be included.

Needle Pointer

Many knitting patterns have graphed designs. These graphs are sized appropriately for knit stitches, so they will work for duplicate stitching as well. If you find a knitting graph you'd like to "duplicate," be sure to determine how large the design area will be on your sweater before you start stitching.

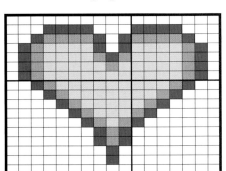

Color Key

X	DMC	ANC	JPC	Colors
	3688	66	3087	Mauve
	3687	68	3088	Mauve Med.
	3685	1028	3089	Darkest Mauve

Stitching Solution

Cross-stitch alphabet or monogram designs are often suitable for use with duplicate stitch. Choose a monogram that is tall and narrow and has no backstitching or other embroidered details. When the design is duplicate stitched, it will be shorter and wider. Color the design on duplicate stitch graph paper first to see how it will look, if desired. For cross-stitch alphabets, see pages 78 and 79.

Starting and Stopping

No hoop or frame is needed for duplicate stitch. Carefully measure your sweater or knitted item to locate the center of the design area. Begin stitching the center of the design at this center point. To begin the first duplicate stitch, leave about 5" of floss at the back of your work and weave it in after stitching is complete. The waste knot or loop stitch method may also be used.

Waste Knot

1. Make a knot in the end of the floss. Insert the needle into the knitted fabric from the front at least 1" into the stitching area.

2. Come up at the position of the first stitch, and stitch the first few rows over the floss end as shown above.

3. Leave the waste knot in place until you have made several stitches, then cut the knot off at the front.

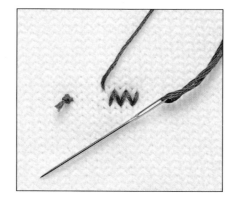

4. Pull the floss end through to the back, thread it through the needle, and weave the floss end through five or six stitches on the back of your work as shown.

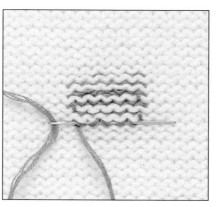

Loop Stitch

1. If you will be stitching with an even number of strands, cut the floss strands to twice the desired length (36 to 40 inches). Separate the floss plies, then take half the number of plies needed and fold them in half.

2. Thread the loose ends through the eye of the needle.

3. Bring the needle up from the back of the knitted fabric at the first stitch, leaving the loop underneath.

4. When you insert the needle back down through the knitted fabric with the first duplicate stitch, take the needle down through the loop as shown. Pull the floss to secure the loop.

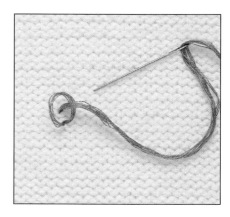

Ending a Thread

1. Leave at least 2½" of floss for ending. To end the thread, run the needle vertically under several stitches at the back of your work, then turn and weave under several stitches in the opposite direction. Clip the floss end.

2. When you finish a section of color and move to a new section of the same color, do not carry the thread across more than ½" of an unstitched area. If the area is stitched, run the needle under the stitches. If it is unstitched, end the thread and begin again in the new area.

Stitches

All duplicate stitches are worked basically the same, with the floss or stitching fiber duplicating the knitted stitch. There are differences in stitching technique depending on the direction in which each row of duplicate stitches is pointing.

Stitch Variations

Duplicate Stitching from Right to Left

To make the first duplicate stitch, bring the needle through the knitted fabric from the back to the front at the base of the first "V." Insert the needle in the upper right point of the "V" and bring it out at the upper left point of the "V" (a). Insert the needle in the base of the "V" again. To make the next stitch to the left, bring the needle out at the base of the next "V" to the left (b). To continue the row, insert the needle in the upper right point of the "V," which is the same as the upper left point of the previous "V." Bring the needle out at the upper left point of the "V" (c). Repeat (b) and (c) to complete the row.

Needle Pointer

If you'd like to add more detail to your duplicate stitch design, try graphing your design with some half stitches along the edges. These serve the same purpose as fractional stitches in cross-stitch, softening the edges and making the design look more realistic. To stitch half duplicate stitches, stitch only one side of the V-stitch.

Stitching Solution

For your first duplicate stitch project, try a simple design on a knitted item with fairly large duplicate stitches. The duplicate stitched areas will not be as stretchy as the original knit fabric, so it's a good idea not to plan your design for areas of an item that will be stretched often.

Duplicate Stitching from Left to Right

Bring the needle through the knitted fabric from the back to the front at the base of the first "V." Insert the needle in the upper left point of the "V" and bring it out at the upper right point of the "V" (a).

Insert the needle in the base of the "V" again. To make the next stitch to the right, bring the needle out at the base of the next "V" to the right (b). Insert the needle in the upper left point

of the "V," which is the same as the upper right point of the previous "V." Bring the needle out at the upper right point of the "V" (c). Repeat (b) and (c) to complete the row.

Duplicate Stitching from Bottom to Top

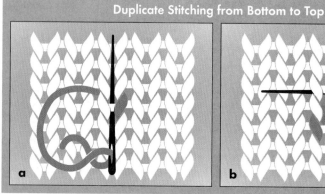

Complete (a) in "Duplicate Stitching from Right to Left" on page 101. Insert the needle in the base of the "V" again, and bring the needle out at the base of the next "V" above (a).

Insert the needle in the upper right point of the "V" and bring the needle out at the upper left point of the "V" (b). Repeat (a) and (b) to complete the row.

Duplicate Stitching from Top to Bottom

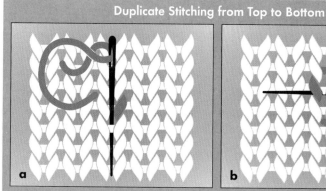

Complete (a) in "Duplicate Stitching from Right to Left" on page 101. Insert the needle in the base of the "V," and bring the needle out at the base of the next "V" below (a).

Insert the needle in the upper right point of the "V" and bring the needle out at the upper left point of the "V" (b). Repeat (a) and (b) to complete the row.

Duplicate Stitching Diagonally Upward

Complete (a) in "Duplicate Stitching from Right to Left" on page 101. Insert the needle in the base of the "V," and bring the needle out at the base of the stitch to the left and one row up (a).

Insert the needle in the upper right point of the "V," and bring the needle out at the upper left point of the "V" (b). Repeat (a) and (b) to complete the row.

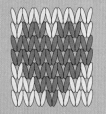

Needle Pointer

To achieve the smoothest results, make sure your stitching fibers are smooth before you begin stitching. Smooth the fibers on a damp sponge or press with a warm iron.

Duplicate Stitching Diagonally Downward

Complete (a) in "Duplicate Stitching from Right to Left" on page 101. Insert the needle in the base of the "V," and bring the needle out at the base of the stitch to the left and one row down (a).

Insert the needle in the upper right point of the "V" and bring the needle out at the upper left point of the "V" (b). Repeat (a) and (b) to complete the row.

Stitching Solution

To add an easy-to-stitch argyle design to a purchased knit sweater, duplicate stitch diagonal rows on the sweater in a diamond pattern. Begin the first rows at the center front of the sweater just below the neckband. Stitch the argyle diamonds in two colors, if desired.

Techniques

Duplicate stitch projects can be dressed up by stitching some of the duplicate stitches with pretty specialty fibers such as metallic threads, silk or satin ribbons, and chenille yarns. Embroidery stitches or small trims may be added for extra interest.

Fancy Fibers

Fancy stitching fibers such as thin ribbons, shiny metallics, and fuzzy yarns add exciting dimension and personality to duplicate stitch designs.

When using these specialty fibers, the most important consideration is care of the finished item. If you would like to be able to hand wash your project, be sure to check the fiber's packaging for cleaning instructions.

Try using soft and fuzzy fibers for duplicate stitching the hair or fur areas on people or animal designs. Add sparkle and shine to holiday designs with shimmering metallic threads or dimensional glittery fibers.

Thin chenille yarn brings a very soft touch to duplicate stitch, while narrow silk or satin ribbons add elegance and old-fashioned charm.

Specialty fibers can be used to stitch an entire duplicate stitch design, or they can be used to accent small areas of a design stitched primarily with six-strand embroidery floss.

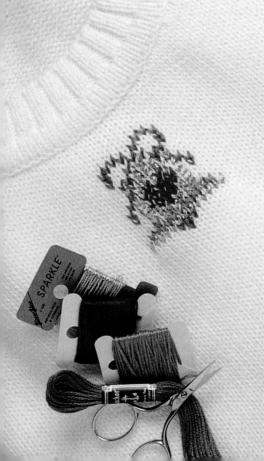

Fancy Touches

Embroidery stitches such as stem stitches, lazy daisy stitches, and French knots can be added to duplicate stitch designs with beautiful results.

Beads, buttons, jewels, pearls, and other small trims can also be added to finished duplicate stitch designs.

Adding Embroidery

1. Complete all of the duplicate stitches.

2. Stitch the flattest embroidery stitches first. Then add the more dimensional embroidery stitches.

3. Use a sharp-pointed crewel needle to add the embroidered details. Stitch through the knitted fabric and completed duplicate stitches, piercing the yarn as needed for proper placement of the embroidery stitches.

Adding Trims

1. Complete all of the duplicate stitches.

2. To make the trims rest on the surface of the knitted fabric rather than disappear between the stitches, sew through the yarn of each knit stitch rather than through the openings between the stitches.

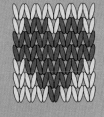

Finishing

Duplicate stitched items are usually as easy to clean and care for as the basic garment itself unless fragile specialty fibers have been used for stitching. Be sure to check the labels of the sweater and all stitching fibers for care instructions.

Cleaning

If your sweater has gotten dirty during stitching, hand wash it before pressing. Pressing can set stains.

If your sweater is washable and the duplicate stitched areas have been worked with cotton floss, your sweater may be hand washed as shown below (left). Hand wash it in cool water using a mild detergent, and lay it flat to dry.

If you have added metallic threads or silk ribbons, dry cleaning is recommended.

Pressing

If the sweater is cotton or acrylic, a gentle steam pressing helps to even out the duplicate stitches and make the design look more "knitted in." After all stitching is complete, lightly steam-press the sweater from the wrong side. Do not let the surface of the iron rest on the knitted fabric. Hold the iron over the fabric as shown below (right), letting the steam penetrate the yarn fibers. Allow the sweater to completely cool and dry before moving it.

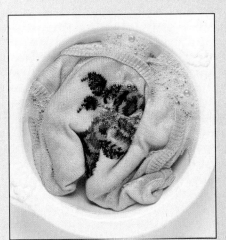

Needle Pointer

If you have a very elaborately stitched duplicate stitch item that represents many hours of your time, it may be best to have it dry-cleaned. Ask your dry-cleaner if your item can be run through the first solution of the day because as it is used, the solution picks up soils and odors.

Stitching Solution

When stitching with ribbon or flat metallic braids, take extra care to untwist the ribbon or braid with each stitch as needed. Each time you take a stitch, smooth the ribbon or braid to make it lie flat on the knit stitch. It should lie flat on the back as well because twists can work their way to the front of your work as the finished item is worn or washed.

Sweetheart Bluebirds Sweater

Cheerful little bluebirds and a shaded heart are easy to stitch on a pretty white sweater. Perfect for spring-time, this project is easy enough for a beginner.

Skill Level

Easy

Size

Design fits any size sweater with a gauge of 5 stitches per inch and 7 rows per inch (5 x 7 gauge)

Materials

White short-sleeved knit sweater with a gauge of 5 stitches per inch and 7 rows per inch (5 x 7 gauge)

Six-strand embroidery floss as indicated in the color key

Tapestry needle

Instructions

1. Using 12 strands of the floss or the number of strands desired for proper coverage and following the chart, center and stitch the heart onto the front of the sweater 1½" down from the center front of the neckband. (See "Starting and Stopping" on page 100 and "Stitches" on page 101.)

2. Stitch the bluebirds to the left and right of the heart.

Something Different

Stitch a perky bluebird or heart onto the cuff of white socks for a fun fashion accent. The way ribbing is stitched on many socks makes it necessary to work the duplicate stitches by turning the sock upside down.

Color Key

X	DMC	ANC	JPC	Colors
	3688	66	3087	Mauve
	3687	68	3088	Mauve Med.
	3685	1028	3089	Darkest Mauve
	809	130	7021	Blueberry Lt.
	797	132	7143	Deep Blueberry
	820	134	7024	Royal Blue Very Dk.
	972	298	2298	Tangerine Med.

Sweetheart Bluebirds Sweater

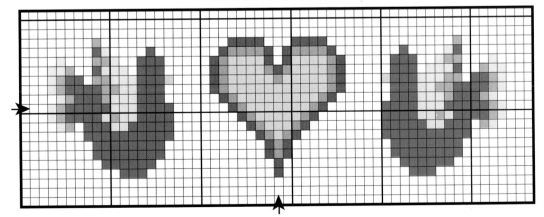

Merry Christmas Ornaments

Brighten your holidays with this trio of ornaments. Stitch a candle, a snowflake, and a bell and trim them with ribbons and jingle bells.

Skill Level

Intermediate

Size

3½" x 3½"

Materials (for one ornament)

Two premade 6" x 6" duplicate stitch sample squares or hand-knit squares (see Chapter 6 on page 144) with a gauge of 5 stitches per inch and 6 rows per inch (5 x 6 gauge)

Six-strand embroidery floss as indicated in the color key

⅓ yard of white ⅛" satin ribbon

1½ yards of white ¼" satin ribbon

3 jingle bells or 1 liberty bell

Fiberfill

Instructions

1. For each ornament, knit two Stockinette stitch squares, each 19 stitches and 21 rows according to the instructions in Chapter 6, beginning on page 144, or use premade 6" x 6" duplicate stitch sample squares.

2. Using 12 strands of the floss or the number of strands desired for proper coverage and following one of the charts, center and stitch one design on one of each pair of sample squares or knit squares.

3. If you are using premade 6" x 6" duplicate stitch sample squares, stabilize the knit fabric by ironing fusible interfacing or commercial stabilizer to the back. Measure, mark, and machine zigzag around a 3½" square area on each square with the design in the center. Trim the squares just outside the zigzag line.

4. With the wrong sides together, pin each pair of squares together. Using matching yarn and a tapestry needle or crochet hook, whipstitch or slip stitch around three sides, covering the zigzag edges on the premade squares. Turn the squares right side out. Stuff them lightly with fiberfill, and slip stitch the open side closed.

5. For each ornament, cut three 18" lengths of the ¼" ribbon. Hand sew the ends of the ⅛" ribbon to the top corners of the ornament, creating the hanging loop. With one piece of the ¼" ribbon, tie a bow at the top of the hanging loop. Holding the remaining two pieces of the ¼" ribbon together, tie a bow and tack it in place at the bottom center of the ornament using the sewing needle and thread. Tie the bells to one or more ends of the bow. Trim the ends of the ribbon as needed.

Stitching Solution

For fancy ornaments, add a real ribbon bow in place of the stitched bow on the bell. Add red beads to the holly below the candle. Create a glittery snowflake by stitching a tiny jewel in place at the end of each point.

Color Key

X	DMC	ANC	JPC	Colors
	White	2	1001	White
	498	1005	3000	Garnet
	796	133	7100	Royal Blue
	699	923	6228	Kelly Green Dk.
	742	303	2302	Tangerine

Bell

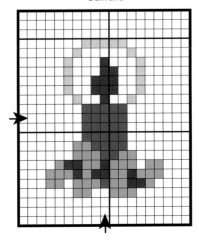

Candle

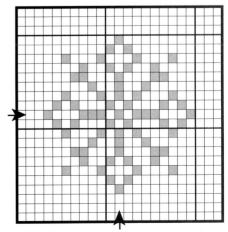

Snowflake

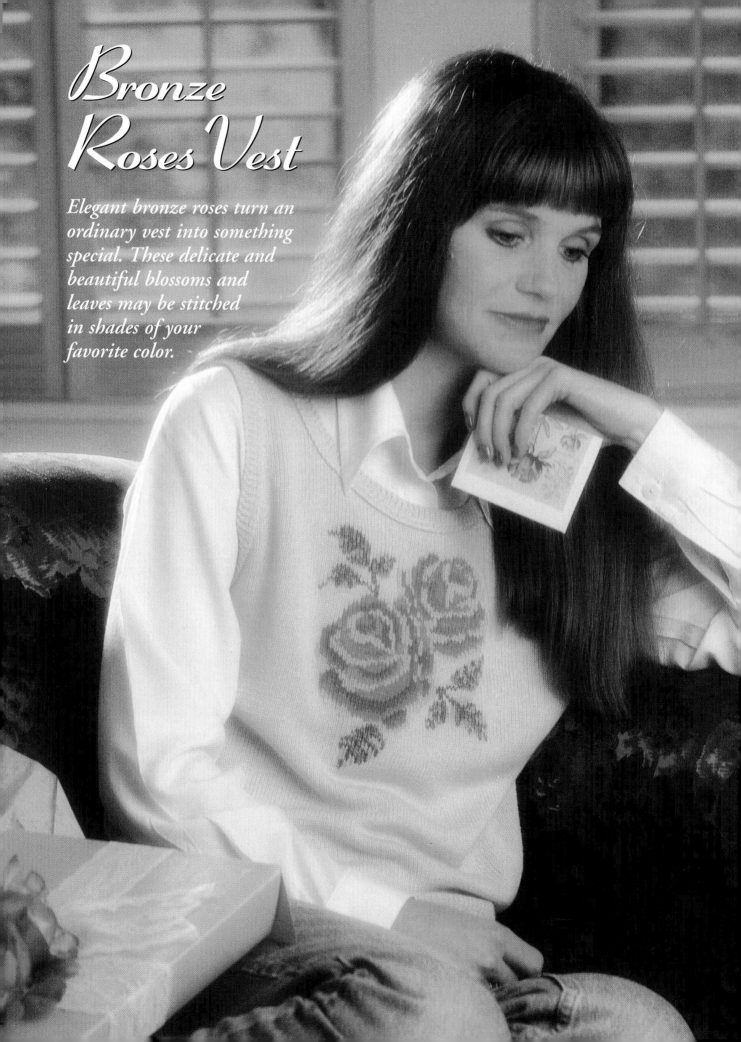

Bronze Roses Vest

Elegant bronze roses turn an ordinary vest into something special. These delicate and beautiful blossoms and leaves may be stitched in shades of your favorite color.

Skill Level

Challenging

Size

Design fits any vest with a gauge of 9 stitches per inch and 11 rows per inch (9 x 11 gauge)

Materials

Knit vest with a gauge of 9 stitches per inch and 11 rows per inch (9 x 11 gauge)

Safety pins

Six-strand embroidery floss as indicated in the color key

Tapestry needle

Instructions

1. Determine the placement of the Bronze Roses Vest design on the front of the vest 1" down from the center front of the neckband, and mark the center with the safety pins.

2. Using five strands of the floss or the number of strands desired for proper coverage and following the chart, center and stitch the rose pattern, working from the center outward.

Bronze Roses Vest

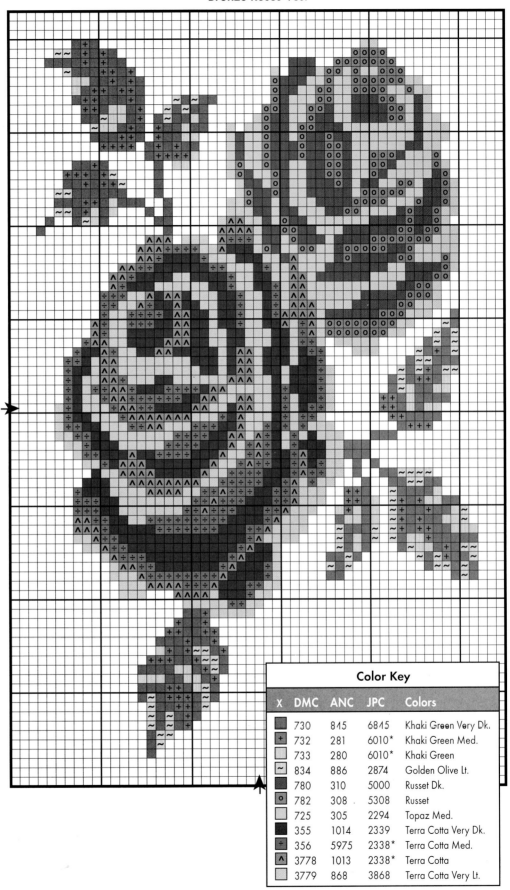

Color Key

X	DMC	ANC	JPC	Colors
	730	845	6845	Khaki Green Very Dk.
+	732	281	6010*	Khaki Green Med.
	733	280	6010*	Khaki Green
~	834	886	2874	Golden Olive Lt.
	780	310	5000	Russet Dk.
o	782	308	5308	Russet
	725	305	2294	Topaz Med.
	355	1014	2339	Terra Cotta Very Dk.
÷	356	5975	2338*	Terra Cotta Med.
∧	3778	1013	2338*	Terra Cotta
	3779	868	3868	Terra Cotta Very Lt.

* This brand of floss does not have two shades of these colors. Use the same shade for both colors.

Embroidery

For centuries, many forms of embroidery have been used to adorn fabrics with decorative threads.

Embroidery encompasses everything that can be done with fabric and a threaded needle. Some types of embroidery are worked on the surface of fabric, with the fibers providing the design. Other types use the threads of even-weave fabric along with the stitching threads to form the design.

Although most stitches have remained basically the same through the ages, today's embroiderer can choose from a wealth of fine fabrics and stitching fibers.

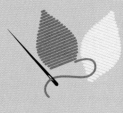

Equipment

Just as there are many different types of embroidery, there are also dozens of fabrics and stitching fibers suitable for embroidery. Whether you are stitching with the simplest cottons or the finest silks, the basic supplies of thread, needle, hoop, and fabric remain the same.

Hoops or Frames

For most types of embroidery, a hoop or a frame is needed to hold the fabric taut as the stitches are worked, preventing puckers.

Fabrics

For most surface embroidery, a densely woven cotton fabric provides a plain surface against which the embroidery stitches stand out. For pulled and counted-thread embroidery, even-weave fabrics are necessary. Linen, hardanger, Jobelan, hopsacking, and even burlap are suitable for these types of embroidery.

Hot Iron Transfer Pencils

Transfer pencils are helpful for transferring embroidery designs to fabric. Be sure to test each type of pencil on fabric to see if marks are removable.

Dressmaker's Carbon Paper

This type of transfer paper has been used for decades for transferring embroidery designs. For large designs, a tracing wheel may be used; for smaller, more detailed designs, trace with a dry ballpoint pen.

Needles
Chenille, crewel, or embroidery needles are sharp-pointed and are used for surface embroidery. Tapestry needles are blunt and are used for counted-thread embroidery.

Needle Pointer

Experiment with different types of thimbles to see which you prefer. Metal, plastic, and leather thimbles are available in a variety of shapes and sizes. To help pull the needle through the fabric in tight spots, grasp it with a deflated balloon over the tip of your finger.

Scissors
Sharp embroidery scissors are useful for clipping threads. Dressmaking shears are needed for cutting fabrics.

Fibers
Six-strand cotton embroidery floss is a popular choice for many types of embroidery. The strands may be separated and recombined as desired. Two-ply crewel yarn is used one strand at a time for fine crewel embroidery. Three-ply tapestry wool, or Persian yarn, is used for many types of embroidery. Pearl cotton comes in sizes 3, 5, 8, and 12 and features a beautiful firm twist. It is used for pulled and drawn thread work. Metallic threads and silk ribbons add sparkle and interest to stitchery. Machine embroidery threads are made especially for machine embroidery, and they produce a satiny, shiny result.

Getting Started

Place your fabric in a hoop, thread your needle, and make a few basic stitches. While you are learning, be sure to focus on maintaining a smooth, even tension in your stitches for beautiful finished results.

Embroidery Basics

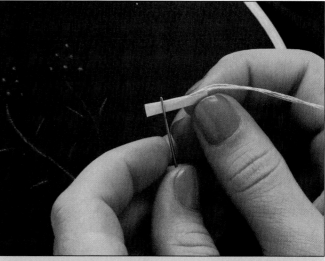

1 To draw freehand embroidery designs on fabric, use a dressmaker's pencil. If you prefer, use a hot-iron transfer pencil or dressmaker's carbon to apply the design.

2 To help make needle threading easy, slip the floss or yarn into a thin, folded strip of paper as shown. Insert the paper into the eye of the needle and pull the paper and floss through.

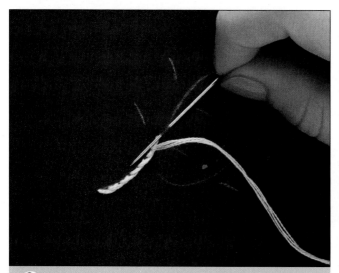

3 Using the embroidery stitches of your choice or those indicated in the pattern, embroider along the pattern designs.

4 Using different fibers for different parts of an embroidery design adds interest and texture. Here, six-strand floss is used for the stem and leaves. Pearl cotton is used for the French knots.

5 When stitching with ribbon, be sure to pull gently on the ribbon with each stitch, so the stitches will lie softly on the fabric. If you pull too tightly, the stitches lose dimension.

6 Add small trims such as sequins, jewels, or beads to your completed embroidered design if desired. Use a beading needle to apply tiny seed beads.

Needle Pointer

If your embroidery hoop does not hold your fabric firmly enough, wrap the bottom hoop with a long strip of cotton fabric and secure it with a few stitches.

Transferring Patterns

Transferring an embroidery design to fabric may be accomplished by one of several different methods. Dressmaker's carbon paper is suitable for marking smooth fabrics, and the paper comes in a variety of colors from light to dark. Many patterns are available in hot-iron transfer form, or you can make your own patterns with a special hot-iron transfer pencil. When using any marking method, transfer the thinnest line possible, so you can cover all of the transferred markings with embroidery stitches.

Dressmaker's Carbon Paper

1. Place the dressmaker's carbon paper colored side down on the right side of the fabric. Place the pattern right side up over the carbon paper, making sure the design is positioned over the fabric correctly. Pin in each corner (a) or use tear-away sewing tape.

2. Use a dry ballpoint pen to trace the design (b), or roll a tracing wheel over the pattern lines (c).

Dressmaker's Carbon Paper

a

b

c

Hot-Iron Transfer

1. Cut the transfers apart. Follow the transfer instructions to test the transfer on a scrap of your fabric.

2. Position the transfer on the right side of the fabric. Pin, if desired, at the corners or in places the iron will not rest, or use heat-resistant tape to affix your transfer to the fabric.

3. Using the iron temperature suggested on the transfer package, press one area of the transfer for a few seconds without moving the iron as shown. Lift up the corner of the pattern to make sure the design is transferring properly.

4. Lift the iron and press another area without moving the iron. Continue until all of the pattern has been transferred as shown.

Hot-Iron Transfer Pencil

1. Using a graphite pencil or fine-line permanent marker, trace the embroidery design onto tracing paper.

2. Turn the traced design face-down, and using a sharpened hot-iron transfer pencil, trace the design (a).

3. Place the hot-iron transfer tracing against the right side of the fabric. Pin, if desired, at the corners or in places the iron will not rest.

4. Follow Steps 3 and 4 for "Hot-Iron Transfer" to transfer your design (b).

Stitching Solution

To protect your embroidery fabric and keep it clean as you stitch, place one or two layers of tissue paper over your fabric and mount both the fabric and the paper in the embroidery hoop. Carefully tear away the center of the tissue paper to expose the stitching area. Keep your hands on the tissue paper as much as possible while you stitch.

EMBROIDERY

Dressmaker's Pencil

1. Use a sharpened dressmaker's pencil to draw freehand designs on fabric.

2. Select the white end of the pencil for medium to dark fabrics, and use the blue end of the pencil on white or light fabrics.

3. Stitch over the pencil marks.

Needle Pointer

Use air- or water-soluble marking pens for marks that are removable. Air-soluble dressmaker's carbon paper is also available. Air-soluble marks disappear after anywhere from a few hours to a day or two, depending upon the humidity. Water-soluble marks may be removed by dampening the fabric with plain water. Avoid using these products on heirloom projects.

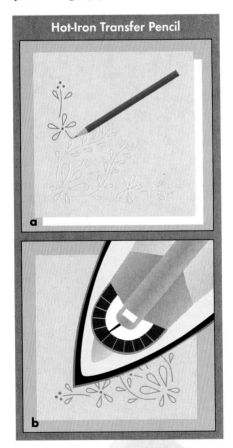

Hot-Iron Transfer Pencil

a

b

Dressmaker's Pencil

Preparing to Stitch

Before beginning to stitch, finish the edges of embroidery fabric with zigzag stitches or treat the edges with a fray preventer.

It's important to use an embroidery hoop when stitching most forms of embroidery. The hoop will hold the fabric taut and smooth while you stitch so that the stitches do not pull the fabric out of shape.

Select a hoop proportional to the size of your design.

Using a Hoop

1. Place the embroidery fabric over the inner ring of the embroidery hoop.

2. Place the outer ring of the hoop over the inner ring with the fabric between, and adjust the screw on the hoop so that the rings fit together snugly.

3. Push the outer ring down over the inner ring smoothly, and pull on the fabric as needed until it is taut in the hoop as shown, tightening the screw as needed.

Preparing Yarns and Threads

Yarns and threads have a grain just as fabrics have and are slightly smoother in one direction than in the other. The thread will retain its smoothness as you stitch if you thread the needle so that you are stitching with the grain. To stitch with the grain, thread the needle with the end that comes off the outside of the ball or skein as shown. This end will be the short end of your strand if you are stitching with one thickness of yarn.

To separate strands of embroidery floss or Persian wool for stitching, cut strands about 18" long, then follow the instructions in Step 1 for "Preparing Floss" on page 72.

Because red floss tones can bleed, it's best to colorfast them by soaking them in a solution of 1 tablespoon of white vinegar and 1 cup of water. Allow the floss to air dry before stitching.

A needle threader is helpful for threading needles with thick yarns and threads.

Stitching

It's best never to use knots in embroidery. This is true for most other forms of needlework as well. Knots can show from the front when the stitching is complete, especially if you're working the embroidery on thin fabric or if the piece will be framed. Instead, secure the threads under your stitches on the back of the fabric to achieve a smooth look.

Securing Threads

1. To begin the first thread in an embroidery piece, bring the

needle up from the back of the fabric and pull it through, leaving about 2" of thread at the back of the fabric.

2. Hold the thread end at the back with your fingers as you begin to stitch, and work over it with the first few stitches.

3. When about 4" of thread remains, pull the needle to the back of the fabric. Run the needle under about 2" of stitches on the back, and clip the thread.

4. To begin a thread after some embroidery has been worked,

draw the needle and thread under a few existing stitches, bringing the needle out near the point of the first new stitch.

Stitching the Design

For the most attractive embroidery, try to cover all of the pattern markings as you stitch.

For patterns that have portions of the design overlapping other portions, stitch the underlying parts first. Then stitch the uppermost parts, overlapping the stitches slightly.

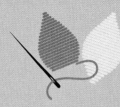

Needle Pointer

Chalk marks or dressmaker's pencil marks may fade or disappear as you stitch. These marks may be reapplied as needed during stitching. For best results on large designs, use dressmaker's carbon or a hot-iron transfer pencil.

Reposition the fabric in the hoop as needed so that you will be stitching in the center of the hoop as much as possible. Be sure to pull the fabric as needed to keep it smooth and taut in the hoop.

Remove the hoop each time you lay your stitching aside to prevent hard-to-remove hoop marks from remaining on the fabric after the project is complete.

Stitching Solution

If you wish to store a partially completed embroidery piece for an extended period of time, remove it from the hoop, roll it up, and store it in an acid-free cardboard tube. Rolling is preferable to folding because creases may become permanent. If you must fold a completed piece for storing, wrap it in acid-free tissue paper. As you fold the piece, insert extra layers of tissue between the folds.

Stitches

Although it is possible to make dozens of different embroidery stitches, most are variations of a few basic stitches. As you stitch, try to keep the back of your work as neat as possible.

Surface Embroidery

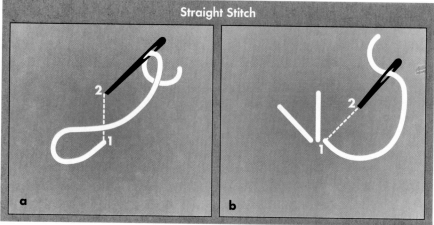

Straight Stitch

a   **b**

Straight stitches are single stitches that can be worked in any direction. Bring the needle up at 1 and down at 2 (a). Worked in groups (b), straight stitches can be used to form flower stems and leaves or other designs.

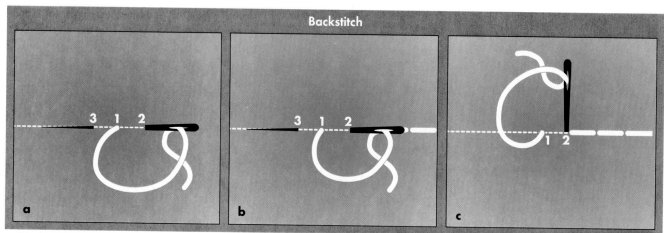

Backstitch

a   **b**   **c**

Backstitches are typically used to outline. Working from left to right, bring the needle up at 1, down at 2, and back up at 3 (a). Repeat, making all stitches the same length (b). For the last backstitch, insert the needle at 2 (c), and pull the needle and the floss through to the back of the fabric.

Stem Stitch

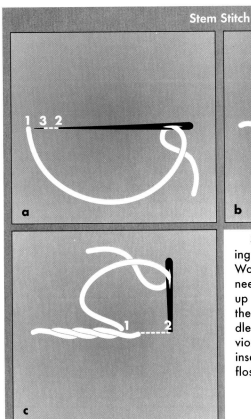

Stem stitches can be used as outlining stitches or to form stems or lines. Working from left to right, bring the needle up at 1, down at 2, and back up at 3 (a). Repeat, making all stitches the same length and bringing the needle up each time at the end of the previous stitch (b). For the last stem stitch, insert the needle at 2 (c), and pull the floss through to the back of the fabric.

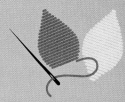

Needle Pointer

///////////////////

Dress up a plain shirt or blouse with simple embroidery stitches such as stem stitches or blanket stitches. Choose a matching or contrasting color of floss, and stitch around the collar, cuffs, and front band.

Split Stitch

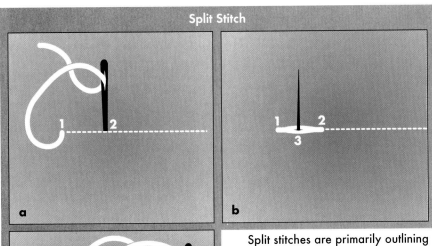

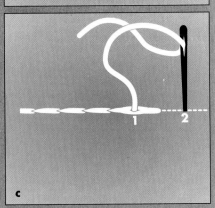

Split stitches are primarily outlining stitches. Working from left to right, bring the needle up at 1, down at 2 (a), and back up at 3, splitting the yarn with the needle as it comes up (b). Repeat, making all stitches the same length and bringing the needle up each time at the end of the previous stitch. For the last split stitch, insert the needle at 2 (c), and pull the floss through to the back of the fabric.

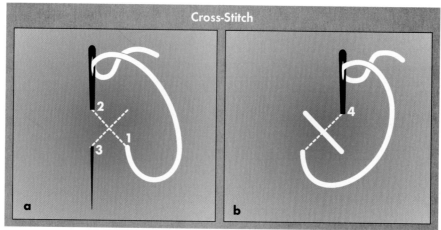

Cross-stitches are usually worked in rows. Bring the needle up at 1, down at 2, and back up at 3 (a). Take the needle down at 4 (b) and pull the floss through to the back of the fabric. When working rows of cross-stitches, work each stitch in the same order so that all top crosses are going in the same direction.

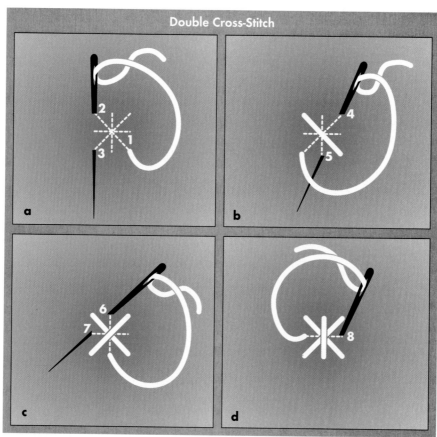

Double cross-stitches may be worked in rows or placed individually. Bring the needle up at 1, down at 2, and back up at 3 (a). Take the needle down at 4 and back up at 5 (b). Take the needle down at 6, back up at 7 (c), and down again at 8 (d). Pull the thread through to the back of the fabric. When working rows of double cross-stitches, make sure to work each stitch in the same order so that the top stitches are going in the same direction.

Long-Armed Cross-Stitch

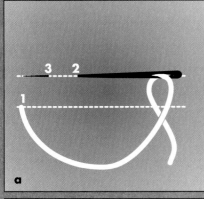

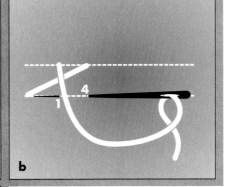

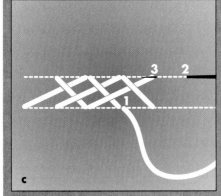

For long-armed cross-stitches, each stitch overlaps the previous one. Working from left to right, bring the needle up at 1, down at 2, and back up at 3 (a). To complete the stitch, go down at 4; to begin the next stitch, come up at 1 (b). Repeat, working stitches evenly and making each stitch touch the previous one at the top and overlap it at the bottom (c).

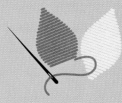

Needle Pointer

Cross-stitches and their variations should be stitched evenly to show off their symmetrical appearance. To help make stitches more even, use an air-soluble marking pen to place a tiny dot at each place where a stitch will begin or end.

Buttonhole Stitch

Buttonhole stitches are used to finish raw edges such as buttonholes. Working from left to right, bring the needle up at 1, down at 2, and back up at 3, taking the floss under the point of the needle as it emerges. Work stitches close together.

Stitching Solution

Embroidery pieces don't need to be limited to threads on fabric. Throughout history, embroidery stitches have been worked on many surfaces and with a wide variety of materials. Leather, parchment, and other natural materials can serve as the background, while stitches may be worked with raffia, leather strips, and metal threads.

Blanket Stitch

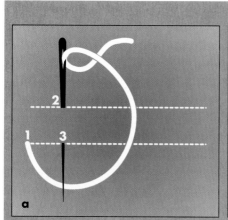

a

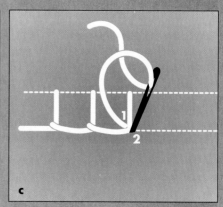

b

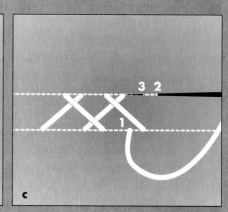

c

Blanket stitches are primarily used to finish edges, but they can be used for outlining as well. Working from left to right, bring the needle up at 1, down at 2, and back up at 3, taking the yarn under the point of the needle as it emerges (a). Repeat, working stitches evenly (b). To make the last blanket stitch, insert the needle at 2 (c), and pull the needle and the floss through to the back of the fabric.

Herringbone Stitch

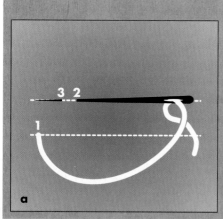

a

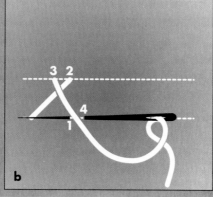

b

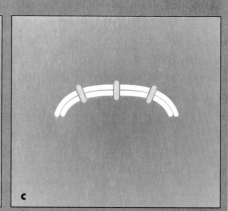

c

Herringbone stitches are used for borders. To make the herringbone stitch, working from left to right, bring the needle up at 1, down at 2, and back up at 3 (a). Making a stitch about the same length as the one just made, take the needle down at 4 to complete one herringbone. To begin the next stitch, bring the needle up at 1, with the space between 4 and 1 equal to the space between 2 and 3 (b). Repeat, working stitches evenly (c).

Couching

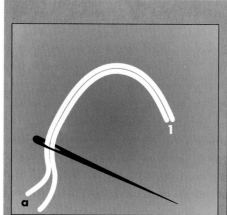

a

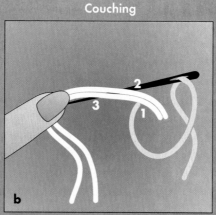

b

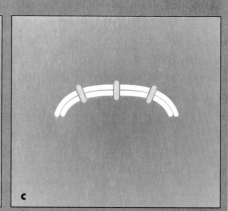

c

Couching may be used for outlining or for creating stems and lines of a design. Bring up the desired number of strands to be couched at 1 (a). Using another needle and the couching floss, come up at 1 and go down at 2, taking a small stitch over the threads to be couched. Come up at 3 (b). Positioning the threads as desired, continue to take small stitches to secure the couched threads. At the end, pull all threads to the back of the fabric (c).

Satin Stitch

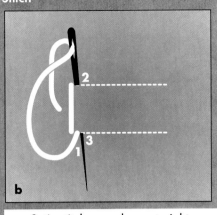

a

b

c

Satin stitches are long, straight stitches placed side by side to cover an area. Bring the needle up at 1, down at 2, and back up at 3 close to the bottom of the first stitch (a). To begin the next stitch, take the needle down at 2 close to the top of the first stitch, then back up at 3 close to the bottom of the second stitch (b). Repeat to cover the area (c).

Padded Satin Stitch

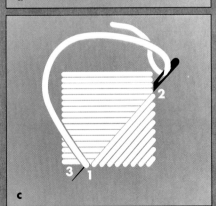

a

b

c

Padded satin stitches form a raised area for added dimension. Begin by outlining the area with split stitches (a). Work satin stitches over the area (b). Then work another layer of satin stitches over the area, working them in another direction (c).

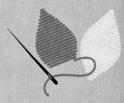

Needle Pointer

For a lightly padded satin stitch, make several rows of small running stitches within the design area. Satin stitch over the running stitches in one direction only.

Long and Short Stitch

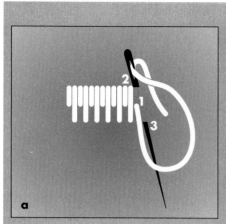 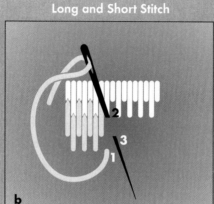 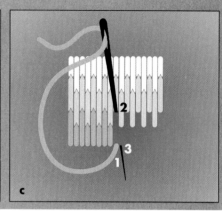

Long and short stitches are used for shading. Beginning with the first color, work a row of stitches, alternating long and short stitches and placing them side by side (a). With the next color, work a row of staggered stitches of equal length below the first row of stitches, piercing the bottom of each stitch in the first row as you work (b). Repeat with more colors as desired. In the last row, alternate the long and short stitches to make the bottom of the stitched area even (c).

French Knot

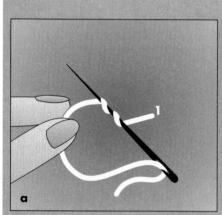 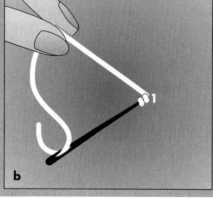 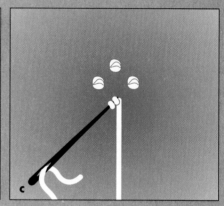

French knots are used to create texture. To make a French knot, bring the needle up through the fabric at 1. Holding the floss securely with your left hand, wrap it around the needle two or three times (a). Pulling the floss taut with your left hand, insert the needle back into the fabric very near 1 (b). Pull the floss through to the back of the fabric, maintaining the tension on the floss with your left hand until the knot rests on the fabric (c).

Feather Stitch

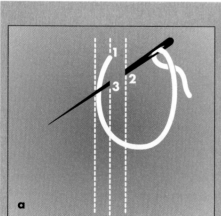 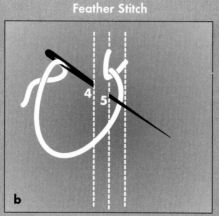 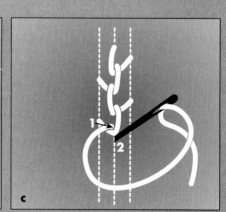

Feather stitches make an attractive border embellishment. Working from top to bottom, bring the needle up at 1, down at 2 (slightly lower and to the right), and back up at 3, taking the floss under the point of the needle as it emerges (a). Insert the needle at 4 (slightly lower and to the left) and bring it out at 5, taking the floss under the point of the needle as it emerges (b). To make the last feather stitch, insert the needle at 2 (c), and pull the floss through to the back of the fabric.

Fly Stitch

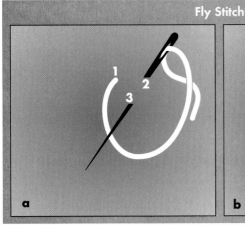

Fly stitches can be used to fill an area or to outline a border. Bring the needle up at 1, down at 2, and back up at 3, taking the yarn under the point of the needle as it emerges (a). Take a stitch over the loop of yarn at 3, inserting the needle at 4 (b).

Bullion Knot

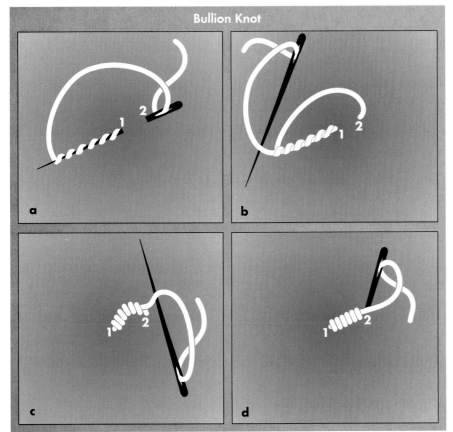

Bullion knots are long, dimensional stitches. Bring the needle up at 1, down at 2, and back up at 1. Wrap the floss around the point of the needle 6 or 7 times (a). Pull the needle through the wraps carefully (b). Pull the floss and needle toward 2, using the point of the needle as needed to evenly distribute the wraps until the stitch lies flat (c). Insert the needle at 2 (d).

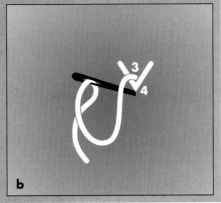

Needle Pointer

To make a thick padded line, first make a row of running stitches along the center of the line. Satin stitch across the running stitches.

Turkey Work

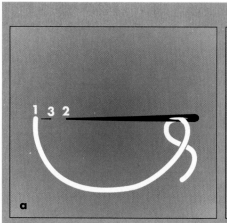

a

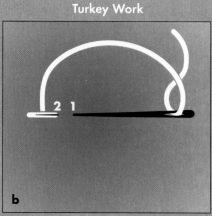

b

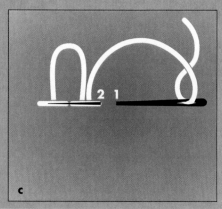

c

Turkey work is similar to backstitching, except stitches are pulled up and looped. Loops can be trimmed for a fur-like effect. Working from left to right,

bring the needle up at 1, down at 2, and back up at 3 (a). Take the needle down at 1 and back up at 2, carrying a loop of floss above the stitch (b).

Carrying the floss below the stitching line, work a backstitch that lies flat, then work another backstitch, carrying a loop of floss above the stitch (c).

Chain Stitch

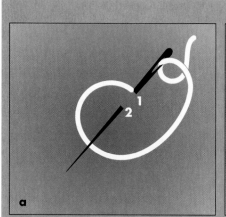

a

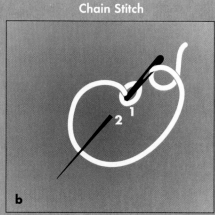

b

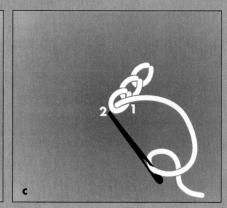

c

Chain stitches can be used for borders. Working from top to bottom or right to left, bring the needle up at 1, then go back down at 1 and up at 2,

taking the floss under the point of the needle as it emerges (a). Take the needle down at the same point and come up again, taking the floss under the

point of the needle (b). To make the last chain stitch, take a stitch over the loop of floss, inserting the needle at 2 (c). Pull the floss through to the back of the fabric.

Lazy Daisy Stitch

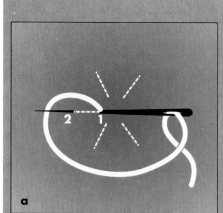

a

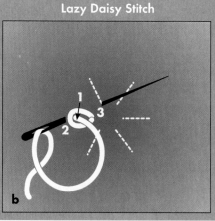

b

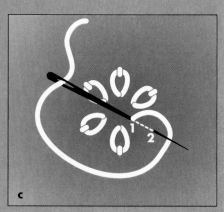

c

Lazy daisy stitches are single chain stitches. Bring the needle up at 1, back down at 1, and up at 2, taking the floss under the point of the needle as it

emerges (a). Take a tiny stitch over the loop of floss and insert the needle at 2 again to complete one lazy daisy, then bring the needle out at 3—the begin-

ning point of the next lazy daisy (b). Lazy daisies can be worked in a circle to form flower petals (c) or used alone for other effects.

Techniques

Traditional embroidery stitches have been used to embellish linens and clothing and to create beautiful wallhangings. Some of these old-fashioned techniques—cross-stitch and ribbon embroidery—are enjoying renewed popularity. Free-motion machine embroidery offers unlimited creative possibilities.

Pulled-Thread Embroidery

Pulled-thread embroidery is a counted-thread technique in which each stitch is pulled tightly enough to draw the fabric threads apart to create open patterns in the fabric.

The four-sided stitch is one of the most popular pulled-thread techniques.

1. Leaving about a 6" tail, bring the needle up from the back at the lower right point of the stitch. Go down at 2 and back up at 3 (a).

2. Take the needle down at 2, and back up at 3 (b).

3. Take the needle down at 2 and back up at 3 (c).

4. Take the needle down at 2, completing the stitch (d). Pull the stitch tightly. If this is the first in a row of stitches, bring the needle out again at 3, as instructed in Step 1.

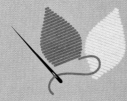

Needle Pointer

If you're following a large, detailed graph, you may find it helpful to mark points on the graph with an air-soluble pen. This helps you keep your place, and marks disappear within 24 hours, leaving the graph looking like new.

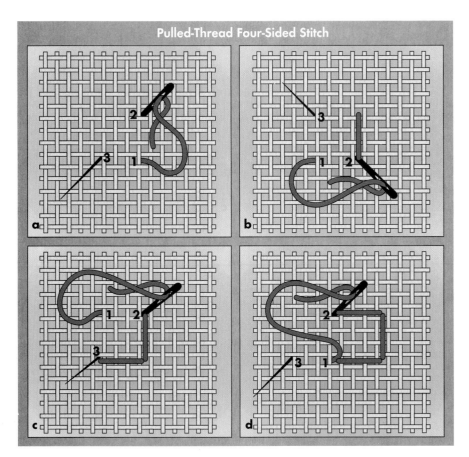

Pulled-Thread Four-Sided Stitch

Ribbon Embroidery

Ribbon embroidery is an elegant and beautiful technique involving dimensional embroidery stitches using ribbons. Silk ribbons are widely used, but satin, rayon, chiffon, cotton, and linen ribbons may also be used. Silk ribbon embroidery has been used since the eighteenth century to adorn clothing, quilts, and decorative accessories.

Ribbons are twisted and turned during stitching to form realistic-looking flowers, buds, and leaves. Regular embroidery stitches such as satin stitches, straight stitches, French knots, and stem stitches may be used with ribbon. There are several stitches and stitch combinations that are exclusive to ribbon embroidery, and they are used for making dimensional flowers, leaves, buds, and other details.

Threading the Needle

1. Cut a 14" length of ribbon. Thread the end through the eye of a crewel needle (sizes 3 to 9).

2. To lock the ribbon onto the needle, pierce the ribbon ½" from one end as shown and pull on the opposite end. The ribbon will rest securely on the eye of the needle and will not come unthreaded as you work.

Stitching

Keep the ribbon flat at all times while making the stitches. After taking each stitch, make sure the ribbon is untwisted, and use the needle to straighten the ribbon as needed.

For stitches where the ribbon is to be wrapped around the needle, be sure the ribbon is flat so that the stitches will be as full as possible.

As you stitch, be sure to pull gently on the ribbon so that the stitches will not be tight and thin. The stitches should lie very softly on the fabric.

Japanese Ribbon Stitch

Bring the needle up at 1. Flatten the ribbon softly against the fabric in the direction the leaf will go. Pierce the ribbon at 2, and draw the ribbon through until soft curls remain at the top of the stitch. Do not pull this stitch too tightly, or the dimension will disappear.

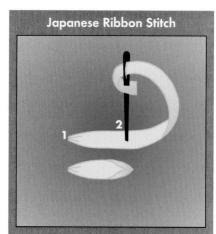

Japanese Ribbon Stitch

Spider Web Rose

Make the "spiderweb" using floss or thin pearl cotton, beginning with a fly stitch and adding straight stitches for a total of five spokes (a). Bring the ribbon up near the center and weave it under and over the spokes (b) until the spokes are covered, keeping the ribbon loose and allowing it to twist as you work.

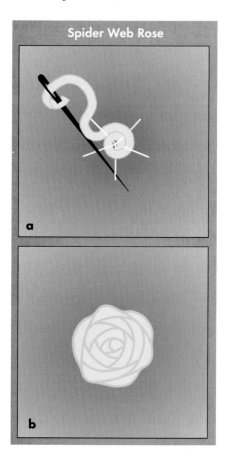

Spider Web Rose

a

b

Plume Stitch

As shown on the opposite page (top), bring the ribbon up at 1 and down ⅛" to ¼" away at 2, forming a loop. Use the tip of the needle or a round toothpick to keep the loop flat. Hold the loop in place and bring the needle up at 3, piercing the ribbon, and form another loop.

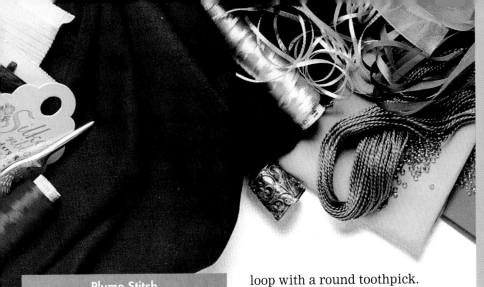

Plume Stitch

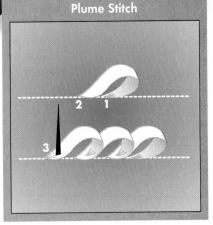

loop with a round toothpick. Bring the needle up at the beginning point again, and form another loop. Repeat until you've made a total of five loop petals. With contrasting floss or ribbon, add French knots to the center of the flower.

Loop Flower

Needle Pointer

For wearables, use closely stitched ribbon stitches such as French knots and lazy daisy stitches. Larger, looser, and more fragile stitches can be used for projects that will be framed.

Decorative Lazy Daisy

Begin by working a soft lazy daisy stitch with the first color of ribbon (see the instructions on page 130). With a contrasting ribbon color, work a straight stitch across the end of the lazy daisy stitch.

Decorative Lazy Daisy

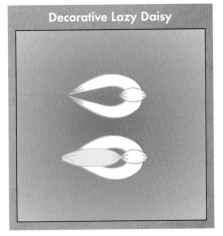

Loop Flower

Bring the ribbon through the fabric, then down ⅛" to ¼" away, forming a loop (see the illustration of plume stitch). Control the

Stitching Solution

Ribbon embroidery can be added to many purchased or home-sewn garments. If you are planning to embellish a purchased item, look for garments with yoke seams or linings that can be loosened to allow you to slip your embroidery hoop inside. When embellishing home-sewn baby garments, it's sometimes best to stitch the embroidery before the garment is cut out from the yardage. For adult garments, embroidery can be added during or after construction.

Machine Embroidery

While medium-weight woven fabrics are easiest to use for machine embroidery, virtually any fabric can be used. Thin or stretchy fabrics should be stabilized first with commercial stabilizer.

Many sewing machines today feature built-in decorative specialty stitches and monogramming designs. Many older-model zigzag machines feature decorative embroidery designs that can be created by using cams or other attachments. These specialty stitch patterns can be used to make many beautiful home accents and wearable items. Free-motion embroidery creates the same effect as hand embroidery, except you use your machine to outline and fill in areas of your pattern.

Preparing Fabric

1. If you're using thin or stretchy fabric, stabilize it with a commercial stabilizer, thin iron-on interfacing, or freezer paper. For more information about stabilizing, see page 24.

2. Transfer the pattern onto the fabric following the instructions on page 118. For nappy fabrics such as terry cloth, trace the pattern onto paper, and pin the paper to the fabric with the design in the proper position.

Preparing the Machine

1. Make sure your machine is clean and oiled, if needed. (If your machine is used frequently for machine embroidery, it will require more frequent cleaning and oiling.)

2. Work a small strip of satin stitches or very close zigzagging on scrap fabric. Loosen the top tension until no puckers appear in the stitching, the top thread pulls to the back slightly, and no bobbin thread shows on the front of your work.

3. Follow your machine's instruction manual for stitching with decorative specialty stitches or monograms.

Free-Motion Embroidery

1. Place the fabric in an embroidery hoop.

2. Lower the feed dogs and remove the presser foot as shown. Lower the presser bar while stitching to engage the tension on the top thread. A darning foot may be used and will help prevent puckering.

3. Set the stitch length to zero, and set the stitch width to a short to medium zigzag for filling in areas. Set the stitch width to zero for making outlines. Experiment to find the proper tension. You will probably have to lower it by two stops.

4. Hold the top thread and bring up the bobbin thread. Then hold both threads as you take a few stitches with your stitch length on zero to secure the threads. Clip the thread tails. Stitch the design, holding the embroidery hoop with both hands.

Rest your forearms on the sewing table as you stitch, and move the embroidery hoop back and forth with both hands.

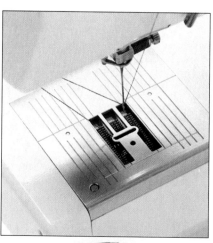

Finishing

After the stitching is complete, clean and press or block the embroidered piece. A gentle hand washing or dry cleaning is recommended to remove oils and dirt.

For embroidered clothing and most embroidery worked in a hoop, pressing is sufficient to remove wrinkles. For pieces that have been stretched out of shape during stitching, blocking is necessary.

Blocking is a fairly simple procedure that will enhance the appearance of your finished embroidery if the fabric has been pulled out of shape.

Cleaning and Pressing

If an embroidered piece is made with washable fabrics and threads, hand wash it according to the instructions for hand washing cross-stitch on page 80. Embroidery may also be dry-cleaned.

After washing, roll the damp embroidery in a clean, white cotton towel and press it according to the instructions on page 80.

Blocking

1. Make a blocking board large enough to hold your embroidered piece according to the instructions for blocking cross-stitch on page 80.

2. If all of the embroidery fibers and fabric are washable, hand wash the embroidered piece. If the fibers are not washable, have the piece dry-cleaned, then dampen it with cold water using a fine-mist spray bottle.

3. Lay the damp embroidered piece on the blocking board, and pin it to shape using the board's grid lines as a guide as shown. Allow the piece to dry.

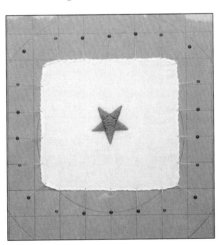

Stitching Solution

It's best to use acid-free materials for framing fine embroidery. Other materials can cause deterioration and discoloration of the fabrics and threads over time. Acid-free materials are available in fine art materials shops and also in some quilting and needlework shops.

EMBROIDERY

Needle Pointer

If you need to rip out a densely stitched area of machine embroidery, try holding the fabric taut and "shaving" the back of the fabric with a few strokes of a disposable razor.

Springtime Napkins

Set a pretty table with colorful embroidered napkins. Traditional flowers and stems brighten the corners of purchased napkins.

Skill Level

Easy

Size

Design area is about 5½" x 5½"

Materials (for one napkin)

Large cloth napkin, about 18½" x 18½"

Six-strand embroidery floss as indicated in the color key

Instructions

1. Following the instructions on page 118, transfer the Springtime Napkins pattern onto the corner of the napkin.

2. Using two strands of floss and satin stitches, embroider the large flower petals in the colors indicated in the pattern.

3. Using three strands of floss and stem stitches and lazy daisy stitches, embroider the stems and leaves as indicated.

4. Using three strands of floss and lazy daisy stitches, embroider the purple flowers.

5. Using three strands of floss and straight stitches and French knots, embroider the remaining flowers and flower centers as indicated.

Something Different

Embroider this springtime floral design on the collar of a pretty Easter dress. Choose pastel floss colors to coordinate with the dress, and outline the large flower in stem stitches for a delicate look.

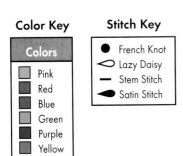

Color Key

Colors	
☐	Pink
☐	Red
☐	Blue
☐	Green
☐	Purple
☐	Yellow

Stitch Key

●	French Knot
◯	Lazy Daisy
—	Stem Stitch
◖	Satin Stitch

Springtime Napkins

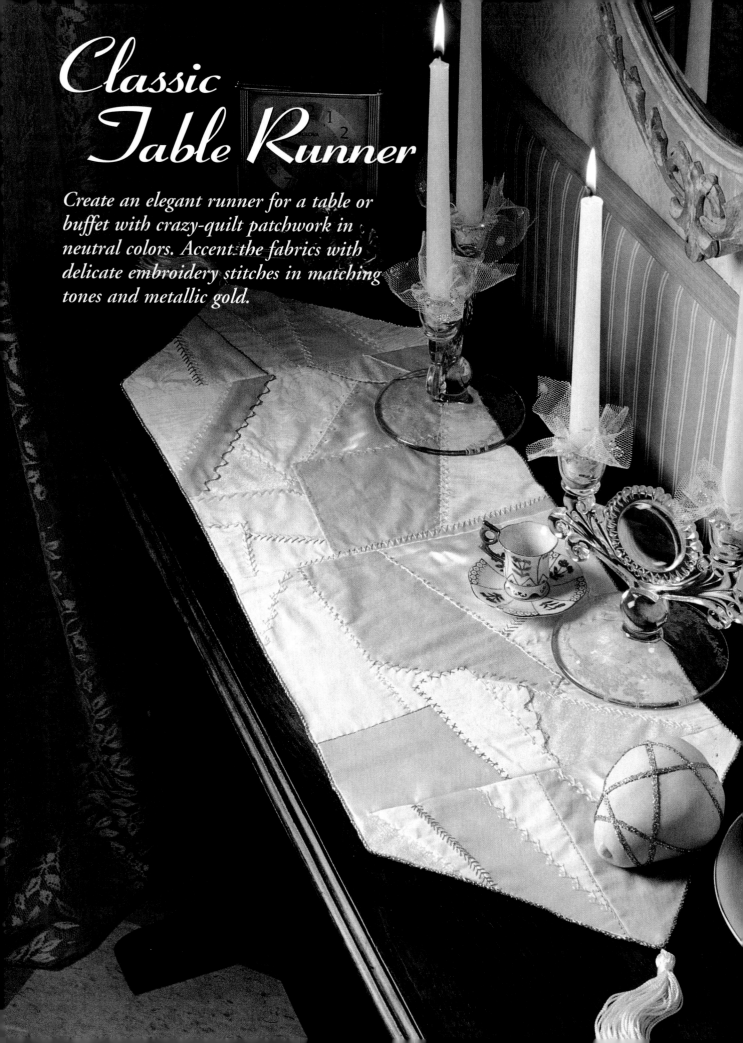

Classic Table Runner

Create an elegant runner for a table or buffet with crazy-quilt patchwork in neutral colors. Accent the fabrics with delicate embroidery stitches in matching tones and metallic gold.

Skill Level

Intermediate

Size

9" x 33" plus tassels

Materials

1 yard of white cotton

Scraps of cotton, satin, silk, moiré, and other fabrics as desired in several colors of white, off-white, beige, and similar colors

2¼ yards of narrow metallic gold cording

2 off-white 4" tassels

White sewing thread

Six-strand floss, thin metallic cording, and metallic thread in several shades of white, off-white, beige, and gold

Instructions

1. From the white cotton, cut two 10½" squares. Adding ½" seam allowances and following the instructions on page 13 for enlarging the pattern, cut two Runner End Piece patterns. Press the fabric scraps.

2. Following the instructions on page 188 for "Crazy Patchwork," cover the squares and end pieces with the scraps.

3. Using a rotary cutter, cutting mat, and see-through ruler if desired, trim the squares to 9½" x 9½". Trace the Runner End Piece pattern, adding ¼" seam allowances. Pin a paper pattern to each patchwork end piece, then trim each end piece to the pattern shape. Press all pieces from the front and the back.

4. Using ¼" seam allowances and with right sides together, sew the squares together, then sew an end piece to each end. Press the seams open.

5. Using two strands of floss, one strand of metallic cording, and one or two strands of metallic thread, work decorative embroidery along each patchwork seam line. Use straight stitches, stem stitches, cross-stitches, chain stitches, feather stitches, blanket stitches, French knots, and herringbone stitches. Do not embroider along seams attaching squares and end pieces. Press from the back.

6. To cut out the runner lining, use the runner front as a pattern. Pin the runner front wrong side down to the remaining white cotton with the length of the runner perpendicular to the grain line of the cotton. Cut out the lining to match the runner front.

7. Position the runner front and runner lining with right sides together. Using a ¼" seam allowance and leaving an opening along one side for turning, sew around all of the edges of the runner. Trim the corners, turn right side out, and press. Hand sew the opening closed.

8. Using the sewing machine threaded with invisible nylon thread or a needle and gold thread, sew gold cording around the outside of the runner. To sew by machine, use a narrow zigzag stitch and hold the cording to the edge of the runner as you stitch, overlapping the ends slightly and taking ½" tails to the back of the runner. To sew by hand, whipstitch the cording in place. Hand stitch the tails to the back.

9. Sew the tassels to the table runner points.

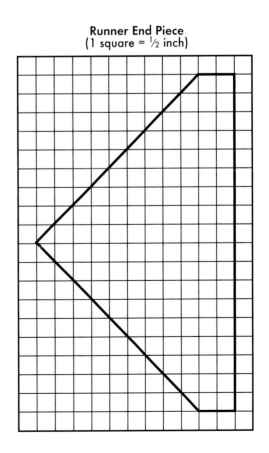

Runner End Piece
(1 square = ½ inch)

Samantha the Cat

This precious feline is right at home in any decor from country to Victorian. She's made with crewel embroidery stitches, then stuffed and adorned with a perky ribbon collar or bow tie.

Skill Level

Challenging

Size

9" x 13"

Materials

Two 16" squares of medium-weight off-white cotton, such as duck or sailcloth

Dark gray, medium gray, and beige tapestry wool

Tiny amount of white tapestry wool or embroidery floss

Fiberfill

Bow tie or 24" of ribbon (optional)

Instructions

1. Following the instructions on page 118, transfer the Samantha the Cat pattern on pages 142 and 143 onto one square of the fabric, tracing the overlapping area of the pattern only once.

2. Use one strand of tapestry wool throughout. Using dark gray and satin stitches, stitch the center of each eye. Using dark gray and stem stitches, outline the eyes. Using white and a small straight stitch, add a highlight to each eye.

3. Using both colors of gray and long and short stitches, stitch the bridge of the nose, placing the colors as indicated in the pattern. Using beige and satin stitches, stitch the tip of the nose and the tongue.

4. Using dark gray and stem stitches, stitch the mouth, extending the lines under the nose as indicated by the heavy lines on the pattern.

5. Using dark gray and stem stitches, stitch the leg and foot

outlines. Using medium gray and satin stitches, stitch the triangular areas on the feet.

6. Using long and short stitches and the colors indicated in the pattern, stitch the cat's stripes and all of the remaining areas. Begin stitching each stripe at the center and work outward.

7. Press the finished piece from the back. With the right side of the embroidery facing the right side of the cotton square, pin the pieces together around the outside of the cat. Using short stitches and leaving a 3" opening

along the side for turning, sew along the outside pattern line. Turn right side out and press.

8. Stuff the cat, using a chopstick or dowel to push bits of stuffing into the ears. Do not stuff too firmly; the cat should be flat and not too rounded.

9. Hand sew the opening closed.

10. If desired, cut the tie ends from the bow tie and pin the tie to the cat's neck area, or wrap the ribbon around the cat's neck and tie a bow.

Something Different

Create a Victorian kitty by wrapping ribbon and lace around the neck. Add a ruffled jabot made from a piece of gathered lace, and top it off with an antique earring "brooch."

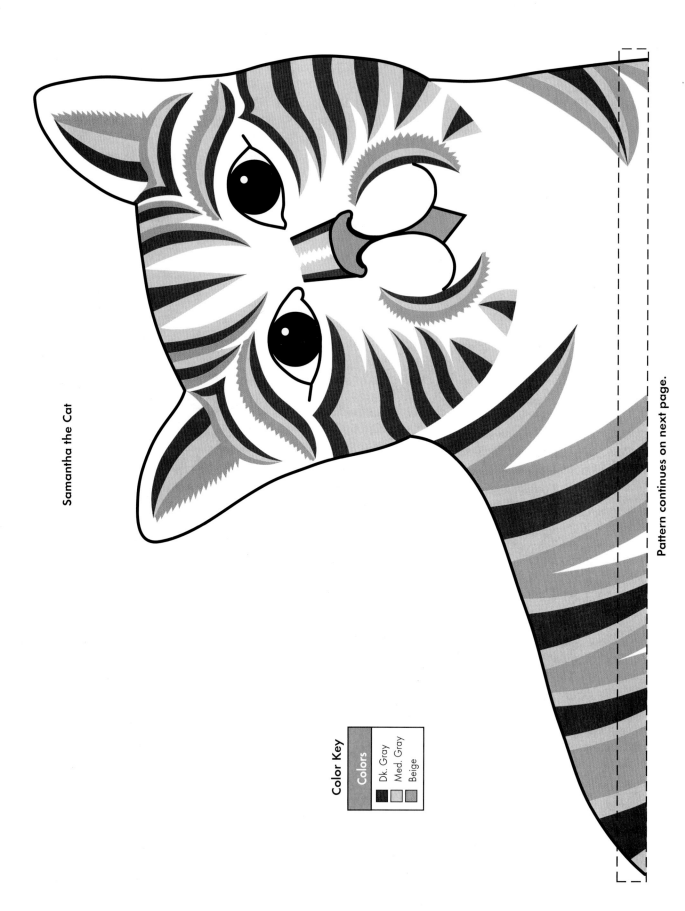

Samantha the Cat

Color Key

Colors	
■	Dk. Gray
□	Med. Gray
▨	Beige

Pattern continues on next page.

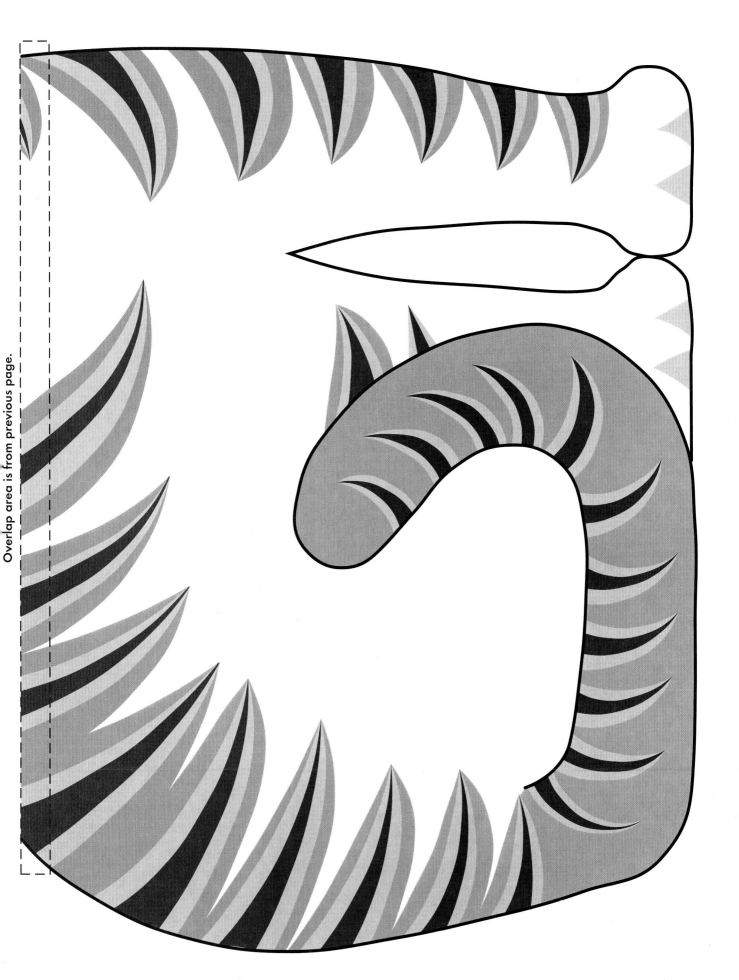

Knitting

Knitting has been used to fashion clothing and blankets since very early civilization. The basic forms for the styles of knitting that are popular today have their roots in the British Isles, including many of the islands off the coast of Ireland. Knitting stitches, which began as hallmarks of particular regions and clans, are appreciated now purely for the beauty of their textural interest and design.

Many traditional wool yarns are available today, as well as a huge selection of yarns in other natural and synthetic fibers.

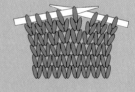

KNITTING

Equipment

There is a wide range of knitting yarns available to suit every taste and budget. With your chosen yarn, a pair of knitting needles, and familiarity with a few basic stitches, you're ready to begin. Other accessories are helpful as you move on to larger and more intricate projects.

Yarn

From simple acrylic or wool to lush silks and textured blends, yarns for knitting encompass all types used for crocheting and then some. When selecting yarn for a sweater or other knitting project, an important consideration is its washability. Most yarn labels have care instructions and recommendations for knitting needle size.

Plastic Rings and Stitch Count Markers

Placed on needles, plastic rings and stitch count markers are used to indicate points, such as increase or decrease. Plastic rings may also be used to make yarn-covered buttons.

Yarn Bobbins

These are used in multicolored knitting. Each bobbin, wrapped with a different color yarn, dangles from work as knitting progresses.

Knitting Gauge Rulers

These rulers have a right-angled opening through which stitches and rows can be accurately measured. Most knitting gauge rulers also have holes for checking needle size.

Stitch Holders

Similar to large safety pins, stitch holders are used to temporarily hold stitches while knitting shaped areas such as necklines and shoulders.

THE BOYE NEEDLE COMPANY

INSTRUCTIONS: To check your gauge, cast on 20 to 30 stitches, using needle size recommended in instructions. Knit 3" in pattern stitch. Smooth out swatch and pin down, but don't stretch. Place Boye 2" stitch measure over swatch and count number of stitches across and number of rows. If you have more stitches and rows than called for in the instructions, use larger needles. If you have fewer, use smaller needles. Knit new swatches and re-check until gauge is correct.

KNITTING GAUGE
6" RULER

Boye

2" STITCH MEASURE

Tapestry Needles
Sometimes called yarn needles, these large sewing needles are used for weaving in loose ends and sewing seams.

Crochet Hooks
Picking up dropped stitches and joining seams can be accomplished with crochet hooks.

Point Protectors
These are rubber tips that slip on the end of a needle to prevent stitches from slipping off.

Knitting Tally
This small tool slips on the end of the knitting needle, or it can be kept nearby, to keep track of the number of rows as they are knitted.

Regular Knitting Needles
Regular knitting needles are straight and have a point on one end. They are used for flat knitting and come in various lengths in sizes 0 through 15.

Double Pointed Needles
These short, straight needles have points on both ends. They come in sets of four and are used together to make seamless knitted tubes for items such as socks and mittens.

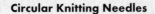

Circular Knitting Needles
Made of plastic or nylon, circular knitting needles have two points connected by a thin cable. The needles are available in various lengths and many sizes and are most often used for making sweaters and other garments with many stitches.

Cable Stitch Holders
These needles are used while making cables. They temporarily hold a few stitches either to the back or front of the work.

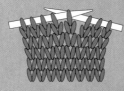

KNITTING

Needle Pointer

With a circular needle, you can stitch around the entire circumference of a sweater up to the bottom of the arm-holes, eliminating side seams. This method also saves time because you do not have to turn your work at the end of each row.

Getting Started

Casting on is a foundation for the first row of knitting. One of the most important things to remember while learning to knit is to keep the cast-on stitches loose. You can do this by casting on with a set of needles that is one size larger than recommended. After casting on, switch to the correct needle size and begin knitting.

Casting On

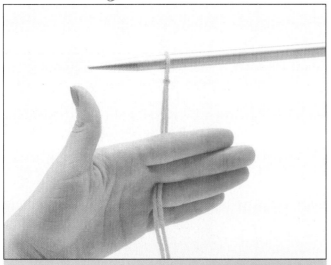

1 Measure 1" of yarn for each stitch you plan to cast on. Make a slip knot according to the instructions on page 40. Slide one knitting needle into the knot. Slip the yarn between the middle and ring fingers of your left hand.

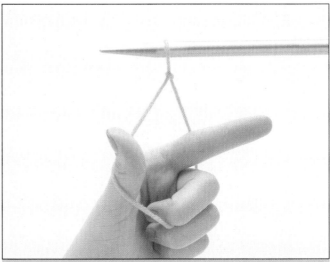

2 With the short end of the yarn over your thumb, slip your thumb and forefinger between the yarn strands. Curl your remaining fingers to hold the yarn.

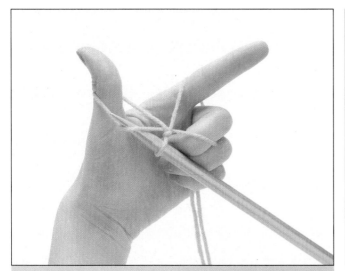

3 Bring the needle forward. Insert the end of the needle from the front to the back under the bottom of the strand that goes around your thumb.

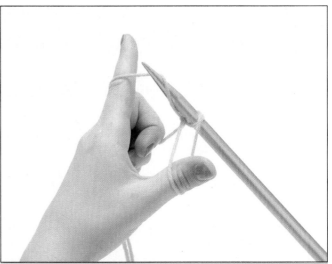

4 Take the needle up to the right of the strand that goes over your forefinger, and insert the needle under the strand from the right.

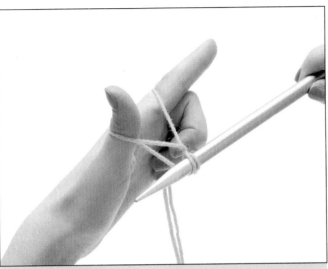

5 Take the needle and yarn through the loop on your thumb, forming the first cast-on stitch on your needle.

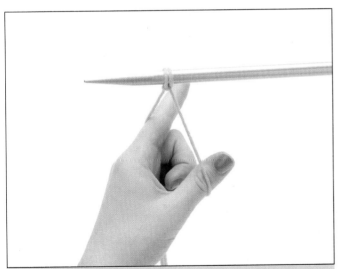

6 Let the loop slip from your thumb. Insert your thumb under the front strand of yarn and pull (not too tightly) to secure the stitch on the needle.

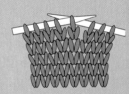

Needle Pointer

For a soft edge, use the cast-on method shown here. For a firmer edge, use the two-needle cast-on method shown on page 152.

Reading Instructions

Knitting instructions are written with abbreviations for most-often-used terms and are punctuated with parentheses, brackets, and asterisks to indicate sections of the pattern that you should repeat.

Punctuation Marks

( ) Parentheses enclose a sequence of instructions. Following the parentheses will be an indication of how many times this sequence is repeated. For example, "(k2, p4, k2, p6) 4 times" means to follow the instructions enclosed in the parentheses a total of four times.

* Asterisks may appear alone or in pairs and are often used in combination with parentheses. When used in pairs, asterisks serve essentially the same function as parentheses, with one exception. The instructions of what to do with the sequence enclosed between asterisks may appear directly after the last asterisk or later in the pattern. For example, "*p 4, (k6, psso, k6) twice*, p12; repeat from * to * 4 times" means to work through the instructions, then repeat only the instructions between the asterisks four times.

[ ] Brackets are used to further clarify sequences of instructions, usually in combination with parentheses and asterisks. In addition, instructions are usually written for one size, with pattern changes for additional sizes enclosed in brackets.

Stitch Count At the end of some of the rows in knitting instructions, a number is enclosed in parentheses. This is the stitch count, or number of stitches you should have on your needle.

Abbreviations These marks shorten instructions and make them easier to follow. At right is a list of the most commonly used abbreviations.

Abbreviations

alt	alternate
beg	beginning
cbl	cable
cn	cable needle
dec	decrease
dp	double pointed
inc	increase
k	knit
lp	loop
p	purl
patt(s)	pattern(s)
psso	pass slip stitch over
rem	remaining
rnd	round
rep	repeat
sk	skip
Skp	slip 1, knit 1, pass slip stitch(es) over knit stitch(es)
sl	slip
sl st	slip stitch
ssk	slip, slip, knit decrease
st(s)	stitch(es)
St st	stockinette stitch
tog	together
yb	yarn in back
yf	yarn in front
yo	yarn over

Selecting Needles

When making knitted baby items or other lightweight garments, choose baby weight or sport weight yarn and knitting needles up to size 5. For most knitted adult garments, accessories, and afghans, worsted weight yarn is the best choice, and it can be knitted on needles from size 5 to 9. Heavy jackets, sweaters, and afghans may be knitted with bulky yarn and needles from size 10 to 15.

Needle equivalences are not exact and may vary depending on the published source. At right is a list of the most commonly used equivalences.

Needle Sizes

U.S.	Metric
0	2.00 mm
1	2.25 mm
2	2.75 mm
3	3.25 mm
4	3.50 mm
5	3.75 mm
6	4.00 mm
7	4.50 mm
8	5.00 mm
9	5.50 mm
10	6.00 mm
10½	6.50 mm
11	8.00 mm
13	9.00 mm
15	10.00 mm

Checking Gauge

Gauge is very important, especially for garments. Needle size is the key to correct gauge.

1. Make a 6" × 6" sample piece using the needle size and stitch indicated.

2. Without stretching the swatch, pin it flat and count the stitches and rows. If your swatch has more or fewer rows or stitches per inch than stated in the gauge, make the swatch again with smaller or larger needles.

Controlling Yarn Tension

For even stitches, the same amount of yarn should be released from your fingers with each stitch. Control the yarn tension by wrapping the yarn around the fingers of your right hand as shown. Lift the yarn and make each stitch with the index finger of your right hand.

Holding Yarn

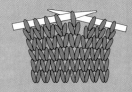

Needle Pointer

If your hands feel rough, and your yarn doesn't slide smoothly through your fingers, apply lotion or hand cream before picking up your knitting. Wait a few minutes for the cream to absorb, or it may be transferred to your yarn.

Stitches

Every knitting stitch is a variation of two simple stitches, the knit stitch and the purl stitch. With combinations of these two stitches, stitch patterns are created.

Basic Stitches

Two-Needle Cast On

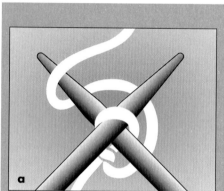

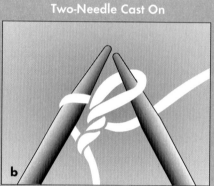

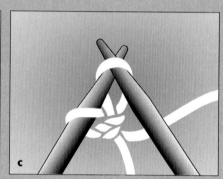

Make a slip knot about 3" from the end of the yarn and slip the knot onto the needle. Hold this needle in your left hand, and insert the other needle through the loop from the front to the back. Bring

the yarn counterclockwise between the needles to the front (a). With the right needle, draw the strand through the loop on the left needle, forming a stitch on the right needle (b). Slip the stitch

onto the left needle (c), and gently pull on the yarn to secure the stitch. To make another stitch, insert the needle through the new stitch from the front to the back, and repeat (b) and (c).

Knit Stitch (k)

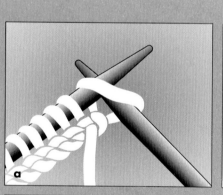

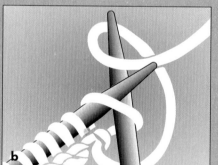

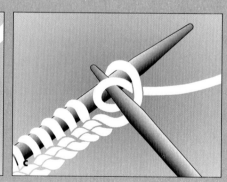

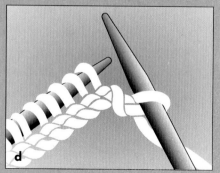

Hold the needle with the cast-on stitches in your left hand. With the yarn at the back of your work, insert the right needle into the first stitch from the front to the back (a). With your right forefinger, take the yarn

counterclockwise around the right needle and between the needles (b). Draw the yarn through the loop on the left needle, forming a new stitch (c). Slip the stitch off of the left needle (d).

Purl Stitch (p)

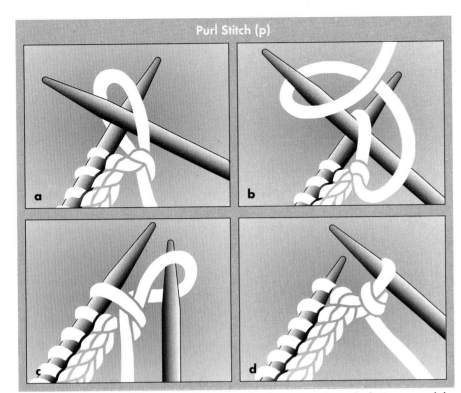

Hold the needle with the cast-on stitches in your left hand. With the yarn at the front of your work, insert the right needle into the first stitch from the back to the front (a). With your right forefinger, take the yarn counterclockwise around the right needle and between the needles (b). Draw the yarn through the loop on the left needle, forming a new stitch (c). Slip the stitch off of the left needle (d).

Stitching Solution

To recycle yarn from last year's half-finished knitting project, unravel the yarn, dampen it, and wind it around the back rungs of a wooden chair. Do not wind the yarn too tightly, or it will lose some of its loft. Allow it to dry completely before removing it from the chair.

Unraveled knitting yarn with the kinks left in makes wonderful hair for cloth dolls and stuffed animals.

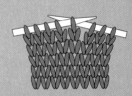

Needle Pointer

Many beginning knitters purl more loosely than they knit. If you find yourself doing this, try to keep more tension on the yarn for purl rows. If the problem is severe, you may want to switch to smaller needles for the purl rows.

Stitch Patterns

Garter Stitch

Knit all rows. Both sides of the fabric will look alike.

Stockinette Stitch (St st)

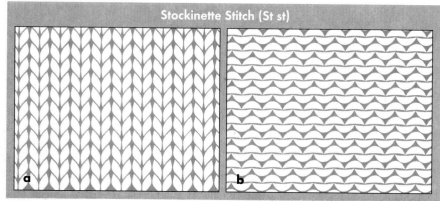

Knit one row, then purl one row. Repeat these two rows, knitting all right-side rows and purling all wrong-side rows. The front of the knitted fabric forms

V-stitches (a), and the back has small ridges (b). The stitch is called reverse stockinette stitch if the back of the fabric is used as the right side.

Stitching Solution

If the stitches at the ends of your stockinette stitch rows are looser than the rest of the stitches, try slipping the first and last stitch of every knit row onto the right needle without knitting. Or, after making the first stitch each time, stop and tug on the yarn to make the stitch extra tight.

Seed Stitch

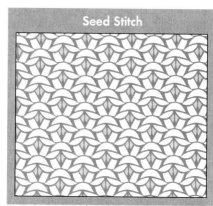

For the seed stitch, cast on an odd number of stitches. Knit 1, (purl 1, knit 1) across. Repeat this pattern for every row. Both sides of the knitted fabric will look alike.

Ribbing

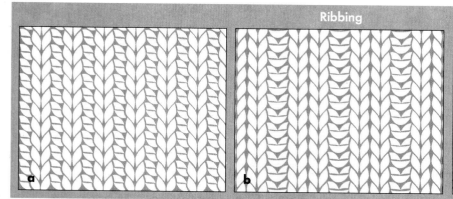

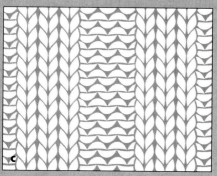

Ribbing patterns vary according to the width of the rib. On an even number of stitches, for a narrow ribbing , (knit 1, purl 1) across (a). Repeat for each row. For wider ribbings, (knit 2, purl 2) across (b) or (knit 3, purl 3) across (c).

Repeat for each row. Both sides of the ribbing will look the same for either narrow or wide ribbings.

Basketweave Stitch

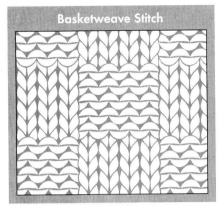

Cast on a number of stitches divisible by 8. For Rows 1, 2, 3, and 4, (knit 4, purl 4) across. For Rows 5, 6, 7, and 8, (purl 4, knit 4) across. Repeat these 8 rows for the pattern. Both sides of the knitted fabric will look the same.

Cables (Cbl)

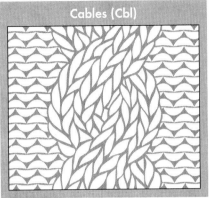

Where a cable occurs, slip half of the stitches in the cable onto a cable needle stitch holder and hold it either to the front or the back of the work. If the cable needle is held to the front of the work, the cable will twist to the left. If it is held to the back of the work, the cable will twist to the right. Knit the other half of the stitches in the cable, then knit the stitches from the cable needle. Cable patterns vary in size, shape, and number of stitches. This cable has 6 stitches, and the cable is worked in stockinette stitch with the background stitches in reverse stockinette stitch.

Bobbles

On the right side, increase the indicated number of stitches in the indicated stitch (see "Increasing" on page 156). Turning the work each time, knit, purl, then knit only the increased stitches (3 rows). Then decrease the stitches to the original 1 stitch (see "Decreasing" on page 158). This illustration shows a completed bobble made by increasing 3 stitches, working the bobble in reverse stockinette stitch on a stockinette stitch background.

Eyelets

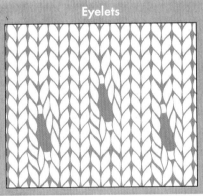

The easiest type of eyelet is a chain eyelet. To make this simple eyelet, make a yarn over, then knit the next 2 stitches together. The yarn over adds a stitch, and knitting two together decreases a stitch, so the resulting number of stitches is the same. (See "Decreasing" on page 158.) On the next row, treat the yarn-over loop as a stitch.

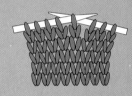

KNITTING

Needle Pointer

Garments made with acrylic yarns can be machine washed and dried. Turn the garment inside out while washing, and place it in a pillowcase or net bag to prevent snags. You may wish to hand wash and dry your acrylic garment for longer life, as many acrylic yarns may pill when machine washed and dried.

Techniques

Increasing and decreasing can be used to create patterned stitches or to shape garments and other projects. Special needles and various stitch combinations are used to knit interesting textures and special effects.

Increasing

In order to shape the pieces of a garment, increases must be added. Increases are also an important part of many stitch patterns.

There are several methods of increasing. The most popular are knitting a stitch twice, yarn over, and knitting between stitches. Each method has a different purpose.

Knitting a stitch twice, sometimes called the bar or raised method of increasing, produces a small raised area on the right side of your work and is not always a good choice in open areas of stockinette stitch. However, this raised area is not obvious at the edge of the work.

The yarn over increase method is used for making lacy and openwork knitting patterns because small holes are created with each increase.

Knitting between the stitches is the most invisible of all methods, and it is used for garment shaping.

Knitting a Stitch Twice

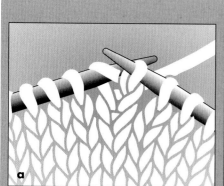

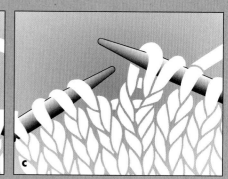

Knit 1 without slipping the stitch off of the left needle (a). Insert the right needle into the back loop of the same stitch and knit again (b). Slip the stitch off of the left needle onto the right needle (c).

Yarn Over Increase (yo)

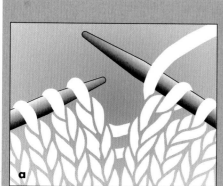
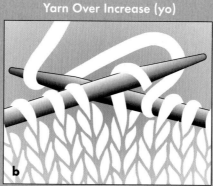
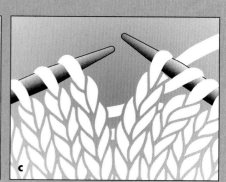

Bring the yarn to the right side of the work and loop the yarn around the right needle (a). Knit or purl the next stitch, wrapping the yarn as usual (b). Slip the stitch to the right needle (c). On the next row, treat the yarn-over loop as a stitch.

Knitting between Stitches

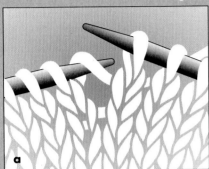

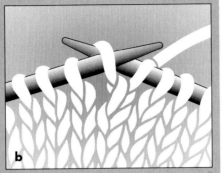

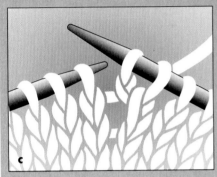

With the left needle, pick up a loop between the stitches (a). Knitting through the back loop, knit the loop as if it were a stitch (b). Slip the stitch from the left needle to the right needle (c).

Stitching Solution

To measure the width of a section of a sweater—the back, front, or sleeve—while it is still on your knitting needles, knit the piece on an extra-long circular needle. Place point protectors onto the needle tips and spread the knitting out completely flat to measure, making sure the needle is long enough to hold all of the stitches flat. If the knitted piece is still too wide for the needle, thread a tapestry needle with crochet cotton and carefully slip the stitches off of the needle and onto the cotton. After measuring, slip the circular needle back into the stitches.

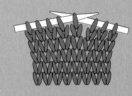

Needle Pointer

It is best not to increase or decrease in the very first or very last stitches in a row because it is impossible to weave a neat and invisible seam over these stitches. If a pattern says to increase or decrease at the beginning or end of a row, make these changes one or two stitches in from the edge.

Decreasing

Decreasing is used for shaping garments and is also an important part of many patterned stitches. The two basic methods for decreasing are knitting two stitches together and passing a slip stitch over.

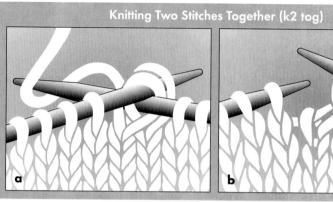

Knitting Two Stitches Together (k2 tog)

Insert the right needle into two stitches on the left needle (a). Knit them both at the same time as if they were one stitch (b).

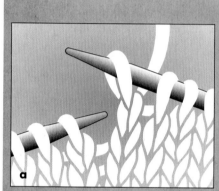
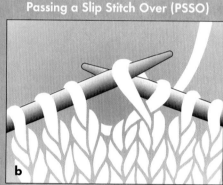
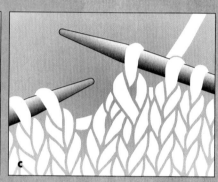

Passing a Slip Stitch Over (PSSO)

Slip the next stitch to the right needle without knitting. Knit the next stitch (a). With the left needle, pick up the slipped stitch from the right needle and pass it to the left over the knitted stitch and right-needle point without twisting (b, c).

Dropped Stitches

If you notice a dropped stitch several rows back and the stitch has been unraveling, you can pick it up with a crochet hook. Dropped stitches may be picked up on either the knit or the purl side.

1. Choose a hook size appropriate to the yarn. For knit stitches, or on the right side of stockinette stitch, insert the hook in the loop and pull the yarn "bar" above the loop through the loop (a).

2. Pull the next yarn "bar" through the loop on the hook; repeat up to the knitting needle; slip the last loop onto the needle.

3. For purl stitches, or on the wrong side of stockinette stitch, loop the dropped stitch through the back of and over the next yarn "bar." Pull the yarn bar through the loop (b); repeat up to the needle. Slip the last loop onto the needle.

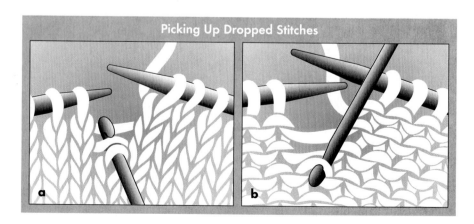

Picking Up Dropped Stitches

Correcting Mistakes

If an error involves only a stitch or two, remove only these from the needle, unravel, and reknit them following the instructions for "Dropped Stitches."

If an error involves many stitches or rows, take all of the knitting stitches off the needles and carefully unravel one row at a time until you have unraveled to the row just past the mistake. Slip all the knitting stitches back onto the left needle and reknit.

Correcting Mistakes

Binding Off

To remove the stitches from the needles and create a finished edge, you bind off.

1. With all of the stitches on the left needle, knit 2.

2. Insert the left needle into the front of the first stitch on the right needle (a). Lift this stitch over the second stitch knitted and the point of the right needle (b), leaving one loop on the right needle.

3. Knit 1; repeat (a) and (b) to bind off. For a more finished edge, knit the knit stitches and purl the purl stitches when binding off.

4. To finish the last stitch, clip the yarn about 6" from the end and pull the yarn end through the stitch.

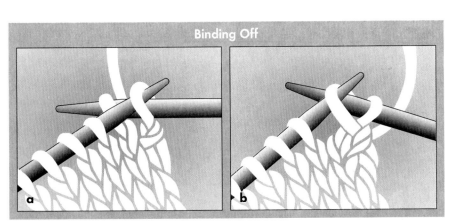

Binding Off

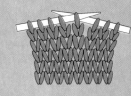

Needle Pointer

If you discover you have a mysterious extra stitch in your knitting, try to figure out where it was created. Often, extra stitches are added by forgetting to bring the yarn to the front when purling. This creates an extra yarn over, which is a technique used for increasing and leaves a hole in the fabric. If you discover a yarn-over hole in your knitting, try darning it from the back with matching yarn. If the repair job is almost invisible, there really is no need to rip out your work and correct the mistake.

Knitting in the Round

In order to form seamless tubes, use double pointed needles for knitting in the round. Four double pointed needles are used, with the stitches divided on three needles and the fourth needle used for making the stitches.

1. To cast on in the round, cast on the required number of stitches on one double pointed needle, then slip one-third of the stitches on each of two double pointed needles.

2. Form a triangle with the three needles, and place a stitch marker at the end of the cast-on stitches as shown. Make sure the knitting isn't twisted. With the fourth needle, knit the first stitch on the next needle to close the circle.

3. Knit the remaining stitches on the first needle. Now use the first needle, which no longer has any stitches on it, to knit the stitches on the second needle. Repeat for the third needle.

4. Use the slip stitch marker to mark the start of each round.

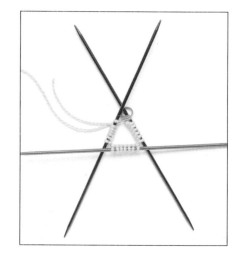

Color Knitting

There are several methods for knitting with more than one color of yarn. Fair Isle knitting patterns look very intricate, but they are fairly easy to knit because only two colors are used in each row as shown below. The strands not in use are carried across the back of the work as shown on the right.

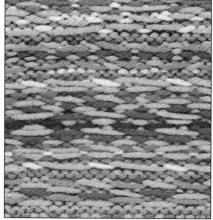

When a knitting design features small, isolated areas of color, knitting bobbins can be used. Knitting bobbins hold small amounts of yarn and help keep yarns from tangling. When bobbins are used, yarn is not carried across the back. Instead, each section of color has its own bobbin.

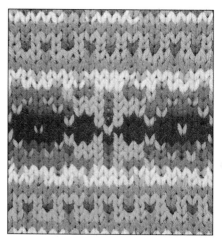

When knitting with more than one color, the yarn must be twisted each time a new color is picked up. This is a small but crucial step that will prevent holes from forming at the point where the color changes.

As you pick up the new color, twist both colors together once at the back of your work. Holding the new color, work the next stitch.

Lace Knitting

These stitch patterns look difficult, but most are actually quite simple. The pretty openwork patterns are formed by increasing, usually with yarn overs, and decreasing elsewhere in the pattern so that the number of stitches remains constant.

Lace designs have always been among the most popular of all knitting techniques. Many of today's patterns have roots dating back to nineteenth-century Scotland and the Shetland Islands.

Aran Knitting

Sometimes called Irish fisherman knitting, this technique features interesting cables, bobbles, and other textured patterns. It is usually worked with one color of yarn, traditionally off-white. Authentic Irish fisherman sweaters are knitted with raw wool, which retains many of its natural oils, making the heavily textured sweaters even warmer. Today, aran patterns are knitted with many types of yarn, and they are also used to make afghans, baby items, and many accessories.

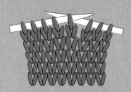

KNITTING

Needle Pointer

When making a garment or afghan using aran knitting stitches, remember that a sample of this type of knitting will be shorter and narrower than the same number of rows and stitches of stockinette stitch.

Weaving in Loose Ends

1. Thread one loose end into a size 16 or 18 tapestry needle.

2. Weave the end through the back of matching color stitches for several inches along the edge as shown, then turn and weave back in the other direction. Be sure to hide the loose end in the stitches. Do not pull the loose end tightly. If the loose ends are in the middle of your work, weave them in carefully through the back of several stitches or rows.

3. Clip the yarn end and stretch the area slightly. The yarn end will disappear into the stitches.

Cleaning and Blocking

Finished knitted pieces may be cleaned and blocked before assembling the item, or the completed knitted item may be cleaned and then blocked. Blocking a piece before assembly will shape it to the desired measurements before it is sewn together.

Blocking a finished garment is useful when you need to shape an item to a specific finished size.

Cleaning

1. Following the instructions on the yarn label, gently wash the knitted pieces.

2. Rinse the pieces well, then squeeze out the excess water gently and without wringing, and lay the pieces flat on large towels out of direct sunlight.

Blocking

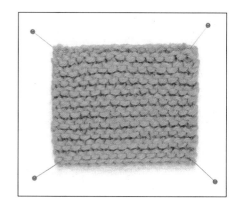

1. Arrange the knitted pieces right side up on the towels. Using your hands, press the pieces to smooth the stitches flat and to even out the edges. Measure to make sure the pieces are the correct size, making sure sleeves and other matching pieces are the same. Make sure seams that will be sewn together are exactly the same length.

2. Secure the pieces in place at the edges with rustproof pins as shown, if desired. Pins may leave marks on some knitted fabrics, so take care to place the pins in the edges or in areas that will be part of the seams.

3. If the pieces are made with synthetic yarn, lightly steam press the pieces by holding the iron above the stitches and allowing the steam to penetrate the fibers as shown. Do not rest the iron on the knitted pieces. Do not steam mohair or other natural fibers. Allow the knitted pieces to dry completely before moving them.

Joining

There are several methods for joining knitted pieces. The sewing and crochet methods are best if an item is knitted with fine or medium-weight yarn. The weaving, or grafting, method does not add bulk and works well for items knitted with heavy or bulky yarn.

Sewing Method

1. Thread a tapestry needle using the yarns from the project.

2. Sew the seams together using a backstitch or slip stitch over one or two stitches as shown. As you stitch, match the pattern.

Crochet Method

1. Choose a crochet hook size appropriate for the yarn (see "Selecting Hooks" on page 43).

2. Slip stitch the seams together as shown. (For instructions on joining with a slip stitch, see page 55.)

Stitching Solution

A loose stitch in the body of your work can be tightened. Use the point of a knitting needle to pull the stitch from the back until it looks like the other stitches. Then, working toward the nearest edge, pull the fullness into the next stitch and so on until you reach the edge. The resulting loop at the edge of the knitting can be sewn into the seam later.

Weaving (or Grafting) Method

1. Each piece should have the same number of stitches. Do not bind off; slip the stitches off of the needles, and lay the pieces right side up with seam areas butting.

2. Thread a tapestry needle with yarn from the project.

3. Insert the needle from the bottom to the top into the first stitch on the bottom left piece.

4. Insert the needle from the top to the bottom into the next stitch on the right piece as shown, then bring the needle up in the next stitch on the same piece.

5. Insert the needle from the top to the bottom into the next stitch on the left piece, then bring the needle up in the next stitch on the same piece. Stitches may be woven while still on the knitting needles.

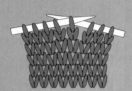

Needle Pointer

Sometimes flawed yarn can cause a discolored stitch or two in your project. If you first notice the discolored area after the project is finished, don't despair. The area can be stitched over with duplicate stitch and new yarn to create a flawless appearance. See Chapter 4, beginning on page 92, for duplicate stitch instructions.

Toasty Mittens

Knit a pair of soft and cozy
mittens in her favorite color.
They're so warm and pretty,
she'll never forget them!

Skill Level

Easy

Size

Size indicates measurement in inches around the palm. Instructions are written for size 6½, with sizes 7 and 7½ in brackets.

Materials

3 oz. knitting worsted weight yarn

Knitting needles sizes 5 and 7, or sizes needed to obtain proper gauge

Gauge

With larger size needles, Stockinette Stitch: 20 sts and 24 rows = 4".

Instructions

With smaller needles, cast on 29 (31, 33).

Right Mitten Cuff

Row 1: P1, (K1, P1) across.
Row 2: K1, (P1, K1) across.
Repeat Rows 1 and 2 until the piece measures 2½" [2¾", 3"].

Mitten Body

Row 1: With larger needles, K across, increasing 5 [7, 7] sts evenly spaced. (34 [38, 40] sts)
Row 2: P across.
Row 3 (begin raised pattern and shaping): P5 [6, 6], K6 [6, 7], P5 [6, 6], place a ring marker on the right needle, increase twice, place another marker on the right needle, K across. (36 [40, 42] sts)
Row 4: P to the marker, slip the marker, P to the next marker, slip the marker, P5 [6, 6], K6 [6, 7], P5 [6, 6].
Row 5: K to the marker, slip the marker, increase, K to within one st of the next marker, increase, slip the marker, K across. (38 [42,44] sts)

Row 6: P across, slipping the markers as you come to them.
Rows 7 to 12 (7 to 12; 7 to 14): Repeat Rows 3 to 6, then 3 and 4 again [Rows 3 to 6, then 3 and 4 again; Rows 3 to 6 twice]. (44 [48, 52] sts)
Continue the pattern established in Rows 4 through 7, repeating without increases until piece measures about 4¾" [5", 5¼"]. End with a wrong-side row.

Thumb

Row 1: Work in established pattern to the marker and slip the 16 [18, 19] sts just worked onto a st holder. Pick up a loop between sts to add one st, K to the marker. Remove the marker; pick up a loop between sts to add one st. Slip the remaining 16 [18, 19] sts onto a st holder. (14 [14,16] sts)
Work even in St st until the thumb measures about 2" [2¼", 2½"]. End by working a P row.
Next Row: K2 tog across. (7 [7, 8] sts)
Cut the yarn, leaving a long end for sewing the seam. Using a yarn needle, weave the yarn end through the remaining sts, slipping the sts off the needle. Pull firmly and weave the thumb seam.

Mitten Back

The patterned section of the work on one side of the thumb is the back of the mitten.

With the thumb facing you, slip the sts from the back of the mitten onto a knitting needle. Work in the pattern established in Rows 4 to 7 without increases until the piece measures about 7" [7½", 7¾"]. End with a wrong-side row.

Shaping

Row 1: K2, sl 1 as if to K, K1, psso, K across to within 4 sts of end of row, K2 tog, K2. (14 [16, 17])
Row 2: P across.
Repeat Rows 1 and 2 three [four, five] times. (8 [8, 7] sts)

Next Row: K2 tog across. For the largest size, K2 tog across, K last st.
Cut the yarn, leaving a long end. Using a yarn needle, weave the yarn end through the remaining sts, slipping the sts off the needle and pulling firmly. Take a small stitch to secure the end of the mitten.

Mitten Palm

With the thumb facing you, slip the sts from the palm of the mitten onto a knitting needle. Work even in St st until the piece measures about 7" [7½", 7¾"]. End with a wrong-side row.
Repeat the "Shaping" instructions as for the mitten back.
Weave the mitten seams.

Left Mitten

Work as for the right mitten through Row 2 of "Mitten Body."
Row 3 (begin raised pattern and shaping): K16 [18, 19], place a ring marker on the right needle, increase twice, place another marker on the right needle, P5 [6, 6], K6 [6, 7], P5 [6, 6]. (36 [40, 42] sts)
Row 4: P5 [6, 6], K6, [6, 7], P to the marker, slip the marker, P to the next marker, slip the marker, P across.
Row 5: K to the marker, slip the marker, increase, K to within one st of the next marker, increase, slip the marker, K across. (38 [42,44] sts)
Row 6: P across, slipping the markers as you come to them.
Row 7: K to the marker, slip the marker, increase, K to within one st of the next marker, increase, slip the marker, P5 [6, 6], K6 [6, 7], P5 [6, 6]. Continue the pattern established in Rows 4 to 7, repeating without increases until the piece measures about 4¾" [5", 5¼"]. End with a wrong-side row.
Finish the left mitten, following the instructions in "Thumb," "Mitten Back," and "Mitten Palm."

Braided Cable Scarf

Try out some new stitches with this warm and fashionable scarf in fuzzy bulky yarn.

Skill Level

Intermediate

Size

11½" x 48" plus fringe

Materials

9 oz. fuzzy bulky yarn
Knitting needles size 10, or size needed to obtain proper gauge
Cable needle

Gauge

Stockinette St: 12 sts and 20 rows = 4"

Instructions

Cast on 38 sts.
Rows 1 to 7: (K1, P1) across.
Row 8: (K1, P1) 3 times, K26, (K1, P1) 3 times.
Row 9: (K1, P1) 3 times, P26, (K1, P1) 3 times.
Row 10: (K1, P1) 3 times, K10, sl next 2 sts onto a cable needle and hold at back of work, K2, K2 from cable needle, K12, (K1, P1) 3 times.
Row 11: Repeat Row 9.
Row 12: (K1, P1) 3 times, K12, sl next 2 sts onto a cable needle and hold at front of work, K2, K2 from cable needle, K10, (K1, P1) 3 times.

Something Different

Knit a 3¾" wide and 20" long strip of seed stitch with yarn that matches the scarf. Twist the strip once and sew the ends together for a stylish, warm headband.

Repeat Rows 9 to 12 until the scarf measures about 46" from beginning.
Repeat Rows 1 to 7. Bind off.

Fringe

For each fringe, cut two strands, each 8½" long. Follow the instructions on page 58 for attaching fringe to the scarf. Trim the ends evenly.

Stitching Solution

If you'd like to make this scarf an extra-easy beginner's project, try making it without the cable. Work the seed stitch rows according to the pattern for Rows 1 to 7. Then repeat Rows 8 and 9 until the scarf measures about 46" from the beginning. Repeat Rows 1 to 7 and add the fringe.

Fair Isle Pillow

Fair Isle knitting looks complicated, but only two colors are used in each knitted row. This decorative pillow will warm up your favorite reading spot.

Skill Level

Challenging

Size

Fits a 14" pillow form

Materials

2 oz. gold knitting worsted weight yarn

½ oz. each burgundy, dark rose, light rose, light purple, medium purple, and dark purple knitting worsted weight yarn

Knitting needles size 8, or size needed to obtain proper gauge

Crochet hook size G

14" pillow form

Gauge

Stockinette St: 15 sts and 18 rows = 4"

Instructions

Pillow Front

With burgundy, cast on 53.

Row 1: K across.

Rows 2 to 33: Following the graph from the bottom to the top, working one stitch for each square on the graph, and carrying each color of yarn not in use at the back of your work, work in St st (K each right side row and P each wrong side row).

Rows 34 to 63: Read the knit rows of the graph (odd-numbered rows) from right to left and the purl rows (even-numbered rows) from left to right.

Following the graph and working the rows from the top to the bottom from Row 32 back to Row 1, continue in St st.

Row 64: With burgundy, K across. Bind off.

Pillow Back

With gold, cast on 53.

Rows 1 to 64: With gold, work in Stockinette St.

Assembly

Block the pieces. Holding the wrong sides together and using the crochet hook, single crochet the pieces together around three sides (see page 58); insert the pillow form and continue to single crochet, joining around the remaining side. End off.

Color Key

Colors
☐ Lt. Rose
▨ Dk. Rose
■ Burgundy
☐ Lt. Purple
▨ Med. Purple
■ Dk. Purple
☐ Gold

Fair Isle Pillow

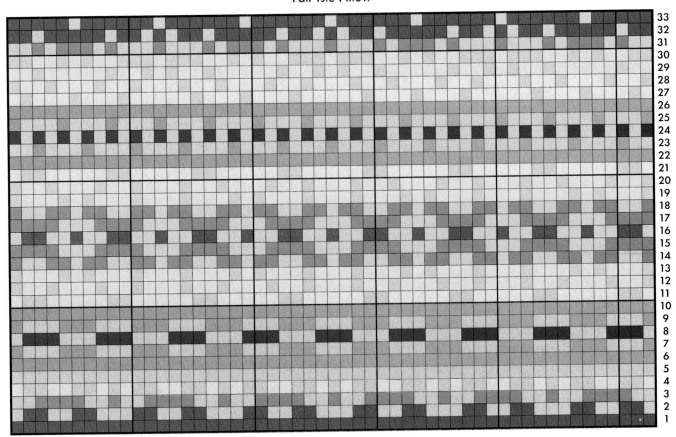

Patchwork Quilting

Quilting, the technique of joining layers of fabric together with a simple running stitch, is centuries old. When patchwork is combined with quilting, the results can be anything from subtle and traditional to stunning and contemporary.

Hand piecing and hand quilting are enjoyed by quilters around the world. These timeless techniques are used with the sewing machine and technological advancements such as the rotary cutter and basting gun. An ever-increasing supply of fabrics and tools offers today's quilter many options.

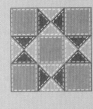

Equipment

Scissors, fabric, needle, and thread are the basics for patchwork quilting, but there are many more tools and materials available. Select tools according to your own needs, and change them as needed as your skills develop.

Thimbles

A thimble is essential for pushing the needle through the layers of fabric and batting when hand quilting. A thimble also can be worn on one finger of the hand that is held under the quilt. Thimbles are made of metal, plastic, or leather.

Markers and Pencils

Sharp pencils are used for tracing around templates onto fabric. Depending on the fabric color, use silver, white, yellow, light blue, or other colors for marking. A chalk marker is helpful for marking quilting lines on your quilt. Many types of markers and pencils are manufactured especially for use in quilting.

Batting

Available in cotton, woolen, synthetic, or blends, batting is the middle layer of the quilt.

Ruler, Yardstick, and Measuring Tape

These tools are used to measure fabrics, batting, bed size, and other items during the quilting process.

Quilting Hoop or Frame

A quilting hoop is like a big embroidery hoop, and it works in the same manner. A round hoop is best for holding the layers of fabric and batting at an even tension for hand quilting. Many types and sizes of quilting frames are manufactured today and are great for holding a quilt in progress.

Rotary Cutter, Cutting Mat, and See-Through Rulers

A rotary cutter is a fabric cutting tool that has a round razor blade attached to a handle. It is used with cutting mats and large, clear plastic rulers that are marked with precise measurements for quick and accurate cutting.

Templates and Stencils

Templates and stencils can be purchased or made from plastic or thin cardboard. Templates are thin, durable shapes that are used as patterns for marking patchwork pieces. Quilting stencils and templates are used to mark quilting patterns on the finished quilt top.

Iron

A steam iron and a padded ironing surface are indispensable for making quilt blocks.

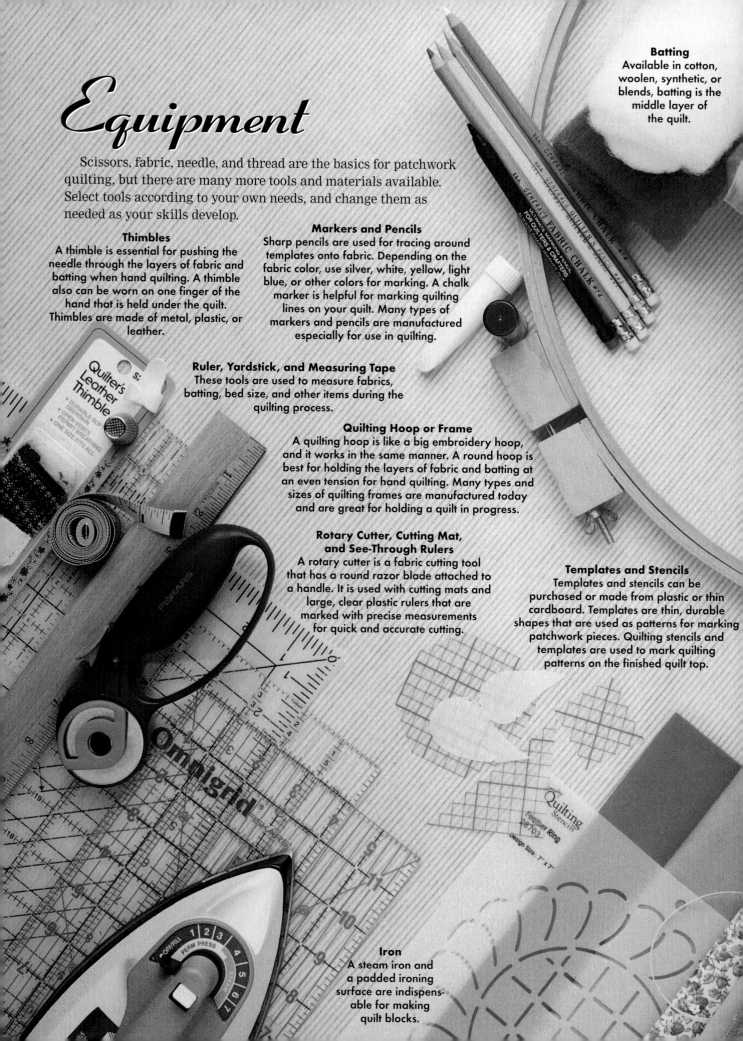

Beeswax
Drawing thread through a cake of beeswax before quilting adds strength. For white quilts, paraffin may be used instead.

Threads
For all hand sewing and hand piecing, 100 percent cotton quilting thread is the strongest. For machine piecing, use good-quality cotton or polyester-wrapped cotton thread. Many fibers are suitable for machine quilting, including invisible nylon thread, cotton and poly/cotton thread, and machine embroidery thread.

Needle Pointer

To make a handy combination pressing, cutting, and storage area for your quilting supplies and projects, purchase wire storage drawer units from a building-supply store. Mount an inexpensive hollow-core door on top of the drawer units, and cover one end of the newly created table with padding fabric stretched tightly and stapled to the back of the door. Place a large cutting mat on the other end of the door.

Needles
Sharps are used for hand piecing and hand sewing. For quilting, use betweens, which are short needles made especially for quilting. For basting, use a long embroidery, doll-making, or milliner's needle.

Seam Ripper
A seam ripper is helpful when machine-sewn stitches must be removed.

Safety Pins
Small, rust-proof safety pins can be used to pin-baste a quilt.

Fabrics
Most quilters today prefer 100 percent cotton fabrics. Quilts can also be made of wool, linen, and blends. Crazy patchwork quilts are traditionally made of scraps of velvet, silk, satin, and other luxurious fabrics.

Scissors
Good-quality dressmaking shears should be reserved for cutting fabric only. Paper-cutting scissors are necessary in some types of patchwork, and small, sharp embroidery scissors are used for clipping threads and trimming seams.

Straight Pins
Long, narrow quilter's pins are easy to use for pinning together layers of fabric, although any slim straight pin may be used.

Getting Started

Cutting out patchwork blocks, sewing them together, and then layering the finished piece with batting and backing are the basics of patchwork quilting. Traditional techniques such as hand quilting can be combined with newer techniques such as rotary cutting and machine piecing.

Patchwork Quilting Basics

1 Align the fabric and the ruler with the cutting mat's lines, and use the rotary cutter to cut the strips. Allow for a standard ¼" seam allowance when cutting the strips and subsequent pieces.

2 To cut pieces from the strips, stack the strips and lay them horizontally on the mat. Make sure the fabric and the ruler are lined up with the mat's lines, and cut strips into squares or other shapes.

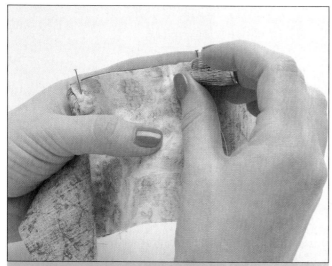

3 Hand piecing is a good method to use when sewing pieces that require intricate matching. Pin the pieces with the wrong sides together and take small running stitches to hand piece them.

4 Whether a finished piece is one block or an entire quilt, the assembly process is the same. Layer the finished patchwork on top of batting and backing, and baste the layers together.

Needle Pointer

If you are right-handed, make cuts with the rotary cutter to the right of the ruler as shown in all of the examples in this book. If you are left-handed, hold the ruler in place with your right hand and make the cuts to the left of the ruler with your left hand.

5 To begin quilting, knot the thread and insert the needle into the quilt top about an inch from where the first stitch will be. Bring the needle out at the first stitch, and tug the thread to pop the knot under the fabric.

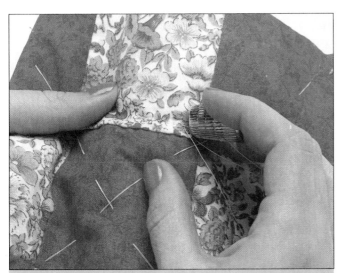

6 A quilting stitch is a small running stitch made through all layers of the quilt. Evenness of the stitches is more important than the size, but both evenness and stitch size will improve with practice.

Selecting Fabric Colors

Choosing colors is a very personal part of the quiltmaking process. Some people prefer bright, clear colors, while others prefer pastels or muted shades. As you plan your quilt, think about which colors and combinations appeal to you in your home decor and your clothing.

Coordinating Theme

Choose one patterned fabric with lots of colors, then pick solid colors and prints to match. Be sure to notice even small amounts of color used in the main print, and add companion fabrics to bring out these colors.

Monochromatic Theme

To plan this type of quilt, choose light, medium, and dark values of one color. This type of quilt can be very attractive if you are careful to choose a variety of prints and shades of each color value.

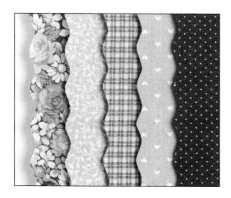

Graduated Theme

A graduated color scheme with progressions of a color from light to dark can create quilts that seem to glow. These quilts are often very artistic and create an illusion of depth.

Scrap Theme

If you want to use a wide variety of scrap fabrics for your quilt, choose one or two colors to use frequently, perhaps as an element in each block or as sashing. Placement of color values is important in a scrap quilt. Try to place the dark, medium, and light colors in the same position on each block.

Advancing and Receding Colors

Warm, bright colors tend to advance, or "jump out at you," from a quilt's surface, while dusty colors, pastels, cool colors, and darker colors tend to recede. One good way to see which colors will advance is to stack bolts of fabric on a table. Turn away from the fabric, then turn and look at the fabric, then turn away again. Which colors remain in your mind? These are the colors that will be most prominent in your quilt.

A single accent color can often add extra personality to a quilt. Select a striking accent color, and experiment with adding small amounts of this color in your project.

Adding Dark Colors and Neutrals

Adding one or two dark colors to your quilt will give it depth and allow the lighter and brighter colors to advance.

Neutral colors such as white, off-white, gray, and black provide a backdrop for stronger colors. These colors give the eyes a resting place on the quilt, and like dark colors, neutral colors allow the stronger colors to come forth.

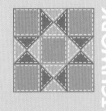

The Color Wheel

The color wheel can be helpful when choosing color for patchwork quilting projects. For pleasing color schemes, select colors that are opposite or next to each other on the color wheel.

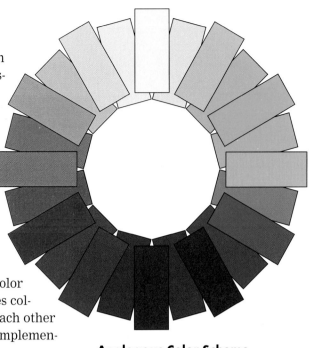

Complementary Color Scheme

A complementary color scheme is one that uses colors that are opposite each other on the color wheel. Complementary colors naturally seem more intense when used together. Combinations of pale shades and more intense shades of complementary colors can be used separately or together.

Analogous Color Scheme

An analogous color scheme uses colors that are next to each other on the color wheel. Quilts made in these themes are usually restful to the eyes and very attractive.

Selecting a Pattern

There are several factors to consider when you choose a patchwork pattern. Is it important to choose a pattern that you can complete quickly using quick-cutting and machine-piecing methods, or do you prefer hand piecing? Is the beauty of the design more important than how quickly you can make the quilt? Would you like to purchase all new fabrics for your quilt, or would you prefer to use your collection of fabric scraps?

It's important to keep in mind what steps of the quiltmaking process you enjoy. If piecing intricate patchwork is most enjoyable to you, the quilting design may be of secondary consideration. If you enjoy hand quilting, you'll want your design to feature large areas of plain fabric in which to quilt.

Patchwork Block Patterns

Most patchwork patterns are based on a square grid. The grid may have a total of 4, 5, 7, 9, or even 25 squares. Other patchwork patterns are made by repeating one motif over and over.

Four-Patch Blocks

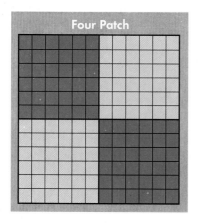
Four Patch

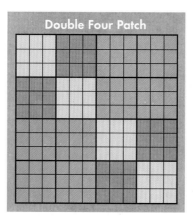
Double Four Patch

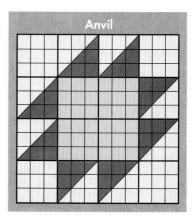
Anvil

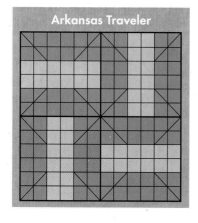
Arkansas Traveler

Bachelor's Puzzle

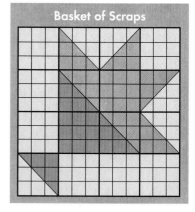
Basket of Scraps

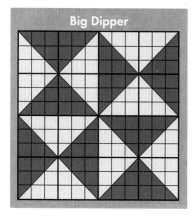
Big Dipper

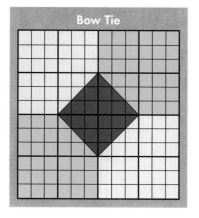
Bow Tie

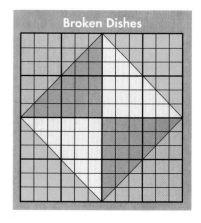
Broken Dishes

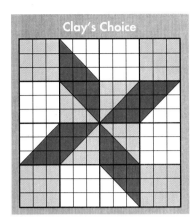

Clay's Choice

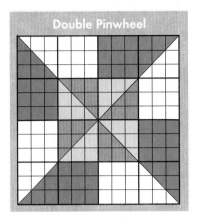

Double Pinwheel

Drunkard's Path

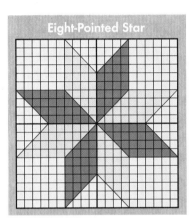

Eight-Pointed Star

Fritchie Star

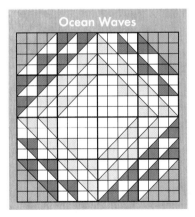

Ocean Waves

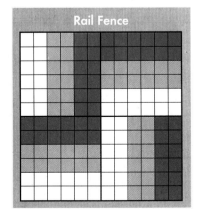

Rail Fence

Spools

Needle Pointer

Sometimes blocks may be slightly out of square when they are complete even if you carefully measured and pieced them. Use a rotary cutter, cutting mat, and large, square ruler to trim your blocks' edges slightly before piecing them together.

Five-Patch Blocks

Bull's Eye
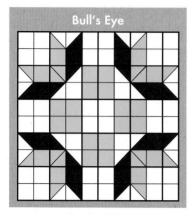

Churn Dash
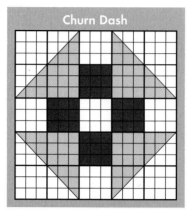

David and Goliath

Duck and Ducklings
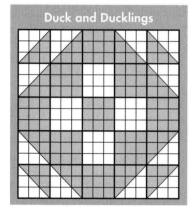

Farmer's Daughter
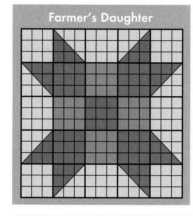

Fruit Basket

Goose in the Pond
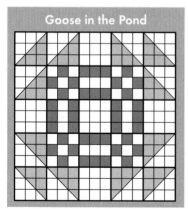

Grape Basket

Philadelphia Pavements
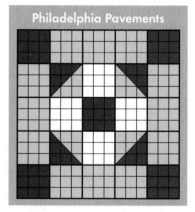

Pine Tree
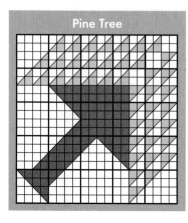

Sister's Choice
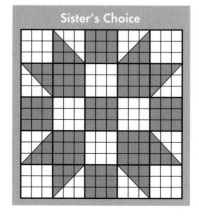

Wild Goose

Seven-Patch Blocks

Bear Paw

Country Roads

Hens and Chickens

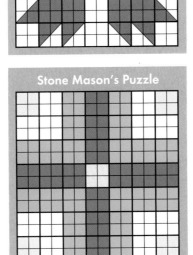

Peony

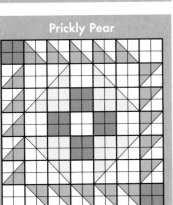

Prickly Pear

Stone Mason's Puzzle

Needle Pointer

A good way to expand your fabric collection is to buy fat quarters. These precut sections of fabric are cut specially for quilters and fabric crafters, and they are twice the length and half the width of an ordinary ¼ yard of 44"-wide fabric. These handy 18" x 22" pieces are often sold as collections of a range of coordinating colors or prints.

Stitching Solution

If you have wall space available in your sewing area, make a quilt planning wall. Staple large pieces of white or off-white flannel directly to the wall or over large pieces of thin plywood or foam insulation and attach them to your wall. Quilt blocks will stick to the flannel without pins, allowing you to arrange and rearrange your blocks and settings as you wish and view them from across the room.

Nine-Patch Blocks

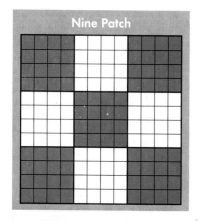
Nine Patch

Double Nine Patch

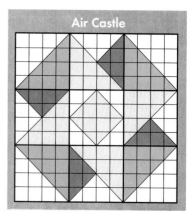
Air Castle

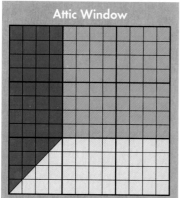
Attic Window

Aunt Sukey's Choice

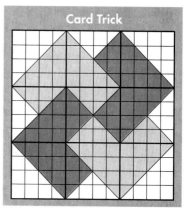
Card Trick

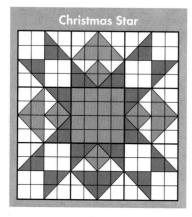
Christmas Star

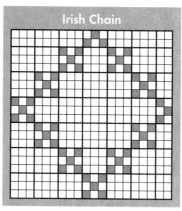
Irish Chain

Jacob's Ladder

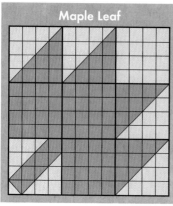
Maple Leaf

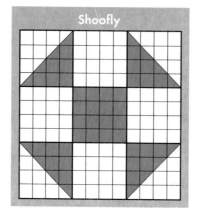
Shoofly

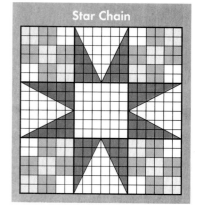
Star Chain

Other Patterns

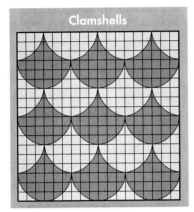
Clamshells

Grandmother's Flower Garden

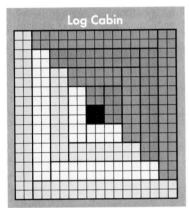
Log Cabin

Schoolhouse

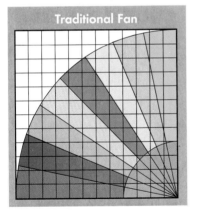
Traditional Fan

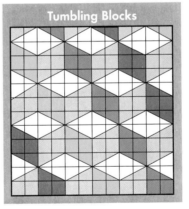
Tumbling Blocks

Needle Pointer

Grandmother's Flower Garden, Clamshells, and other patterns are often called One-Patch patterns because each patch is the same. Many quilters like to use these patterns in charm quilts—quilts in which no two patches are made from the same fabric.

Stitching Solution

To accurately sew the long edge of a triangle to the edge of a square, fold the edges of both the triangle and the square in half and mark the centers with straight pins. Align the pins, pin the pieces together, remove the pins, and sew the seam. Use extra care not to stretch the bias edge of the triangle when sewing. Press the seam allowance toward the darkest fabric, and then trim the points off the triangle to reduce bulk.

Patchwork Techniques

Patchwork can be created with any combination of old and new techniques. Pieces can be cut out individually using templates, or they can be cut in multiples using rotary-cutting tools. Blocks can be pieced together by hand or machine.

Drafting Patchwork Patterns

You may prefer to draft your own quilt patterns rather than use traditional patterns. Pattern drafting is a simple process and can be used to copy blocks from an existing quilt, create new designs, or create traditional designs in different sizes.

Traditional Designs

1. Using plain paper, a pencil, and a ruler, draw the basic grid for your quilt block. The grid can be a four patch, five patch, nine patch, or other size. At this stage, the sketch can be done on plain paper or on ¼" graph paper.

Four Patch

Five Patch

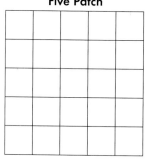

Nine Patch

Seven Patch

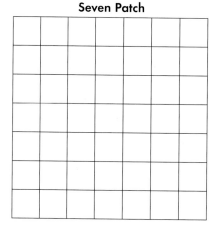

2. To create the pattern, divide each segment of the basic grid into squares, triangles, or curved shapes as shown above (right). Using a sharp pencil and a ruler, draw the pattern actual size on ¼" graph paper. The outside line of the grid is the finished size of the block and should form a square. Choose a finished size that divides easily into an equal number of squares on the graph paper, depending on whether your design is a four patch, nine patch, or other basic pattern. For example, the Monkey Wrench block is a nine-patch block. It can be drawn 30 x 30 squares, with each segment of the block's grid 10 x 10 squares. This creates a finished block of 7½", with each segment of the block measuring 2½". This pattern will be used to make templates for cutting out the pieces of the block, as explained in "Using Templates."

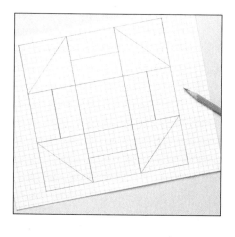

3. Photocopy or draw the grid several times. Using colored pencils, fill in the segments of the pattern as shown until you have an arrangement that is pleasing. Try not to pay too much attention to color at this stage, and focus instead on placement of dark, medium, and light values. Try coloring the design in different color combinations, and try placing the dark, medium, and light values in different places on the design.

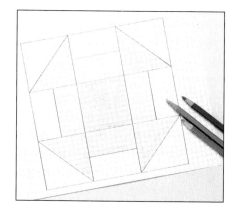

Using Templates

Templates are durable patterns that can be used over and over to mark shapes on fabric. Templates can be purchased in a variety of shapes and sizes, or they can be easily made using template plastic or thin cardboard.

Making Templates

1. Using a full-size pattern drafted on ¼" graph paper (see "Drafting Patchwork Patterns"), trace the shapes from the pattern onto a new sheet of graph paper or ¼" gridded template plastic. Use a fine-line permanent marker for marking patterns on template plastic.

2. If you are using paper, glue the paper shapes to thin cardboard. When the glue is dry, carefully cut out the templates, cutting just inside the marked line.

3. If you are using template plastic, cut out the shapes. A rotary cutter, cutting mat, and see-through ruler are helpful for cutting the straight sides on the templates.

4. Using the marker, write the pattern name, template number if applicable, and the direction of the grain line on each template. The grain lines are parallel to the outer edges of the quilt block.

Marking and Cutting

1. Press the fabrics to be marked.

2. Position the templates on the wrong side of the fabric, making sure the templates are at least ½" apart and ½" from the fabric edges. Align the grain lines on each template with the fabric grain line, which runs parallel to the selvage edge.

3. Choose a marking pencil according to the fabric color. A silver quilter's pencil or regular graphite pencil shows well on most fabric colors. A white or yellow pencil may be used to mark dark colors. Holding the template firmly in place, trace carefully around the templates. Cut out the pieces, adding a ¼" seam allowance to all edges.

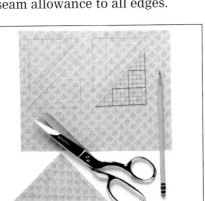

Stitching Solution

For quick and easy template patchwork, trace your template designs onto freezer paper, tracing one template for each piece needed. Cut out the templates carefully. Position the templates at least ½" apart on the right side of your fabric, with the paper's shiny side down. Iron in place, then cut out the patchwork pieces.

Needle Pointer

Create new patchwork designs by folding a square of paper diagonally, horizontally, and vertically several times. Open out the paper and draw a design using some or all of the folds as guidelines.

Rotary Cutting

Rotary-cutting tools and methods increase the speed and accuracy of cutting patchwork pieces. Templates are not necessary with this method. A self-healing cutting mat, one or more see-through rulers marked in ⅛" and ¼" increments, and a rotary cutter are needed.

1. Press the fabric to be cut and fold it, aligning the selvages evenly.

2. Lay the fabric on the cutting mat, with the selvages at the top and the fold along one of the mat's horizontal lines. The raw edges on the right side of the fabric should be lying on the mat. If the mat is not big enough to hold the entire width of the fabric, carefully fold the fabric again, aligning the edges and folds along the horizontal lines.

3. To square up the raw edge of the fabric, lay the edge of the ruler along one of the vertical lines on the cutting mat, aligning them perfectly and with the edge of the ruler close to the raw edges of the fabric as shown.

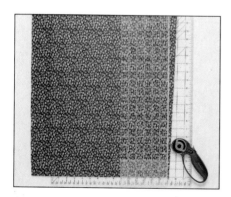

4. Press down on the ruler firmly with your left hand. With the rotary cutter in your right hand, place the blade upright against the edge of the ruler. Hold the cutter firmly as you roll the blade away from you along the entire length of the fabric.

5. To cut a fabric strip, measure the width needed using the grid lines on the mat and see-through ruler. Align the edge of the ruler along the proper line on the mat as shown. Make sure all of the fabric edges are still aligned with the lines on the cutting mat and then make the cut.

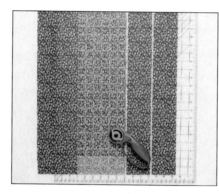

6. To cut square or rectangular pieces from a strip, lay the strip crosswise on the cutting mat as shown above (right), aligning the bottom and right edges of the fabric strip with the lines on the cutting mat. Using the see-through ruler, measure and cut the pieces as in Step 5.

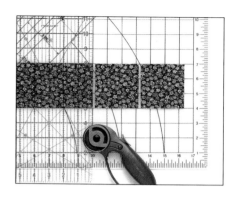

7. To cut a triangle from a strip, align the ruler's 45-degree angle mark along the bottom edge of the strip. Make sure all fabric edges are aligned with the mat's lines, then make the diagonal cut as shown. Then make a vertical cut as in Step 6 to complete the triangle.

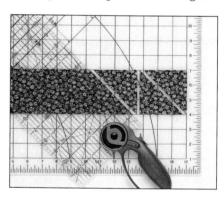

Stitching Solution

A color value filter, which is a red rectangular piece of plastic, can help you to see dark, medium, and light values more clearly. This tool is available in quilt shops and through mail-order catalogs. The same effect can be achieved by viewing your fabrics or quilt blocks through red florist's cellophane. When fabrics are viewed through these tools, the colors become indistinguishable. You'll only see dark, medium, and light.

Hand Piecing

Although any type of quilt can be hand pieced, this method is especially useful for joining small pieces and accurately matching points in patchwork.

1. Thread a sewing needle with an 18" or shorter length of good-quality thread that matches your fabric. If desired, run the thread through a cake of beeswax to strengthen it and to prevent tangling as you stitch.

2. Hold the patchwork pieces with the right sides together and with the marked lines and corners matching, and pin them together. Sword pinning is helpful for perfectly aligned points and seam lines. To sword pin, insert the pin from the wrong side of one patchwork piece exactly on the point or seam line to be matched. Then insert the pin into the corresponding point on the other patchwork piece, and leave the pins dangling in the fabric in this fashion while hand piecing. Insert a pin or two in the normal manner as needed to hold the pieces together as shown above.

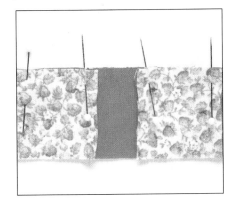

3. Knot the thread at one end. Starting ¼" from the edge of the fabric, sew the pieces together with a small, even running stitch. Make the stitches as even as possible, and take two small backstitches at the end of the seam. Sew only seam line to seam line as shown, leaving the ¼" seam allowances free. When joining pieces with seams, do not stitch the seam allowances down. At each seam, insert the needle through the seam allowance and continue sewing the seam, leaving the seam allowances free as shown.

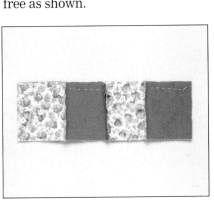

Needle Pointer

If your ruler slips too much on your fabric, you can keep it in place by gluing tiny dots of sandpaper to each corner of the ruler. Precut dots are packaged for this purpose and are sold with quilting supplies.

Pressing

After each pair of pieces or strips of patchwork segments are pieced together, press the seam allowances to one side, pressing toward the darkest fabric as shown.

Press from the wrong side first in order to make the seam allowance lie in the correct direction. Then turn the piece over and press it from the right side to make sure there is no pleat on the seam line.

Machine Piecing

Before beginning to machine piece patchwork, it is important to make sure you can machine sew a perfect ¼" seam. Although you may be getting about a ¼" seam by lining up the edge of your fabric with the edge of the presser foot, take a few minutes to make sure that distance is exactly ¼". If your ¼" seam is even as little as ¹⁄₁₆" off, it can make your blocks substantially uneven.

The Perfect ¼" Seam

1. Cut along one line on a sheet of ¼" graph paper, or using a ruler, mark two lines ¼" apart on a plain piece of paper and cut along one of the lines.

2. Lay the paper under the presser foot of the sewing machine. With the presser foot up, pierce the line with the needle as shown, then lower the presser foot. If the edge of the paper does not line up with a line on the sewing machine or with the edge of the presser foot, you may want to place several layers of masking tape along the edge of the paper to give your fabric pieces an edge to ride against.

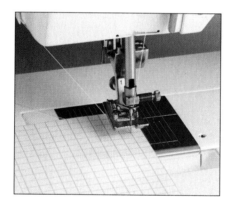

3. If your machine has an adjustable needle position and the opening of the feed dogs is under the ¼" line, move the needle to the left until you find a ¼" mark you can follow.

Chain Piecing

Pieces and rows can be sewn together one after the other without raising and lowering the presser foot or cutting the thread between each seam.

1. Start stitching on a scrap of fabric, then feed sets of patches under the presser foot one after the other, feeding each as closely as possible behind the previous pair.

2. End the "chain" by stitching across a scrap of fabric.

3. Remove the chain of patchwork sections from the sewing machine and cut them apart as shown.

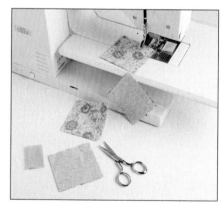

Crazy Patchwork

1. Cut a foundation block of muslin or other lightweight fabric at least 1" larger on all sides than your finished block size.

2. Cut random shapes from patchwork fabrics. Traditional crazy patchwork is sewn with luxurious fabrics such as velvet, satin, and silk. Although crazy patchwork may be pieced by hand, machine piecing is easier and smoother.

3. Place one shape with at least four sides right side up near the

Needle Pointer

Ribbon embroidery offers beautiful techniques for use on crazy patchwork. See pages 132 and 133 for a selection of stitches and instructions for how to make the embroidery stitches.

center of the foundation block. Lay another shape wrong side up on top of the first shape, aligning one edge. Stitch along the aligned edge with a ¼" seam as shown.

ished measurements plus a ⅜" seam allowance. Machine stitch ¼" from all of the edges as shown. Crazy patchwork can then be sewn together.

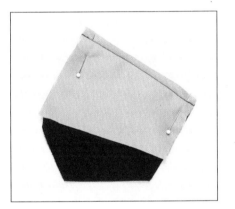

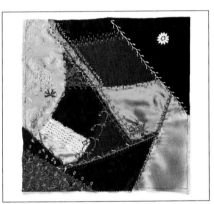

4. Fold the top shape back and press. Lay another shape on top, wrong side up, with one edge aligned with another edge of the first shape. Stitch the shape in place, turn it over, and press as before.

5. Continue adding shapes in this manner until the foundation block is covered with patchwork. Add embroidered embellishments by hand or machine as desired. (See pages 122 through 130 for a selection of embroidery stitches.) Trim the edges of the block to the fin-

Stitching Solution

When drafting patterns, try using ¼" graph paper with blue lines, available in office-supply and discount stores. When this paper is photocopied, only the pattern lines that you have drawn will show on the copies. The blue lines will not photocopy, enabling you to see only the finished design.

Strip Piecing

With this method, strips of fabric are sewn together, then cut, then sewn together again. Strip-piecing methods are very accurate because sewing and pressing are completed before the final shapes are cut, reducing distortion.

Nine-Patch Blocks

1. Using the rotary cutter, cutting mat, and see-through ruler, cut three equal strips of each fabric. Arrange and sew the strips together into two units as shown. Press the seam allowances.

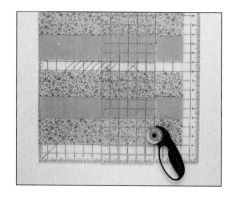

2. To make two coordinating nine-patch blocks, cut three segments from each strip unit that are the same width as the original strips.

3. Arrange the nine-patch segments, alternating dark and light colors for each block as shown, and sew the strips together to form blocks. Press the seam allowances.

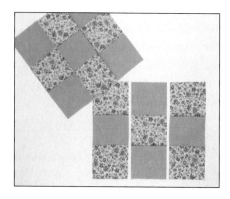

Grid Piecing Triangles

1. Draw a grid of squares on the wrong side of fabric. Make each square ⅞" larger than a finished patchwork square made up of two triangles.

2. Draw a diagonal line through each square and mark stitching lines ¼" from each diagonal line as shown.

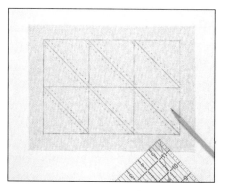

3. Pin this piece of fabric right sides together with another piece the same size, and stitch carefully on the stitching lines. Cut on all of the solid lines to make half-square triangle units.

4. Separate the triangle points by pulling away any threads that remain, and press the triangle squares open. Trim the points as shown.

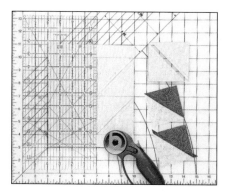

5. To make quarter-square triangle units, make the squares in the original grid 1¼" larger than the finished quarter-square units.

Make half-square triangle units following Steps 2 through 4. Cut each finished half-square triangle unit in half diagonally across the seam. Sew the halves of alternating units together as shown to create quarter-square triangle units as shown. Press, then trim the points.

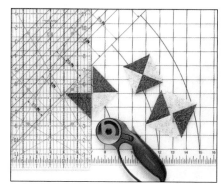

Bias-Strip Piecing Triangles

1. Layer rectangles of two fabrics on the cutting mat. Trim the rectangles to square the edges as needed, and align the rectangles with lines on the cutting mat. Align the bottom of the rectangles with the ruler's 45-degree angle line as shown. Cut bias strips ½" wider than the finished half-square triangle units.

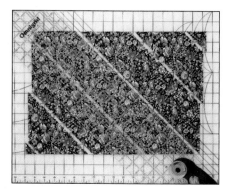

2. Arrange the strips into two units as shown on the opposite page (top left), alternating fabric colors. The bottom left of each unit should be a different color.

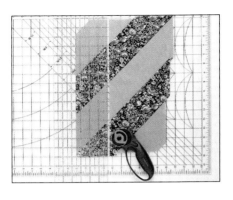

3. With right sides together and using a ¼" seam, sew the strips together. Press.

4. Place the 45-degree angle line of one ruler along one seam as shown. Butt the edge of another ruler against the left edge of the first ruler as shown, and once it is perfectly aligned, remove the first ruler.

7. To cut units, align the 45-degree angle line of the ruler along the seam line and cut along one edge. Then measure the desired unit width, and cut again. Reposition the ruler on the next seam line and cut again for the next unit as shown.

Needle Pointer

When making projects using strip-pieced triangles, you will often have extra triangle units. Save these and stitch units together from several projects for fun patchwork designs.

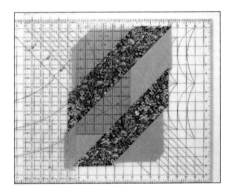

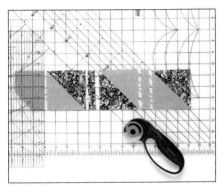

5. Using the rotary cutter, carefully trim the raw edges of the unit as shown. Discard the trimmed edge.

8. To make quarter-square triangle units, follow Steps 1 through 7, cutting all of the strips ⅞" wider than the width the finished quarter-square unit will be.

9. Cut the finished half-square triangles in half as shown. Sew the halves of alternating squares together into units as shown. Press the seam allowances and trim the points.

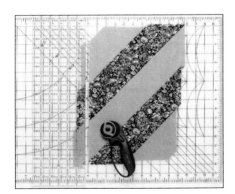

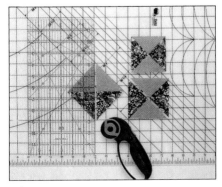

6. Cut strips ½" wider than the desired width of the finished triangle square as shown. Before cutting each strip, repeat Steps 4 and 5.

Setting Blocks Together

The arrangement of the blocks is called the setting. The blocks can be arranged with or without alternate blocks and sashing.

Side by Side

In this setting, the blocks are aligned next to each other as shown and then stitched together. With this arrangement, the eye may see different patterns where the blocks join together.

Sashing and Cornerstones

Sashing strips are strips of fabric sewn between side-by-side blocks. Sashing sets the blocks apart and provides unity for scrap patchwork designs. To add sashing, cut narrow strips the same length as the width of the blocks. Cut the cornerstone squares the width of the sashing strips as shown.

Alternating Plain Blocks

In this setting, the pieced blocks are alternated with plain blocks in a checkerboard fashion as shown. This style reduces the total number of pieced blocks required. If you plan to quilt intricate designs in the plain blocks, the blocks should be a solid color.

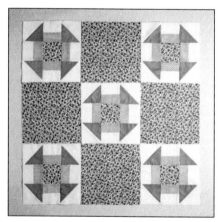

Alternating Pieced Blocks

By alternating your pieced blocks with another simpler, pieced pattern, a new design is created as shown.

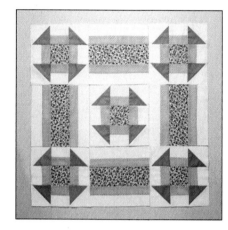

Diagonal Setting

The blocks can be stitched together as shown, with or without alternating blocks.

Adding Borders

Borders frame a quilt, intensify certain colors in the quilt, and can be used to increase the overall size of the quilt. Borders can be added in a variety of ways, including the straight set and mitered techniques.

Measuring for Borders

Measure the length and the width of the quilt, taking the measurements through the horizontal and vertical center of the quilt, not along the edges. Opposite sides of a finished quilt top are often slightly different sizes, so making the borders to fit the measurements taken in the horizontal and vertical center of the quilt will help your quilt remain square and have 90-degree corners.

Straight Set Borders

1. Cut two strips equal to the quilt's center length and two strips equal to the quilt's center width plus the side borders and seam allowances as shown.

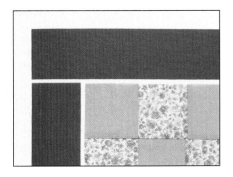

2. Sew the side strips to the quilt, then press. Sew the top and bottom strips in place as shown, easing to fit as necessary.

Mitered Borders

1. Sew the border strips together lengthwise. The strips should be a few inches longer than the center length or width of the quilt plus the width of the borders as shown.

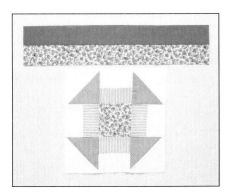

2. Center the top strip and stitch it in place as shown, beginning and ending ¼" from the edges. Repeat for the remaining edges, leaving the corners loose as shown.

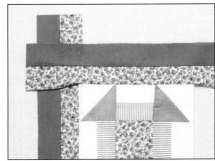

3. Fold the quilt diagonally and align the border strips as shown. Align the 45-degree angle line of a ruler on the stitching line, and mark a line from the end of the stitching to the edge of the border as shown.

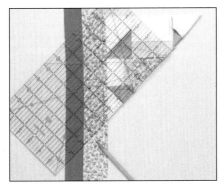

4. Pin the borders together and sew along the marked line. Trim the seam and press. Repeat for the other corners. Press.

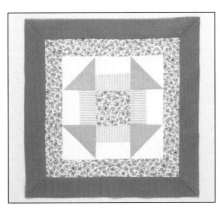

Needle Pointer

When adding sashing and cornerstones, sew strips of completed blocks and sashing together and press. Sew the remaining strips of sashing and cornerstones together and press. Then sew the two types of strips together to form the complete quilt top.

Quilting Techniques

After the patchwork top is finished, it can be quilted. Quilting, whether by hand or machine, refers to the process of connecting the top, batting, and backing layers of a quilt. Depending on your desired result and the amount of time you wish to spend quilting, a variety of techniques and materials are available.

Selecting Batting

A wide selection of batting is available for every quilting need. Low-loft batting is best for patchwork projects that will be hand quilted, while high-loft, or fluffier, batting is best for projects that will be tied or tacked. (See page 200 for tying instructions.)

Bonded polyester batting is easy to quilt and does not shift inside the quilt sandwich. Quilting lines on a project made with polyester batting can be spaced about every 4" to 6".

Cotton batting is desirable because it is a natural fiber, and needlepunched low-loft cotton battings are easy to quilt. Cotton bat-

ting should be preshrunk before using. To preshrink, gently soak the batting and allow it to air dry. Quilting lines on a project made with cotton batting must be spaced about every 1" to 2" to prevent the batting from shifting as the quilt is used and washed.

Cotton and polyester blended battings are also available. These battings, as well as all other types, work equally well for machine quilting and hand quilting.

Unbleached cotton batting sometimes has brown areas that may show through white or light-color areas. White battings are best for quilts with white areas.

Dark gray battings are available for dark quilts.

The batting sheet should be several inches larger than your quilt on all sides. Batting can be pieced by butting straight edges together and whipstitching with thread as shown.

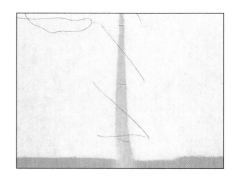

Making the Quilt Back

Some quilting fabrics are available in 90" and 180" widths, and if you use these for the quilt back, you can eliminate seams in most cases. These fabrics can be used vertically or horizontally as needed. Most cotton fabrics are 44" wide, and using this width necessitates piecing the backing fabric for all quilt sizes except crib size. Before sewing the backing sections together, wash, dry, and press the fabric. Use a rotary cutter, cutting mat, and see-through ruler to remove the

selvages. Carefully fold the fabric as needed to make it fit on your cutting mat. The usable width of the fabric will be about 40" to 42".

The pieced quilt back should be about 2" to 4" larger on all sides than the quilt top.

1. To make a quilt back for a twin-size quilt that is less than 80" long, piece the fabric horizontally as shown for the most economical use of the fabric. If desired, the fabric can be pieced vertically and the excess trimmed from the long edges.

2. To make a quilt back larger than 40" x 80", piece the fabric vertically. The seam may run through the center of the backing, or one length can be cut in half vertically and the two halves sewn to the sides of the full length as shown on the opposite page (top left).

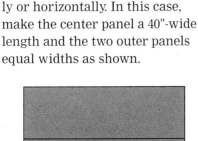

3. To make a quilt back wider and longer than 80", three lengths of fabric must be sewn together. The pieces can be joined vertical-ly or horizontally. In this case, make the center panel a 40"-wide length and the two outer panels equal widths as shown.

Marking Quilting Lines

There is no need to mark straight quilting lines or lines that will follow the stitching in the patchwork before the quilt layers are basted together. Intricate quilting designs and other free-flowing lines should be marked before basting. Straight lines can be guided using ¼" quilter's masking tape after the quilt is basted. (See "Using Masking Tape" on page 199.)

A fine, hard-lead mechanical pencil works well for marking quilt lines on light-color fabrics. This type of pencil does not have to be continually sharpened as you mark, and the line it produces is almost as thin as thread.

Other marking tools include chalk wheels, soap slivers, colored pencils, and kitchen products such as cornstarch or cinnamon. Many markings will fade of flake off during quilting and must be reapplied as you quilt.

1. Press the completed quilt top.

2. Using quilting stencils or templates and a marking tool, mark the design on the entire quilt as shown.

3. To create a stencil for use with cinnamon or cornstarch, trace the quilting design onto a paper bag. With an unthreaded, large needle in your sewing machine, sew along the lines.

4. Position the stencil and apply cornstarch or cinnamon over the holes with a clean powder puff or medium-size, soft paintbrush as shown.

Needle Pointer

As yet, there is no perfect marking tool that will cover all quilting needs. The marking tool you choose should either wash out completely or be very light and thin enough to be mostly covered with quilting thread. Ironing over marked lines may make them difficult to remove. Be sure to test your tool before marking your quilt.

Basting

Before a quilt can be hand or machine quilted, the top, batting, and backing layers are basted together with thread or safety pins. Basting is necessary when quilting with or without a hoop, but it is not necessary when quilting in large floor frames.

Safety-pin basting is easiest for projects that will be machine quilted or quilted without a hoop. Thread basting is best for projects that will be quilted in a hoop.

Projects can also be basted using a basting gun, which shoots thin plastic strips through the layers.

1. Lay the prepared quilt back right side down on a large, flat surface such as a table or the floor. Tape the fabric down in several places along the sides, top, and bottom.

2. Layer the batting on top of the back and the quilt top right side up over the batting. Smooth all layers gently.

3. To thread baste, pin the layers together with long straight pins about every 12". Then, beginning in the center of the quilt, baste the layers using a long sewing needle, a long running stitch, and a double strand of thread. Thin crochet cotton can also be used as basting thread. Baste outward from the center in concentric circles, or baste a large *X* on the quilt. Add the remaining basting lines as shown, adding more vertical and horizontal lines for larger quilts.

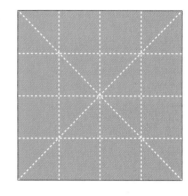

4. To safety-pin baste, insert safety pins into the quilt as shown, beginning in the center and pinning about every 6".

5. To baste using a basting gun, follow the manufacturer's instructions for the gun you choose.

Machine Quilting

The two types of machine quilting are straight-line quilting and free-motion quilting. Straight-line quilting follows the lines in the patchwork or a grid pattern. Free-motion quilting allows you to quilt around curves and create designs with the quilting stitches. Stipple quilting is a method of free-motion quilting that produces small, close, random lines.

Straight-Line Quilting

1. Thread the machine with fine cotton thread in the top and the bobbin or with nylon "invisible" quilting thread in the top.

2. Attach a walking foot, or even-feed foot, as shown to your sewing machine. This special foot allows the layers of fabric to feed evenly under the presser foot as you machine quilt.

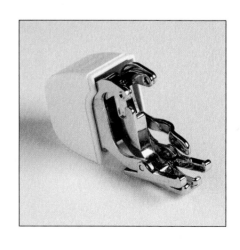

3. Place the center of the quilt under the presser foot. (It is helpful to practice machine quilting on a sample piece of fabric, backing, and batting before you begin quilting a larger project.)

4. Begin and end each line of stitching with several tiny stitches. Use a stitch length of about 8 stitches per inch. It may be necessary to loosen the tension in order to achieve smooth stitches.

5. Quilt one area at a time, removing the basting pins or threads as you go. Roll the quilt as needed to help it fit under the sewing machine.

3. Lower the feed dogs. This allows you to move the quilt freely from side to side under the needle.

4. Follow Step 3 of "Straight-Line Quilting."

5. Stitch your design, keeping your arms relaxed and holding the quilt with both hands. Move the quilt from side to side as you stitch. Think of the needle as a stationary drawing pencil and the quilt as the paper moving under the pencil to create a design. The speed of the machine and how fast you move the quilt determine how long the stitches will be.

Free-Motion Quilting

1. Follow Step 1 of "Straight-Line Quilting."

2. Attach a darning foot or open darning foot as shown to your sewing machine. This foot allows you to see the stitches clearly, and it also holds the quilt sandwich down as you stitch.

Needle Pointer

Before beginning any machine-quilting project, install a new needle on your machine and make sure your machine is clean and well oiled.

Stitching Solution

Experiment with a variety of threads for machine quilting. If you want your stitches to show and become part of the quilt's overall design, choose thread colors that contrast with the fabric colors. Even metallic threads are available for machine quilting. Before using any new or specialty fiber, be sure to test the tension and stitch length on a scrap of fabric, batting, and backing. If the fabric puckers or the thread breaks or if the bobbin thread shows through to the right side, loosen the tension. Clear, "invisible" nylon thread is excellent for producing machine quilting that resembles hand quilting.

Hand Quilting

Hand quilting can be done with or without a hoop or frame. If you use a large floor frame for quilting, follow the manufacturer's instructions for mounting the quilt in preparation for hand quilting.

The Quilting Stitch

The quilting stitch is a simple running stitch taken through all layers of the quilt sandwich. It is easy to learn, and its evenness improves with a little practice.

1. Thread a between or quilting needle directly from a spool of hand-quilting thread. This makes the twist of the fibers face the right direction for ease in quilting. Pull out about 18" of thread, clip it, and make a small knot at the clipped end.

2. Begin quilting in the center of your project. With a thimble on your right middle finger, insert the needle into the quilt top about 1" from where you want the first quilting stitch to begin. Bring the needle out at the position of the first stitch, and tug the thread to pop the knot into the middle of the quilt sandwich as shown.

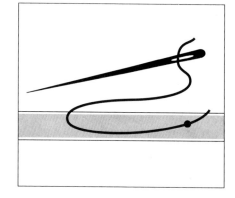

When learning the quilting stitch, strive for evenness. Ideally, the same amount of thread will show in each stitch at the front and the back of the quilt, with the space between the stitches equal to the length of each stitch. Six to 10 stitches per inch is correct, but as you practice, you may be able to get even more stitches per inch. Evenness of stitches is more important than tiny stitches, however.

3. Take several small stitches through all layers of the quilt as shown before pulling the needle through. Rock your right hand as you make the stitches, bringing the needle almost upright each time before inserting the needle back into the quilt. Use the thumb

of the right hand to press the fabric down to the left of the needle as the needle comes back up through the quilt top. Use the thimble on your right hand to push the needle through, and place your left hand under the quilt to feel the needle as it comes through each time. It is helpful to use a thimble on the middle finger of the left hand as well.

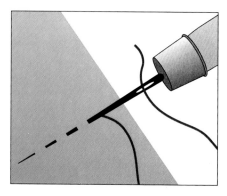

4. To end a thread, take a small backstitch or make a small knot near the fabric and pop the knot into the center of the quilt. Bring the needle out of the quilt top about 1" away, and clip the thread end so that it recedes into the quilt sandwich.

Quilting with a Hoop

1. Starting in the center of the quilt, place the bottom ring of the hoop under the quilt and the top ring over the top, sandwiching the quilt between the hoop's rings.

2. The action of placing the top ring over the bottom will pull the quilt taut, and there is usually no need to pull it any tighter. Hand quilting in a hoop is best accomplished when the quilt is held at a somewhat loose tension as shown on the opposite page (top). This prevents broken and bent quilting needles and also allows you to make smaller, more even stitches.

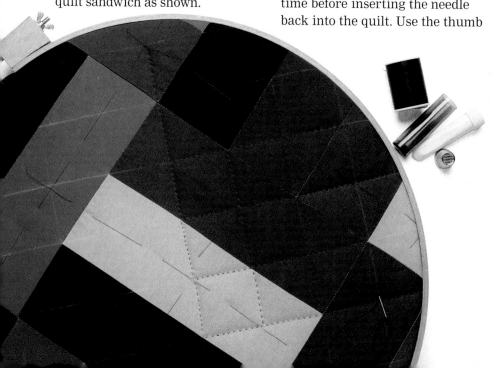

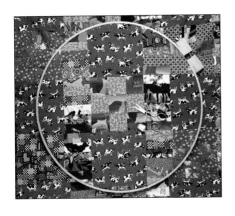

3. As you begin to make the stitches, rock your right hand, bringing the needle almost upright each time before inserting it back into the quilt. Use the thumb of the right hand to press the fabric down to the left of the needle as the needle comes back up through the quilt top.

Quilting without a Hoop

1. To prepare for quilting without a hoop, baste the top, batting, and backing together using thread or safety pins. Baste more closely than you would for quilting in a hoop. Place the pins or basting threads about every 4".

2. Begin quilting in the center of the quilt, rolling the edges of the quilt for easier handling. Pin small sections with long quilter's straight pins as you go as shown. Remove the pins and reposition them as you quilt.

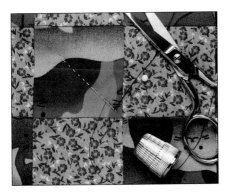

3. Some quilters prefer to use a sharp or a milliner's needle rather than a between for quilting without a hoop. The rocking

action that is necessary for making short stitches when quilting with a hoop or frame is not needed when you quilt without a hoop. Therefore, a short needle is not necessary. A longer needle will allow you to place more stitches on the needle each time before pulling the thread through as shown. The feel of the needle coming through to the back of the quilt is a little different for this technique. A finger guard or thimble on the hand underneath is very helpful.

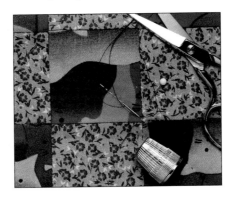

Using Masking Tape

One-quarter-inch quilter's masking tape is a great tool for quilting straight lines.

1. Measure and lay the tape on the quilt top with one edge along your desired quilting line.

2. Quilt along the edge of the tape as shown, then remove the masking tape.

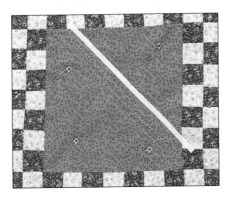

3. Do not leave the tape on the quilt too long or residue may remain. It's best to apply tape and remove it as you quilt.

Needle Pointer

Since hand quilting can be a process that takes hours and hours to complete, it is important that you choose a comfortable chair and work under adequate lighting. It's natural for beginners to tense up and forget to breathe deeply, so remember to relax as you're learning. Hand quilting can be a very relaxing and soothing activity.

Tying and Tacking

Tying and tacking are methods of securing the quilt layers together quickly and without quilting. These finishing methods are suitable for quilts with thick polyester batting. Before finishing a quilt with tying or tacking, baste the quilt layers together with thread or safety pins by following the instructions on page 196.

Hand Tying

1. Following the pattern of the patchwork, plan the location of the ties. Keep the spacing uniform, and plan to place the ties no more than 4" to 6" apart.

2. Thread a large crewel needle with strong crochet cotton, pearl cotton, knitting yarn, narrow ribbon, or other strong thread.

3. Bring the needle down through all layers of the quilt at the tie point, take a small stitch, and bring the needle back up. Cut the thread, leaving enough at both ends to tie a square knot. Tie the knot and trim the ends.

4. If desired, make all of the tie stitches in a row at once, leaving plenty of thread between each stitch to tie the knots. These will look like large, loose running stitches. Clip the thread between the stitches and tie the knots as shown.

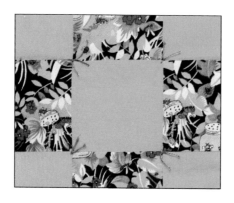

Machine Tacking

1. Follow Step 1 of "Hand Tying." Plan the tacking points either at the edges of the patchwork pieces or in the center of the pieces.

2. To machine tack using a zigzag stitch, set the stitch length on your sewing machine to zero and set the width to a wide zigzag stitch. Thread the needle and bobbin with thread that matches the quilt fabric. Zigzag about ten times at every tacking point as shown.

3. To machine tack using a decorative stitch, practice first on a scrap of quilt fabric, batting, and backing. Set the stitch length and width according to your sewing machine's instructions. Sew the stitch at the tacking points on the quilt as shown.

4. To machine tack using ribbon bows, tie 6" ribbons into bows. Thread your machine with thread to match the ribbon in the top and thread to match the backing in the bobbin. Position a bow, then zigzag over its center as shown.

Binding

French-fold binding provides a double layer of fabric at the quilt's edges for extra durability. It can be made either with strips cut on the straight grain of the fabric or cut on the bias. Bias strips are necessary if the quilt has curved edges.

1. The binding strips should be four times the desired finished width of the binding plus ½" for seam allowances and ¼" to allow for the thickness of the quilt.

2. Measure the quilt's length and width to determine the length of the strips needed. Add 2" to the length of each strip.

3. Using rotary-cutting tools, cut strips. Piece the strips, sewing diagonal ¼" seams.

4. Machine or hand baste ¼" from the edges of the quilt.

5. Fold the strips lengthwise, with wrong sides together, and press.

6. Pin a binding strip to one side edge of the quilt with the raw edges of the binding and quilt aligned. Stitch with a ¼" seam.

7. Trim the backing and binding to ⅛" to ¼" wider than the finished width of the binding. Trim the binding strip even with the ends of the quilt as shown.

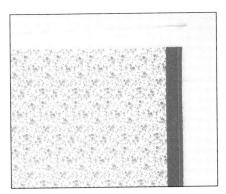

8. Turn the binding strip to the back of the quilt and whipstitch the fold over the seam line as shown.

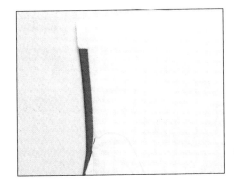

9. Pin, stitch, and whipstitch the binding on the opposite side of the quilt following Steps 6 through 8.

10. Attach the top and bottom binding strips according to Steps 6 and 7, trimming the ends ¼" longer than the width and turning under the edges at the corners before sewing as shown.

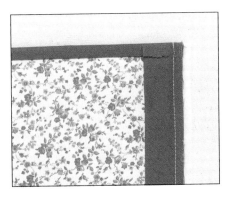

11. Turn the binding strip to the back of the quilt and whipstitch the fold over the seam line. Then whipstitch the ends of the corners closed as shown.

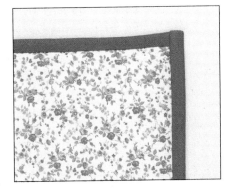

Needle Pointer

When your quilt is finished, add a label to the back indicating your name, the date, and other information as desired. The label can be hand lettered on fabric with a permanent marker, typed on the fabric, or cross-stitched on evenweave fabric. Decorative quilt labels can also be purchased.

Patchwork Breakfast Set

Start your mornings off right with a cheery patchwork tea cozy with a matching place mat and napkin. This pretty ensemble will brighten your table when serving afternoon tea as well.

Skill Level

Easy

Size

Tea cozy is 8" x 12"; place mat is 11" x 18"; napkin is 16" x 16".

Materials

½ yard of blue floral fabric (fabric 1)

1 yard of pink floral fabric (fabric 2)

⅛ yard each of three blue and pink cottons, including calicoes, checks, or patterned prints (fabrics 3, 4, and 5)

½ yard of white cotton (fabric 6)

12" x 30" piece of quilt batting

8" x 12" piece of prequilted white fabric

⅜" button

Sewing and quilting threads to match fabrics

Instructions

Note: All seams are ¼" unless otherwise indicated.

Tea Cozy

1. Using the patterns on pages 204 and 205, make templates A through E according to the instructions for making templates on page 185. Using templates A through E and adding ¼" seam allowances to all of the edges, mark and cut out two A pieces from fabric 1 (reverse one). Mark and cut out one B piece and one 2¼" x 14½" piece from fabric 3; mark and cut out two C pieces from fabric 4, two C pieces and four D pieces from fabric 5, and four D pieces and four E pieces from fabric 6. Cut and piece two 2½" x 14" bias binding strips and one 2½" x 26" bias binding strip from fabric 2. Cut one 2½" x 4" piece from fabric 2.

2. Following the piecing instructions on page 187 or 188 and sewing with ¼" seams, piece the center block for the front according to Diagram A on page 205. Following Diagram B on page 205, sew the longest straight edge of one A piece to each side of the block. Press the seam allowances. Sew the straight edge of the B piece to the top and the 2¼" x 14½" strip to the bottom. Press.

3. Using the pieced front as a pattern, cut the quilt backing from fabric 6. Following the quilting instructions on pages 196 through 199, baste and quilt the tea cozy front.

4. Using the completed front as a pattern, cut the back from the prequilted fabric.

5. Fold the binding strips in half lengthwise with the raw edges even and press. Pin one 14" binding strip to the right side of the bottom of the front, aligning

the raw edges. Stitch with a ⅜" seam. Trim the batting and backing fabric to ½" from the line of stitching, fold the binding to the wrong side, and whipstitch the fold over the seam line. (See page 201 for detailed binding instructions.) Attach the remaining 14" binding strip to the back in the same manner.

6. With the wrong sides facing, pin the front and back together around the curved edges. Stitch with a ¼" seam.

7. To make the top loop, fold the 2¼" x 4" piece of fabric 2 lengthwise, right sides together, and stitch the long edge with a ¼" seam. Pin one end of the strip to the center top front of the tea cozy, aligning the raw edges.

8. Pin the long binding strip to the front along the top curved edge, pinning the strip over the end of the loop strip, aligning the raw edges, and turning the ends

Something Different

Piece, quilt, and bind a simple nine-patch block to make a pot holder to match the breakfast set. Layer two or three thicknesses of batting or fleece in the pot holder to make it heat resistant.

of the strip under ¼" at the ends. Trim the strip as needed. Stitch with a ⅜" seam. Turn the binding to the back of the tea cozy and whipstitch the fold over the line of stitching, turning the remaining end of the loop under ¼" and stitching it in place as you go. Sew the button to the front of the loop.

Place Mat

1. Cut one 10¾" x 11¾" piece and one 1¾" x 10¾" piece from fabric 1. Cut and piece a 2½" bias binding strip from fabric 2 to equal 60" in length.

2. Use a cutting mat, rotary cutter, and see-through ruler to cut the pieces for the patchwork section. Piece them with the strip-piecing method. Cut three 2" x 10" strips each from fabrics 2 and 6. Sew two strips of fabric 2 and one strip of fabric 6 together length-wise into strip unit A, then sew the remaining strips into strip unit B. (See "Strip Piecing" on page 190.) Cut the strips into 2" segments, cutting three segments from strip unit A and four segments from strip unit B. Sew the segments together to match Diagram C in the following order: A, B, A, B, A, B, A.

Or use template E to make the patchwork section using tradition-al cutting and piecing methods. Cut 11 pieces from fabric 6 and 10 pieces from fabric 2. Sew them together following Diagram C.

3. Sew one short edge of the large piece of fabric 1 to the left long edge of the patchwork section, and sew one long edge of the small piece of fabric 1 to the right long edge of the patch-work section. Press the seam allowances.

4. Fold the entire place mat in half vertically and then horizon-tally, matching the corners. Cut

through all four layers, trimming the corners to round them.

5. Using the completed place mat front as a pattern, cut the lin-ing from fabric 6. Following the quilting instructions on pages 196 through 199, quilt the place mat.

6. Fold the binding strip in half lengthwise, with wrong sides together and raw edges even; press. Pin the binding strip to the right side edges of the

place mat, aligning the raw edges. Stitch, using a ⅜" seam, turning the end under ¼" before stitching down, and overlapping the beginning about ¼". Trim the backing and batting to ½" from the stitching line. Fold the bind-ing to the back and whipstitch over the fold.

Napkin

Cut a 16½" x 16½" square from fabric 1. Narrowly fold under and hem the raw edges.

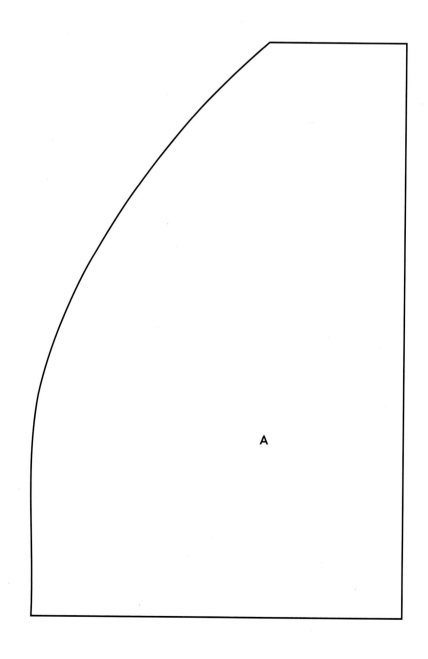

A

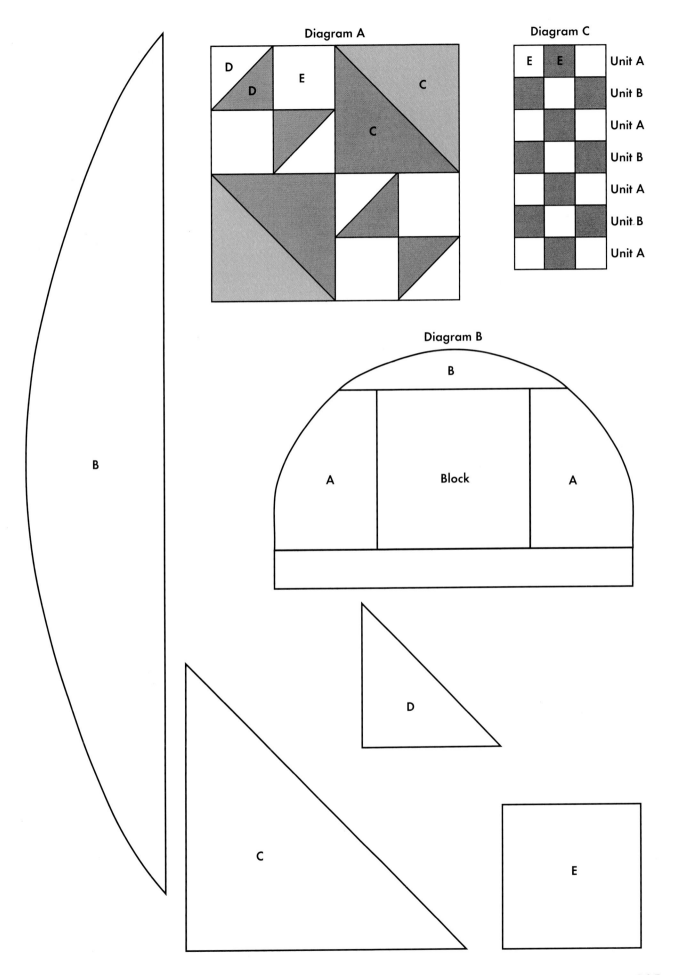

Diagram A

Diagram C

Unit A
Unit B
Unit A
Unit B
Unit A
Unit B
Unit A

D

D

E

C

C

E

E

Diagram B

B

A

Block

A

B

C

D

E

Tulip Jewels Wall Quilt

The colors of precious gems against black make these stylized tulips almost glow. This pieced pattern was inspired by a traditional appliqué floral called Rose of Sharon.

Skill Level

Intermediate

Size

24" x 24"

Materials

¾ yard of print fabric
½ yard of turquoise fabric
⅛ yard of purple fabric
1⅝ yards of black fabric
26" x 26" square of batting
Sewing threads to match fabrics
Black quilting thread

Instructions

1. Using the patterns, make templates A, B, and C according to the instructions on page 185.

2. Using rotary-cutting tools, cut four 6½" squares from the black fabric. Using the templates and adding a ¼" seam allowance to all edges, cut 8 of template B and 4 of template C from the print fabric; 8 of template A, 12 of template B, and 20 of template C from the black fabric; 1 of template A, 16 of template B, and 16 of template C from the purple fabric; and 4 of template B and 24 of template C from the turquoise fabric.

3. For the center block, sew the purple A piece, 4 purple B pieces, 8 print B pieces, 4 print C pieces, and 4 purple C pieces together according to Diagram A. Press.

4. For one tulip block, sew 2 black A pieces, 3 black B pieces, 3 purple B pieces, 1 turquoise B piece, 5 black C pieces, 6 turquoise C pieces, and 3 purple C pieces together according to Diagram B. Press. Repeat to make a total of four tulip blocks.

5. Sew the tulip blocks, the center block, and the four black blocks together according to Diagram C. Press.

6. For the borders, cut four 2¼" x 28" turquoise strips and four 2½" x 28" print strips. For each border segment, sew together one turquoise and one print strip. Following the instructions for mitered borders on page 193 and placing the print border toward the outside, attach the border segments to the quilt and miter the border corners according to Diagram C.

7. Cut a 28" x 28" backing piece from the black fabric. Following the instructions for basting on page 196, layer the backing, batting, and quilt top and baste them together. Following the instructions for quilting on pages 196 through 199 and the instructions for binding on page 201, finish the quilt.

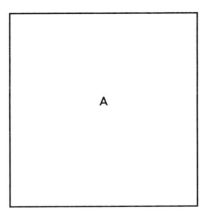

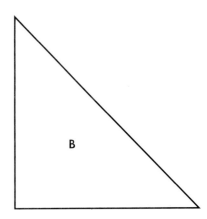

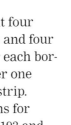

Diagram A

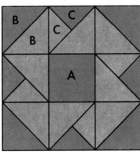

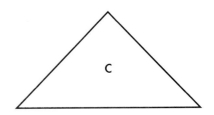

Diagram C

Diagram B

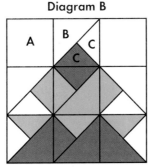

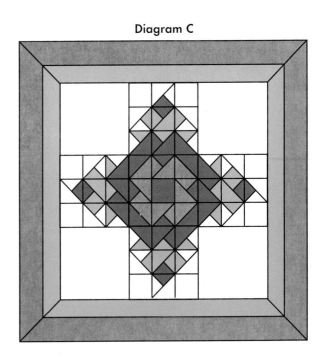

New York Beauty Quilt

The beautiful sawtooth strips, quarter-circles, and eight-pointed stars are a delight to the quilter looking for a challenging project. The intricate geometric design of this pattern is traditionally highlighted in only two colors and white.

Skill Level

Challenging

Size

81" x 81"

Materials

2 yards of light pink solid fabric

4½ yards of light green solid fabric

6 yards of white fabric

6 yards of backing fabric

2½ yards of white fabric for binding

Template plastic

Sewing threads to match the fabrics

White quilting thread

Instructions

1. Using the patterns on page 210, make templates A through I according to the instructions on page 185.

2. Using rotary-cutting tools, cut four 20½" squares from white for the large blocks. For the outer triangular half-blocks, cut four 20⅞" squares from white and cut them in half diagonally. Adding ¼" seam allowances to all edges, mark and cut 24 of template A from green, 24 of template B from pink, 216 of template C from green, 48 of template C from white, and 192 of template D from white.

3. Using rotary-cutting tools, cut sixteen 2¾" x 20½" strips from white for the sawtooth strip units. Adding ¼" seam allowances to all sides, mark and cut 384 of template E from green, 416 of template E from white, and 64 of template F from green.

4. For the star blocks, mark and cut 20 of template G reverse from pink, 20 of template G from green, 20 of template H from white, and 20 of template I from white, adding ¼" seam allowances to all sides.

5. Using rotary-cutting tools, cut two 7⅝" squares from white and cut them in half diagonally for the side triangles. For the corner triangles, cut one 7⅞" square from white and cut it in half diagonally. Cut the resulting triangles in half diagonally again for the corners.

6. For each sawtooth arc section, sew 2 white C pieces, 9 green C pieces, and 8 white D pieces together according to Diagram A on page 211. Make 24 arc sections. Press.

7. To make each large block corner, sew the inner curve of each arc section to one B piece and the inner curve of each B piece to the curve of an A piece, clipping the seam allowances and easing as necessary. See Diagram B on page 211.

8. Matching corners and folding under the outer edge of each sawtooth arc ¼", hand appliqué the sawtooth arc edge of one completed corner over each corner of the large blocks according to Diagram C on page 211. Appliqué one complete corner over the right angle corner of each large triangular half-block. Press, then trim away the excess white fabric from underneath each appliquéd corner.

9. For each sawtooth strip, sew 12 green E pieces, 13 white E pieces, and 2 green F pieces together according to Diagram D on page 211. Make 32 sawtooth strips. Press.

10. To make each sawtooth strip unit, sew two sawtooth strips to one white strip as shown in Diagram E on page 211, making sure the green points face outward on each side. Make 16 strip units. Press.

11. For each star block, sew 4 pink G reverse pieces, 4 green G pieces, 4 white H pieces, and 4 white I pieces together according to Diagram F on page 211. Make 20 star blocks. Press.

12. Sew the large blocks, strip units, star blocks, large half-blocks, side triangles, and corner triangles together as shown in Diagram G on page 211.

13. To make the borders, cut four 3½" x 84" strips each of pink and white. Piece the strips as necessary. For each border, sew one pink and one white strip together. Following the instructions for mitered borders on page 193 and placing the white border toward the outside, sew the borders to the quilt and miter the corners.

14. Following the instructions on page 194 for making the quilt back, the instructions on pages 196 through 199 for quilting, and the instructions on page 201 for binding, finish the quilt.

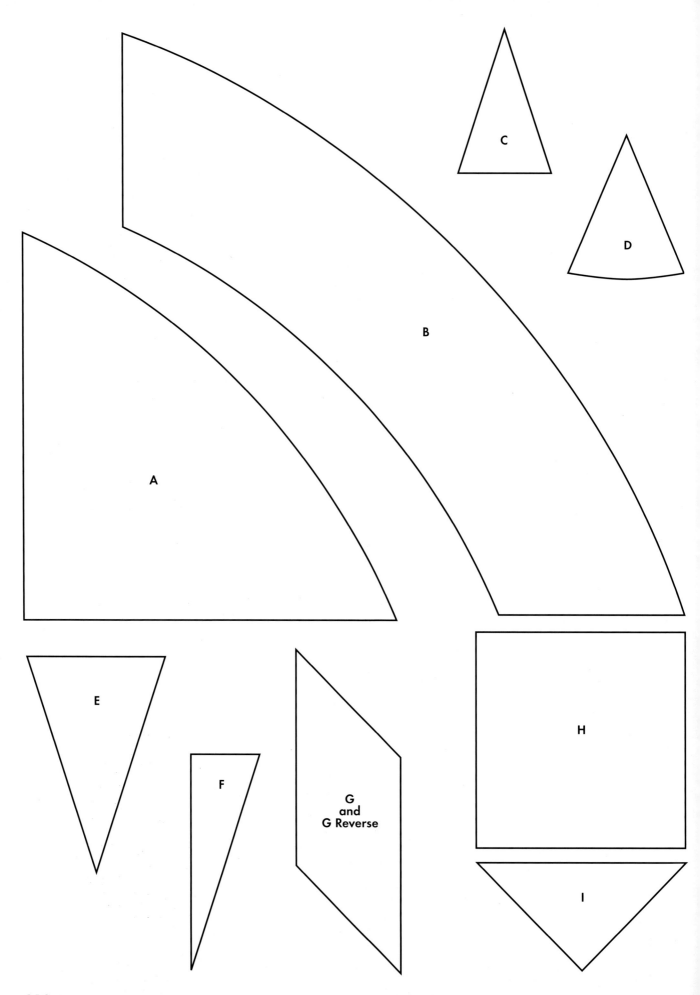

A

B

C

D

E

F

G
and
G Reverse

H

I

Diagram C

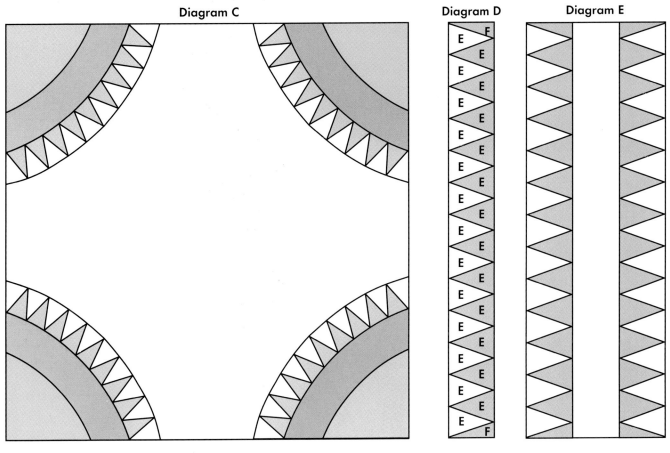

Diagram D

Diagram E

Diagram G

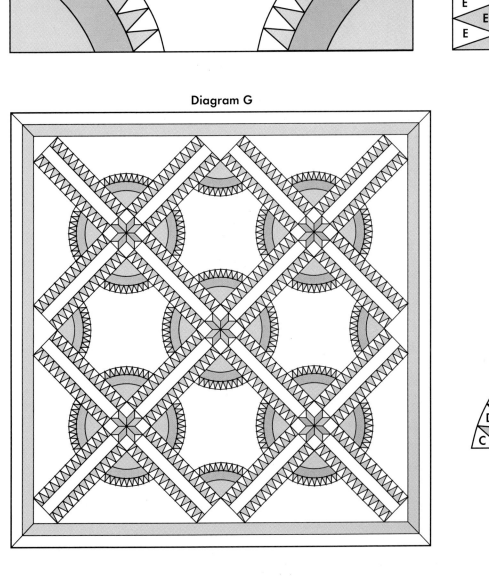

Diagram F

Diagram A

Diagram B

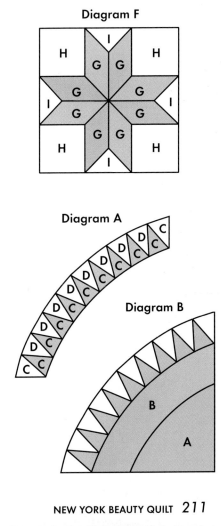

Plastic Canvas Needlepoint

Plastic canvas needlepoint is a very exciting and versatile needlecraft technique. It's so easy to learn that even beginners can enjoy success quickly. The large tapestry needles and easy-to-see plastic mesh make it a favorite of all age groups.

With the wide variety of stitching materials available today, plastic canvas needlepoint is as satisfying to the seasoned stitcher as it is to the beginner. Beautiful, dimensional designs can be created to make home decor items, wearables, and gifts.

Equipment

Plastic canvas is available in a wealth of colors, sizes, and shapes. Although some yarns are manufactured specially for plastic canvas needlepoint, a variety of knitting and crochet yarns, as well as other fibers, can be used for stitching.

Canvas
Plastic canvas comes in 5-count, 7-count, 10-count, and 14-count grids in a variety of colors and shapes. Some plastic canvas is rigid and very sturdy, and some is softer and more flexible.

Marking Tools
A crayon, grease pencil, or fine-line overhead-projection marker can be used to mark plastic canvas before cutting.

Raffia Straw
Natural raffia straw can be used in its natural color or dyed with food coloring to achieve soft, matte colors. Synthetic raffia straw comes in many shiny, jewel-tone colors.

Cording and Braid
Cording is firmly woven fibers that may be pearlized, metallic, or metallic interwoven with colored fibers. Each type of cording comes in about a dozen colors. Metallic braids are flat and come in several thicknesses and more than a hundred colors. These high-quality materials are used as accent colors and for stitching jewelry and similar items.

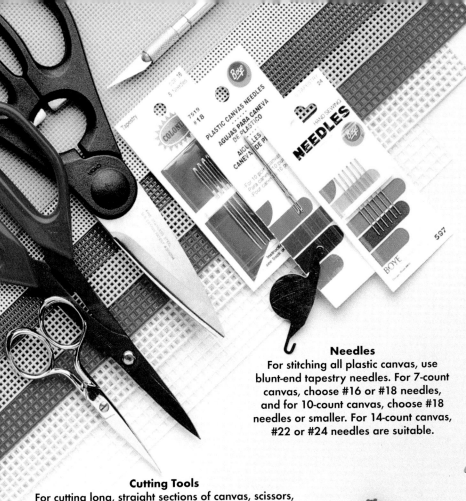

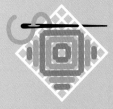

Needles

For stitching all plastic canvas, use blunt-end tapestry needles. For 7-count canvas, choose #16 or #18 needles, and for 10-count canvas, choose #18 needles or smaller. For 14-count canvas, #22 or #24 needles are suitable.

Cutting Tools

For cutting long, straight sections of canvas, scissors, floral cutters, or kitchen shears work well. For cutting detailed areas and for trimming nubs, manicure scissors, a craft knife, or nail clippers are helpful. Bonsai-trimming shears are ideal for cutting plastic canvas, and they are available at specialty gardening shops.

Yarn and Floss

Several brands of nylon, acrylic, and cotton yarns are manufactured specially for stitching 7-count plastic canvas. Four-ply worsted weight yarn can be used as well. Rug yarn can be used for stitching 5-count canvas. Sport weight yarn, #3 pearl cotton, or 12 strands of six-strand embroidery floss can be used for stitching 10-count canvas.

Needle Pointer

After cutting the canvas piece and trimming the nubs, use a fine-grade emery board to remove any remaining bits of plastic from the edges of the piece.

Getting Started

The easy-to-see mesh of 7-count plastic canvas is preferred by most beginners. After the canvas is marked and cut to shape, the first stitch to learn is the continental stitch.

Plastic Canvas Needlepoint Basics

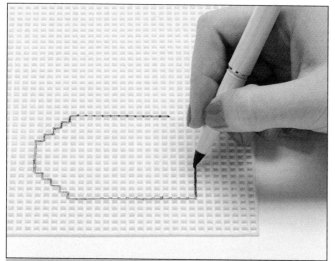

1 Using a crayon, a grease pencil, or an overhead-projection marker and following the pattern graph, mark the plastic canvas along the vertical and horizontal bars.

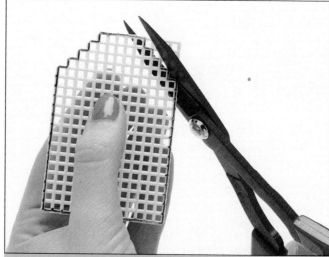

2 Carefully cut out the plastic canvas piece along the marked line, cutting the corners diagonally. Trim all of the nubs, or plastic canvas tips, from the cut edges.

3 Remove all marked lines before stitching with a used dryer fabric-softener sheet for waxy marks and a damp cloth or running water for washable-marker marks.

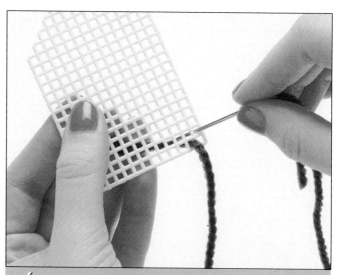

4 To begin stitching, cut an 18" to 24" length of yarn and thread the needle. Hold about 1" of the yarn behind the canvas. Stitch over the yarn end with the first few stitches to secure it.

5 Work continental stitches from right to left by bringing the needle up in the lower left corner of the stitch and taking it down in the upper right. To end a thread, weave it through the back of several stitches.

6 To finish the edges, overcast with one stitch in each hole on the straight edges and with as many stitches as needed to cover the canvas on the diagonal edges and in the corners.

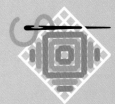

Needle Pointer

For easy-to-make "graph paper" for your plastic canvas designs, place a piece of clear plastic canvas on a photocopying machine. Top with a sheet of white paper and copy. You may have to adjust the lightness or darkness of the copies to get ones that show the canvas but that are light enough to use for designing.

Selecting Canvas

Most plastic canvas projects can be made using standard-size, clear sheets of 7-count canvas. However, plastic canvas is available in many colors, shapes, and sizes, as well as in several hole counts, making the possibilities for plastic canvas designs virtually endless.

Size and Shape

The hole count of plastic canvas is determined by the number of holes per inch. It is easier to count the holes in plastic canvas than the "threads" or lines, and most published instructions give the required dimensions in holes.

The most popular and versatile plastic canvas product is the 7-count 10½" x 13½" sheet. Most plastic canvas projects are made using these standard sheets, which are always 70 x 90 holes.

For larger projects, 12" x 18" (80 x 120 holes) and 13½" x 21½"

(90 x 149 holes) sheets of 7-count canvas are available. Other shapes, including purse forms, place mat ovals, circles, diamonds, and octagons, can be used for some projects.

Ten-count canvas comes only in regular-size sheets. These may vary slightly depending upon the brand, but they are about 10½" x 13½" and about 106 x 136 holes.

For very detailed stitching, 14-count canvas can be used. This canvas is very flexible, looks exactly like perforated paper, and is sometimes called perforated plastic. Any cross-stitch pattern can be stitched on this canvas.

Children's projects, rugs, and many quick and easy designs can be stitched on 5-count canvas. This large-mesh canvas comes in 13¼" x 22" sheets (66 x 110 holes).

Color

Clear canvas is generally used if the entire canvas will be covered with stitches. Colored canvas is used if areas of the canvas are left

unstitched as part of the design. Seven-, 10-, and 14-count plastic canvas, as well as many of the special shapes, are available in clear, white, and a number of colors. Five-count canvas is available only in clear.

Rigidity

Some canvas is rigid and very sturdy, so it is suitable for making boxes and other freestanding or flat items with straight pieces. This type of stiff canvas is not good for making projects that have curved pieces because the canvas mesh may crack while you stitch or after a project has been completed. If you need stiff canvas and don't have it on hand, you can hold together two thicknesses of regular canvas while you stitch.

Rounded items and projects with lots of curves can be made with extra-soft plastic canvas. Although this canvas will not crack when bent, it is more fragile than regular canvas and may tear during stitching if you don't handle it carefully.

Selecting Yarn and Fibers

The most popular fibers for stitching plastic canvas are regular 4-ply worsted weight yarn and nylon plastic canvas yarn. Many stitchers find plastic canvas needlepoint to be the perfect way to use yarn scraps from knitting and crochet projects.

Yarn for 7-Count Canvas

For most plastic canvas projects stitched on 7-count canvas, either 4-ply worsted weight yarn or plastic canvas yarn can be used. Worsted weight yarn is economical and widely available, and it comes in a wide variety of colors. Acrylic worsted weight yarn is more suitable for stitching plastic canvas than wool or cotton yarn because it does not wear out as easily while stitching and because it usually covers the canvas better.

Projects stitched with worsted weight yarn sometimes develop fuzz on the surface of the stitches after the finished item is used. The fuzz can be removed with a garment shaver, but for best results, choose worsted weight yarn only for projects that will not be handled.

Nylon plastic canvas yarn is sturdier than worsted weight yarn, and it has a beautiful shine that enhances the look of most plastic canvas designs. Projects made with this yarn will not develop fuzz, making it the ideal choice for stitching bags, toys, and other items that will be actively used.

Cotton plastic canvas yarn is also very sturdy and gives a beautiful soft, matte look to finished projects. Acrylic plastic canvas yarn is comparable to worsted weight yarn.

Metallic cording and raffia straw may be used for stitching 7-count canvas. Experiment with the cording to see if one or two strands are needed for complete coverage. When using synthetic or natural raffia, flatten each strand before stitching for smoother, more even coverage. When using any type of specialty fiber, it is often necessary to use lengths shorter than 24" to avoid breaking the fiber as you stitch.

Fibers for Other Canvas Sizes

Acrylic rug yarn is a good choice for stitching on 5-count plastic canvas. Fabric strips are also very popular for stitching this large-mesh canvas. To create fabric strips for stitching, cut or tear cotton fabric across the grain into ½" strips.

Finer threads are needed for stitching on 10-count canvas. Sport weight acrylic yarn can be used, as well as #3 pearl cotton or 12 strands of embroidery floss held together. All of these yarns and threads come in a wide variety of colors.

Any fiber that can be used for cross-stitch (see page 68) can be used for stitching on 14-count plastic canvas.

Needle Pointer

If you need to make only one more stitch and your thread is too short, you can avoid starting another thread by using a small steel crochet hook to pull the thread ends through the canvas to make the last stitch. Use a tiny drop of white craft glue to secure the thread end to the back of your work.

Marking the Canvas

In order to accurately cut out the plastic canvas pieces, it is helpful to mark the patterns on the canvas sheets first.

Marking Tools

Many marking tools work on plastic canvas, including crayons, grease pencils, ballpoint pens, and fine-line markers. In order to keep the marks from bleeding onto the yarn as you stitch, you need to remove all marks before stitching.

To remove crayon and grease pencil marks, rub away the marks with a dry tissue or a used dryer fabric-softener sheet.

One of the best marking tools for plastic canvas is a fine-line overhead-projection marker. These markers are sold in office-supply stores and come in several colors. The ink from these markers is not only dark and easy to see but also designed to adhere to plastic and wash away completely in water.

Marking Accurately

1. Plastic canvas graphs are not actual size and should not be used to measure for cutting. Your marked pieces may be larger or smaller than the graph. Count the holes on the printed graph, then count the holes on the canvas to match.

2. Mark all pieces to look just like the graphs as shown, and follow the written instructions for marking straight-sided pieces that may not have graphs. You may find it unnecessary to mark all of the pieces.

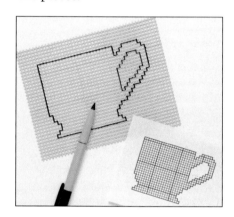

Cutting the Canvas

When cutting plastic canvas, it's important to cut as near to the bar as possible. Cut just outside all marked lines as shown on the right (left), and trim all corners diagonally. Using shears, nail clippers, or smaller scissors, remove all "nubs," or plastic canvas tips, from the cut bars as shown on the right (right). If these nubs remain, the yarn can snag.

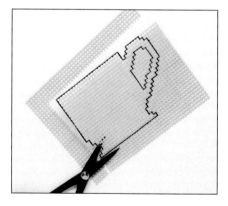

Patterns and Graphs

Before beginning a project, read all of the instructions and look at the graphs and diagrams. Some instructions for cutting, stitching, and assembling pieces refer you to graphs and diagrams, while others give you dimensions for cutting and tell you what color and stitch to use. Graphs are unnecessary for some pattern pieces.

The colors shown on the graphs may not always be the same color as the yarn they represent. This is especially true if there are several shades of one color in a design. In this case, colors on the pattern graph may be very different from the design's actual colors in order to clearly show each color's stitches. Each graph is accompanied by a color key.

To determine which stitches to use, see the printed instructions as well as the graphs. Most plastic canvas stitches are commonly used needlepoint stitches such as those found in "Stitches" on page 222. Some stitches on the graph may be random or unusual, and in this case, make the yarn lie on the canvas just as the line lies on the graph.

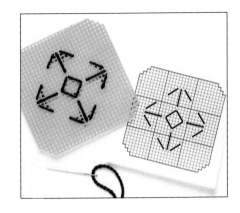

Stitching

Depending on the stitching material, the type of stitch, and the hole count of the plastic canvas, the length of yarn used for stitching plastic canvas should be between 18" and 36". Use shorter lengths with smaller hole counts, wool yarn and other fragile fibers, and small stitches. Use longer lengths of yarn with larger canvas, larger stitches, and most plastic canvas yarn. If you use the correct length of yarn, it will not fray and wear out from the stitching action before it is used up.

1. To begin stitching, thread a tapestry needle with a length of yarn.

2. Holding the canvas in your left hand, bring the needle up from the back at the first hole in the first stitch. Hold about 1" of yarn behind the canvas if you are working short stitches and 3" or 4" for longer stitches. Work over this yarn as you make the first few stitches, securing the end of the yarn.

As you stitch, maintain even tension on the yarn. Loose stitches will look uneven, and too-tight stitches may not cover the canvas completely.

3. To end a length of yarn, weave the end through the back of several matching-color stitches to secure it as shown above. Clip the yarn.

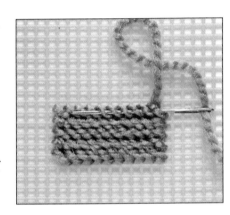

4. When you are finished working one area of color, secure the end of the yarn and begin again at the next area of the same color. Don't carry the yarn across the back because it can show through.

5. To begin a new length of yarn, weave the yarn under the back of a few stitches as shown before beginning to stitch, so the yarn emerges near the point of the first stitch.

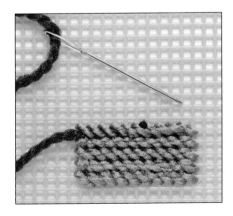

Needle Pointer

To keep the small ends and nubs of plastic canvas under control, trim your projects over an open magazine. When you're finished trimming, the magazine transports the nubs to the wastebasket easily.

Stitches

Many stitches for plastic canvas needlepoint are the same stitches that have been worked for hundreds of years on fabric needlepoint canvas. But you never have to worry about the stitches distorting plastic canvas.

Needlepoint Stitches

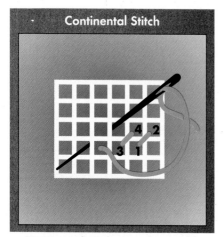

Continental Stitch

Continental stitches can be used for stitching designs or to fill in the background areas. With this stitch, there is more yarn at the back of the canvas than there is at the front, providing excellent coverage of the canvas. It is helpful to turn the canvas completely around to begin each new row.

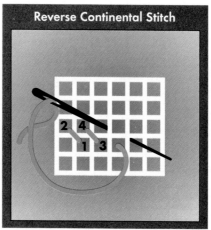

Reverse Continental Stitch

Reverse continental stitches are worked like continental stitches, only in reverse. This stitch is often used on mirror-image areas of a design stitched in continental stitches.

Slanted Gobelin Stitch

Slanted gobelin stitches can be worked in either horizontal or vertical rows over two or more bars.

Stitching Solution

Splitting 4-ply yarn into plies for decorative embroidery stitches on top of needlepoint background stitches is sometimes difficult to accomplish if you are using nylon plastic canvas yarn. Instead of trying to split the nylon 2-ply yarn, use matching six-strand cotton embroidery floss or pearl cotton instead. If you decide to split nylon yarn, be sure to use shorter lengths than normal.

Alternating Slanted Gobelin Stitch

Alternating slanted gobelin stitches can be worked in either horizontal or vertical rows over two or more bars.

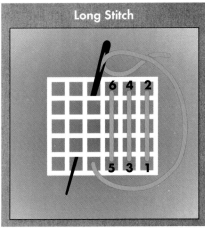

Long Stitch

Long stitches are worked over several bars of the canvas, either vertically or horizontally. The lines of the plastic canvas show between the stitches, so colored canvas is often used with this stitch.

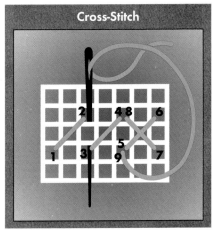

Cross-Stitch

Cross-stitches can be worked over two or more bars. When working several cross-stitches, be sure all of the top crosses face the same direction.

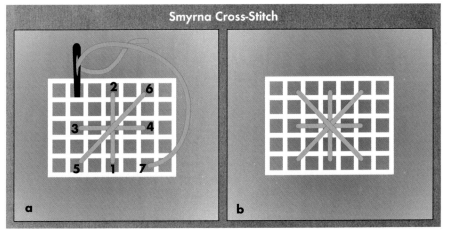

Smyrna Cross-Stitch

Smyrna cross-stitches can be worked over two or more bars. Bring the needle up at odd numbers and down at even numbers (a) to create the finished stitch (b). When working several smyrna cross-stitches, be sure all of the top crosses face the same direction.

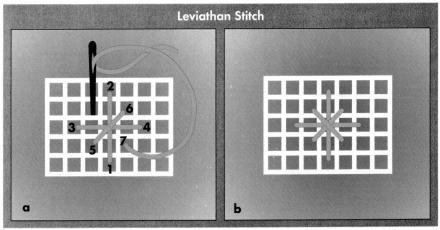

Leviathan Stitch

Leviathan stitches are similar to smyrna cross-stitches, except one portion of the cross is shorter than the other. Bring the needle up at odd numbers and down at even numbers (a) to create the finished stitch (b). When working several leviathan stitches, be sure all of the top crosses face the same direction.

Needle Pointer

Try using the tip of your needle or a plastic hair roller pick to count the holes in your plastic canvas before cutting it.

Satin Stitch

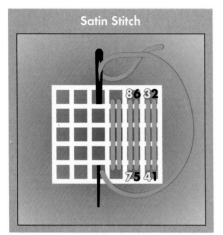

Satin stitches are worked over two or more bars of canvas, either horizontally or vertically. Two stitches are taken in each hole for more dense coverage.

Leaf Stitch

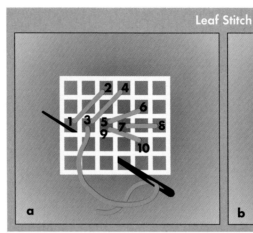

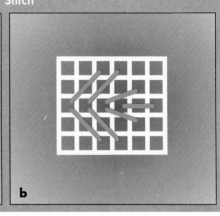

Leaf stitches can be worked with each stitch over two bars (a) or with longer stitches for larger leaves. Bring the needle up at the odd numbers and down at the even numbers to create the finished stitch (b).

Chain Stitch

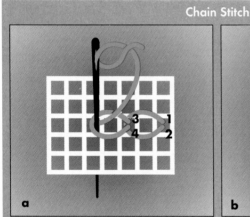

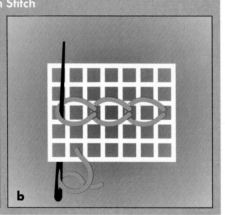

Chain stitches are worked over two or more bars, either horizontally (a) or vertically. Bring the needle up at 1 and down at 2 in the same hole, creating a loop. Bring the needle up through the canvas, through the loop for the beginning of the next chain stitch at 3, and down in the same hole at 4. Work stitches across the row (b).

Running Stitch

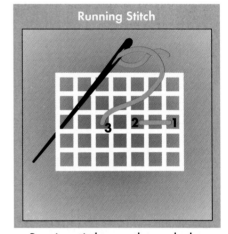

Running stitches can be worked over two or more bars of canvas, either vertically, horizontally, or diagonally. Running stitches can be the same length, or they can vary.

Milanese Stitch

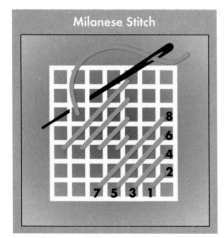

Milanese stitches are generally used as textured filling stitches, and they are worked diagonally. They can be worked in one or more colors.

Byzantine Stitch

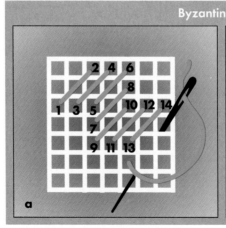

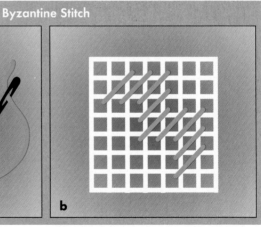

Byzantine stitches are primarily textured filling stitches and can be worked in one color or in rows of different colors. Bring the needle up at the odd numbers and down at the even numbers (a) to create the pattern (b).

Scotch Stitch

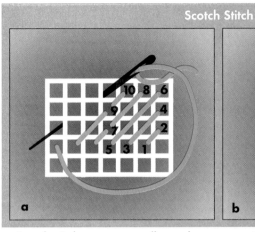

a

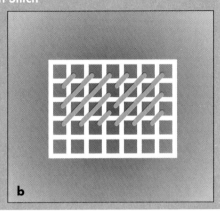

b

Scotch stitches are generally used as textured filling stitches and can be worked in one or more colors. Scotch stitches can be worked as blocks that cover three or more bars. Bring the needle up at the odd numbers and down at the even numbers (a) to create the pattern (b).

Alternating Scotch Stitch

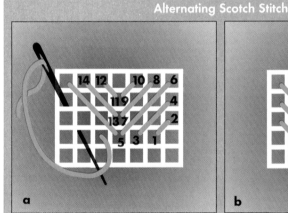

a

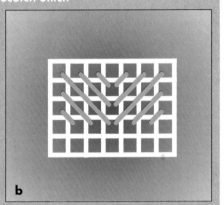

b

Alternating scotch stitches are similar to scotch stitches, except the direction of the stitches is reversed in the adjoining blocks. Bring the needle up at the odd numbers and down at the even numbers (a) to create the pattern (b).

Condensed Scotch Stitch

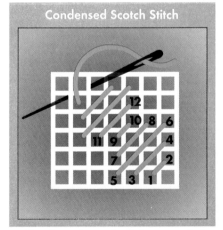

a

Condensed scotch stitches are similar to scotch stitches, except they are worked diagonally with the last stitch in one repeat becoming the first stitch in the next repeat.

Needle Pointer

There are about 45 yards of nylon plastic canvas yarn in each ounce and about 50 yards of 4-ply worsted weight yarn in each ounce.

Stitching Solution

If you are making several pieces of the same design, cut out a master pattern from plastic canvas in a different color than you are using for your projects. Hold the master pattern over the project canvas to cut out the pieces for your projects. This way, you only have to mark the canvas once, and you won't accidentally use your master pattern.

Mosaic Stitch

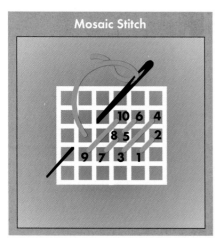

Mosaic stitches are generally used as textured filling stitches. They can be worked all in the same color, in two or more colors, or in a mix of colors.

Condensed Mosaic Stitch

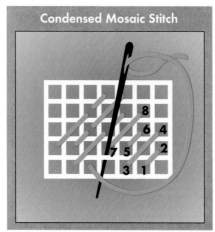

Condensed mosaic stitches are similar to mosaic stitches, except they are worked diagonally with the last stitch in one repeat becoming the first stitch in the next repeat.

Fern Stitch

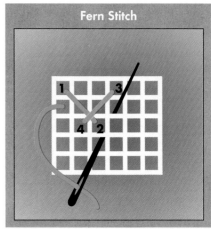

Fern stitches are worked in rows and generally used as textured filling stitches. Fern stitches can be longer or shorter than those shown.

Lark's Head Knot

Lark's head knots provide fringe on plastic canvas, creating hair or fur on toys and animal designs.

Whipstitch

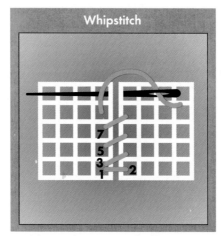

Whipstitches are used to join two or more canvas pieces together at the edges, and they can be worked in matching or contrasting colors.

Braided Whipstitch

Braided whipstitches, a decorative version of whipstitches, are used to join two or more pieces together at the edges.

Stitching Solution

If you make a mistake while stitching, stitches are easy to remove if you clip them first with small embroidery scissors. Carefully clip and remove the stitches. A few wisps of yarn may remain after you pull the stitches out. Remove these by patting the area with the sticky side of a piece of masking tape. "Stitch-remover" scissors feature a blade that is designed to slip under stitches.

Overcast Stitch

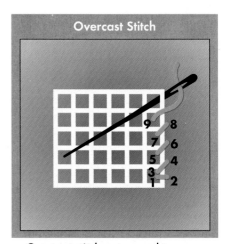

Overcast stitches are used to cover the bare edges of plastic canvas once the design area is complete. They can be stitched in matching or contrasting colors.

Embroidery Stitches

Lazy Daisy Stitch

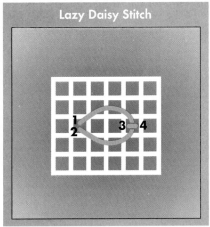

Lazy daisy stitches are embroidery stitches that are generally used to add detail after a design area is stitched. They can be worked over one or more bars in any direction.

French Knot

French knots can be worked over bare canvas or over a stitched design area. They can be worked in one hole or over a bar, and the yarn can be wrapped around the needle two or three times.

Backstitch

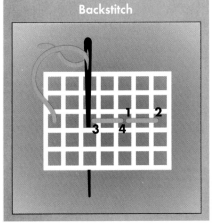

Backstitches are generally worked after the needlepoint areas are complete, and they are used to outline or add detail. Backstitches can be worked in any direction over one or more bars.

Straight Stitch

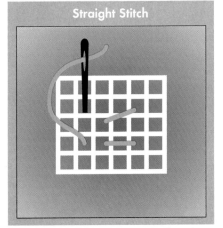

Straight stitches are generally worked after the needlepoint areas are complete, and they are used to add detail. Straight stitches can be worked in any direction over one or more bars.

Needle Pointer

If you accidentally cut or tear a bar of canvas while cutting out pieces or stitching, the canvas can be repaired. Glue the damaged bars together with tiny drops of Super Glue or glue from a hot glue gun. If the damaged area is large, cut a piece of canvas slightly larger than the damaged area. Hold the reinforcement behind your work as you stitch, working through both pieces.

Stitching Solution

When overcasting a long edge, your work will be neater if you use only one length of yarn to stitch the entire edge. Beginning in the center of the edge of your project and with the center of the yarn, overcast the edge to one end. Then overcast the remaining half of the edge with the rest of the yarn.

Techniques

Special effects such as plaid and bargello patterns can be stitched on plastic canvas. Both techniques are easy to learn, and stunning effects can be achieved.

Plaid Patterns

Large or small plaid patterns can be worked on plastic canvas, and you can use two or more colors. The continental stitch is too bulky for use with plaid patterns. The plaid stitch shown creates a less bulky result.

1. Select colors for your plaid design, and determine how many rows of each color you want to use.

2. Stitch all of the vertical rows first using the plaid stitch (a). For the first row, stitch the first stitch and every other stitch to the end of the row. Then turn the canvas, and for the next row, work the second stitch and every other stitch to the end of the row, working in the opposite direction. Continue in this manner, working as many rows as desired of each color until all of the vertical rows are complete.

3. Stitch the horizontal rows using the plaid stitch (b).

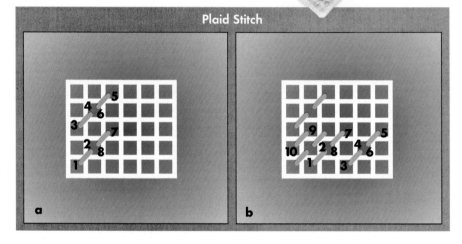

Plaid Stitch

a

b

Beginning with the second color, work the stitch sequence for the horizontal rows in the same manner as the sequence for the vertical rows.

Bargello Needlepoint

Bargello, also called flame stitch, florentine stitch, and Hungarian needlepoint, is a type of needlepoint that usually resembles zigzag or other repeating patterns in shaded colors. The stitches run parallel to the bars of the canvas. Each stitch is usually the same length, although complicated bargello patterns can involve stitches of varying lengths.

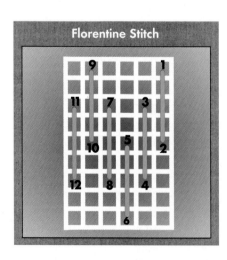

Florentine Stitch

1. To begin a bargello pattern, stitch a row of repeating zigzags or scallops with the stitches the same length and spacing.

2. Repeat the pattern of stitches using a different shade or color for each row until the canvas is filled as shown.

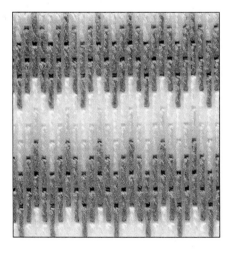

Finishing

Blocking is never necessary for plastic canvas needlepoint. Once the stitching is complete, the item is finished unless it requires assembly or the addition of trims.

Construction and Assembly

Many plastic canvas designs require assembly by gluing or sewing pieces together. In some patterns, placement lines may appear on the graphs or diagrams to show where one piece is to be attached to another as shown.

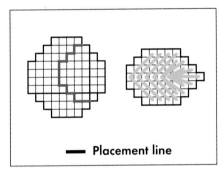

— **Placement line**

Using a Glue Gun

There are several types of glue guns and hot-melt glues on the market. Some guns are designed to operate at cooler temperatures than standard hot glue guns.

When using glue, try to use as small an amount as possible in order to avoid the glue seeping through the stitches to the finished side. Although most glues dry clear, many are shiny when dry.

To combat the inevitable glue strings that appear when using a glue gun, swirl the gun as you lift the tip from the project. Pretend you're making an ice cream cone, swirling the tip slightly to break the glue string. If glue strings remain when your project is finished, fan the completed item with a blow dryer as shown. Glue strings will disappear.

Protecting Your Stitches

You may want to protect your finished plastic canvas project from spills and dirt by spraying it with a fabric protector such as Scotchgard. This type of coating will help the stitched piece repel liquids and resist dust. If you plan to use a spray, be doubly sure to remove all markings from your canvas before stitching, as sprays can cause some marks to bleed through the yarn.

Needle Pointer

Choose a low-temperature glue gun for gluing lace, buttons, and other trims to your plastic canvas designs. The lower temperature glue allows you to position items with your fingers without getting burned.

Tea Time Trivet and Coasters

This whimsical little teapot trivet and coaster set is trimmed in gold and highlighted with a fresh floral design.

Skill Level

Easy

Size

Teapot is 7¾" × 9", and teacup is 3½" × 5"

Materials

2 regular sheets of 7-count plastic canvas

Worsted weight or plastic canvas yarn as indicated in the color key

22 yards of gold metallic cording

Instructions

1. Cut out one teapot and four cups according to the graphs.

2. Using the colors indicated in the color key, stitch the pieces following the graphs. Overcast the handles of the cups and teapot, the bottom and top edges of the cups, and the bottom edge of the teapot using gold metallic cording. Overcast the remaining edges using colors to match the adjacent stitching.

Cup (cut 4)

Teapot (cut 1)

Color Key

	Worsted Weight or Plastic Canvas Yarn
▨	White—20 yds.
▨	Lt. Blue—90 yds.
▨	Lavender—11 yds.
▨	Lt. Green—6 yds.
☐	Pale Yellow—2 yds.
	Metallic Cording
▨	Gold—22 yds.

Ginger Jar

Handy for storing everything from potpourri to tasty treats, this Oriental-style jar is reminiscent of blue willow porcelain patterns.

Skill Level

Intermediate

Size

5½" x 7½"

Materials

Three regular sheets of 7-count plastic canvas

Worsted weight yarn or plastic canvas yarn as indicated in the color key

White craft glue or hot glue gun and glue sticks

Instructions

1. Cut four jar sides according to the graph. Cut four jar corners according to the graph on page 234. Cut one one jar bottom without the opening in the center according to the graph on page 234. Cut two jar bases without the opening in the center according to the graph on page 234. Cut one jar top with the opening in the center according to the graph on page 234. Cut two lid insides according to the graph on page 234. Cut two lid bottoms according to the graph on page 234. Cut two lid centers according to the graph on page 234. Cut three knobs according to the graph on page 234.

2. To make the jar, stitch the sides and corners using continental stitches and the colors shown in the graphs. Fill in the unstitched areas of the sides and corners using white yarn and continental stitches. Stitch the jar top with white yarn and slanted gobelin stitches across the width, and overcast the inside edge. Using white yarn, whipstitch the sides and corners together. Following the photo, whipstitch the top into the correct opening. Then whipstitch the bottom into the other opening.

3. To make the jar base, stack the two base pieces together and overcast them with dark blue through both thicknesses. Glue the base to the jar bottom.

4. To make the jar lid, stitch one lid bottom and one lid center using continental stitches and the colors shown in the graphs. Fill in the unstitched areas of the lid bottom and lid center using white yarn and continental stitches.

Color Key

	Worsted Weight or Plastic Canvas Yarn	
◢	Dk. Blue—20 yds.	
◢	Lt. Blue—56 yds.	
☐	White—90 yds.	

Jar Side
(cut 4)

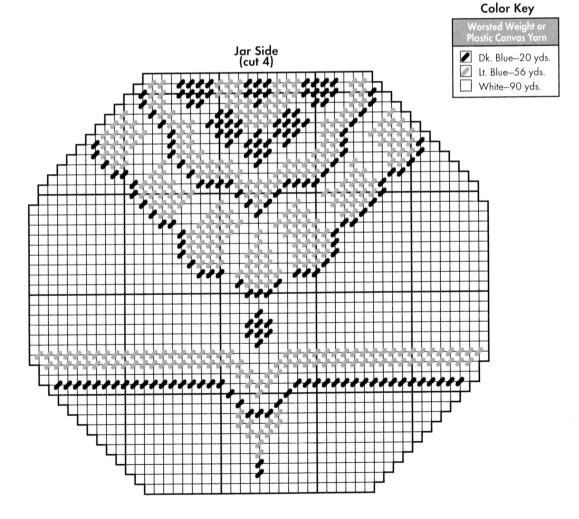

Stack the two lid inside pieces together, and overcast them with light blue through both thicknesses. Stack the two lid bottom pieces together with the stitched piece on top, and overcast them with white through both thicknesses. Stack the two lid center pieces together with the stitched piece on top, and overcast them with light blue through both thicknesses. Stitch one knob piece using dark blue and continental stitches. Stack the knob pieces together with the stitched piece on top, and overcast them with dark blue through all thicknesses. Center and stack the lid inside, bottom, center, and knob, and glue them together.

Jar Top, Bottom, and Base
(cut 1 with opening and 3 without)

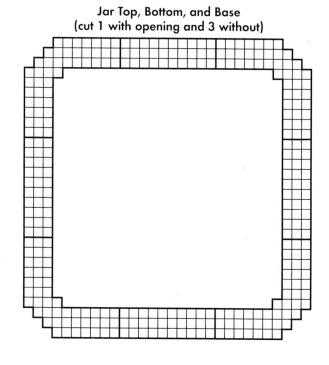

Jar Corner
(cut 4)

Color Key

	Worsted Weight or Plastic Canvas Yarn	
✏	Dk. Blue—20 yds.	
✏	Lt. Blue—56 yds.	
☐	White—90 yds.	

Lid Inside and Center
(cut 4)

Lid Bottom
(cut 2)

Knob
(cut 3)

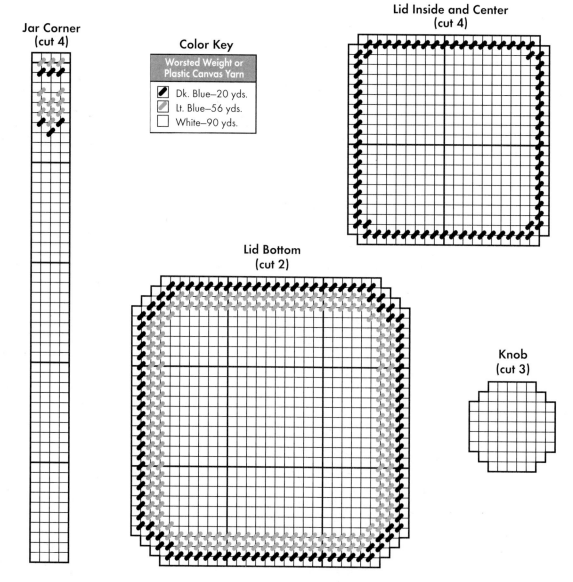

Gilded Poinsettias

Arrange these elegant poinsettias on a mantle or in a container for a beautiful Victorian addition to your holiday celebrations.

Gilded Poinsettias

Skill Level

Challenging

Size

6" to 9" across

Materials

5 sheets of 7-count plastic canvas
Worsted weight or plastic canvas yarn as indicated in the color key
55 yards of gold metallic cording
Seventy-three 6" pieces of 24-gauge floral wire
Green floral tape
40 gold 6 mm beads
Craft glue or hot glue gun and glue sticks

Instructions

1. Cut the required number of each size of bract according to the graphs on the opposite page. Cut 20 centers following the graph on the opposite page.

2. Beginning with one of the smallest bracts, stitch the pink area first according to the graph. Stitch the rose area next according to the graph; do not cut the yarn. Holding a piece of floral wire behind the center opening with 1" extending past the top of the opening and working over the wire with the rose yarn, overcast the center opening.

To do this, insert the needle next to a rose stitch on the right side, carry the thread across the opening and over the floral wire, and insert the needle into the space next to a rose stitch on the left side. Bend the top 1" of the wire down behind the bract. Working over the

floral wire at the stem end of the bract, overcast all of the edges with gold metallic cording.

3. Complete all of the bracts as described in Step 2, stitching seven large bracts according to the graph and stitching three large bracts in green according to the graph for the leaf bract.

4. For each poinsettia center, bend one floral wire in half and insert the ends into the holes of one center piece. Twist the wire ends together firmly.

5. For the smallest poinsettia, hold five center piece wires together. Beginning about 1" below the canvas, wrap all of the wires together three times with floral tape. To create the first tier

of bracts, begin about ½" down from the top of the floral tape, and hold and wrap five smallest bract wires securely against the center wires for a distance of 1". To create the second tier of bracts, hold and wrap five small bract wires against the center wires. Holding all of the wires together, continue wrapping the remainder of wires with tape.

6. For the next poinsettia, make the center, first, and second tiers according to Step 5. About 1" down from the second tier, hold and wrap the gold stem ends and wires of two rose large bracts and three green large bracts. Wrap the gold stem ends securely for the larger bracts so the bottom of the poinsettia will not droop. Wrap the remainder of the wires.

Something Different

Arrange one large poinsettia on a wreath and add gold and rose wire-edged ribbon for a gorgeous holiday door decoration. Add tiny bells or other trims as desired.

7. For the third poinsettia, create the center according to Step 5. Create the first tier using five small bracts, the second tier using five medium bracts, and the third tier using two rose large bracts and two leaf bracts. Wrap the remainder of the wires.

8. For the fourth poinsettia, create the center according to Step 5. Create the first tier using three smallest bracts and four small bracts, the second tier using three rose large bracts and one small bract, and the third tier using three leaf bracts. Wrap the remainder of the wires.

9. Spread and separate the center pieces in each flower. Glue two gold beads to each center piece, placing one bead over each hole. Curve the wires to shape the bracts.

10. Arrange the poinsettias in a container or as desired.

Smallest Bract
(cut 13)

Medium Bract
(cut 5)

Color Key

Worsted Weight or Plastic Canvas Yarn		
	Pink—25 yds.	
	Rose—47 yds.	
	Green—106 yds.	
Metallic Cording		
	Gold—55 yds.	

Small Bract
(cut 20)

Leaf Bract
(cut 5)

Large Bract
(cut 10)

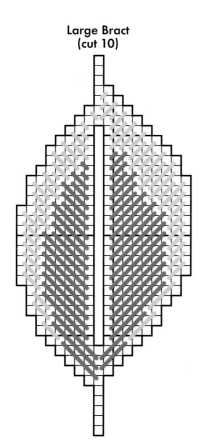

Center
(cut 20)

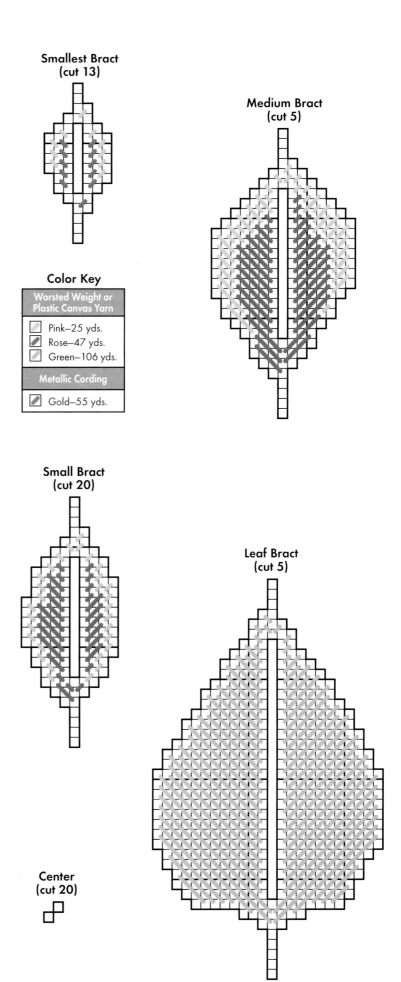

Glossary

Afghan hook: A long crochet hook that is used for working afghan crochet.

Aida: An evenweave fabric manufactured specially for cross-stitch with clearly visible holes into which the needle is inserted.

Appliqué: The hand or machine technique of applying one fabric or trim to the surface of another fabric.

Aran knitting: A knitting technique that involves cables, popcorns, and other textured stitches for warmth and interesting surface design.

Basted appliqué: A hand or machine appliqué method in which the seam allowances are turned under and basted in place before the appliqué stitching is started.

Basting: The process of temporarily stitching fabrics together to hold them in place while the permanent seam is stitched.

Batting: The material used for padding quilts or other quilted projects.

Between: A short needle used for hand quilting.

Bias: The line that runs at a 45-degree angle from the selvage of woven fabrics.

Bias strips: Strips of fabric cut with their edges running at a 45-degree angle to the selvages of the fabric.

Binding: A folded fabric strip that encloses the raw edge of a quilted project.

Binding off: The method of removing stitches from the knitting needles and creating a finished edge.

Blocking: A method of steaming or pressing finished needlework, knitting, and crochet to set it in a desired shape.

Borders: Strips of fabric that are attached to the center section of a quilt to frame the pieced area.

Broomstick lace: A crochet technique that is worked with a large knitting needle or a broomstick to produce large loops that are then crocheted together.

Buttonhole stitch appliqué: The technique of enclosing the edges of appliqué pieces in embroidered buttonhole stitches.

Cable: A knitted textured pattern that looks like raised, woven, or braided cords.

Cable stitch holder: A tool used while making knitted cables for temporarily holding a few stitches either to the back or the front of the knitting.

Casting on: The method for creating the foundation for the first row of knitting.

Chain piecing: A continuous machine piecing technique in which pairs of patchwork pieces are fed through the machine without lifting the presser foot or cutting the thread between each pair.

Chenille needle: A large-eye, sharp pointed needle used for embroidery.

Colorfasting: The process of setting the color in red and dark tones of embroidery floss or fabric by soaking the floss or fabric in a solution of 1 tablespoon of white vinegar and 8 ounces of water.

Color key: The guide that accompanies many needlecraft patterns showing which stitching fiber colors are represented by which graph colors.

Cornerstones: Contrasting squares of fabric pieced into the corners of a quilt where the sashing meets the blocks.

Crewel embroidery: A surface embroidery technique.

Crewel needle: A large-eye, sharp pointed needle used for stitching embroidery.

Crewel yarn: A 2-ply yarn used for crewel embroidery.

Cut-and-sew appliqué: The technique of cutting, turning under, and stitching down an appliqué piece a little at a time after it is basted in place on the background fabric.

Decreasing: A technique used in knitting and crochet for reducing the number of stitches from a row.

Diagonal setting: The setting for a quilt when the blocks are set on point and the rows move diagonally across the quilt.

Double pointed needles: Knitting needles with points on each end that are packaged in sets of four. These needles are used for knitting in the round to make cylindrical knitted shapes.

Dressmaker's carbon paper: A coated paper that is used for transferring needlework patterns to fabric.

Duplicate stitch: Decorative surface embroidery that traces the path of knit stitches.

Evenweave fabric: A fabric with equally spaced vertical and horizontal threads.

Fair Isle knitting: A knitting technique that looks very intricate but is actually quite simple because only one or two colors of yarn are used for each row.

Filet crochet: A type of crochet that involves following a graph for working a series of open and closed blocks to create a pattern.

Free-motion machine quilting: A method of quilting by machine. The feed dogs are lowered and the fabric is moved in any direction during stitching.

Freezer paper appliqué: The technique of using freezer paper as a template for hand or machine appliqué.

French fold binding: A binding that adds a double thickness of fabric to a quilt's edges for durability.

Fusible webbing: A material sold in fabric and craft stores that enables two fabrics or other materials to be attached together when ironed.

Fusing: The process of applying one fabric or trim to the surface of another fabric using a fusible material and an iron.

Gauge: A notation in a knitting or crochet pattern that tells you the number of stitches or rows that should be in each inch of stitched fabric.

Grafting: A technique for joining two pieces of knitting without binding either off for an unbroken stream of knitting across the seam line.

Grain line: The threads that run parallel or perpendicular to the selvage of woven fabric.

Graph: The gridded pattern used for stitching and designing cross-stitch, filet crochet, and other needlework.

Increasing: A technique used in knitting and crochet for adding stitches to a row.

Invisible machine appliqué: A method of machine appliqué in which the edges of the appliqué piece is attached to the background fabric using a narrow zigzag or blind hem stitch and clear nylon sewing thread.

Irish crochet: A type of thread crochet that involves making three-dimensional medallions such as roses, leaves, cording, and shamrocks and attaching them together on a crochet background.

Jacquard crochet: A type of crochet that involves following a graph for changing stitch colors to create a design.

Joining: A crochet technique for attaching the end of a row to the beginning of the same row with a slip stitch. Also the technique of attaching two knitted or crocheted pieces.

Knitting gauge ruler: A knitting measuring tool that features a cutout window to count stitch and row gauge.

Knitting tally: A small tool that slips on the end of a knitting needle or crochet hook to help keep track of the number of rows that have been worked.

Lace knitting: A technique of knitting lace-like openwork patterns by increasing in some places and decreasing in others.

Light box: A glass surface with light underneath that can be used for tracing needlework patterns. A sunny window or a glass coffee table with a lamp underneath can be substituted for an artist's light box.

Loop stitch: The stitch used to begin a thread in cross-stitch, duplicate stitch, and other needlecrafts.

Machine appliqué: The technique of applying one fabric to the surface of another with a satin stitch, buttonhole stitch, or other machine stitches.

Machine embroidery: A method of embroidery that uses the decorative stitches on a sewing machine to create a design or pattern.

Metallic braid: Tightly wound, high-quality stitching fiber that is sold on small spools in dozens of colors. Metallic braids are sized in #8, #16, and #32, with #8 being the thinnest.

Metallic cording: A little thinner than yarn, this cording is sold in 22-yard skeins and is good for stitching plastic canvas needlepoint.

Milliner's needle: A long, thin, small-eye needle.

Needle-turn appliqué: The technique of hand appliqué that involves turning the seam allowance under with the point and shank of the needle as you stitch.

Pa 'ndau: A reverse appliqué technique practiced by the Hmong people of Vietnam that features symbolic swirls and lines.

Paper piecing: The technique of basting cutout appliqué pieces to plain paper patterns for precisely shaped turned-under edges.

Pearl cotton: A stitching fiber with a firm twist that is sized in #3, #5, #8, and #12, with #3 being the thickest.

Perforated paper: A stiff paper with evenly spaced holes that is used for cross-stitch.

Perforated plastic: Fourteen-count plastic canvas that is used for cross-stitch and needlepoint designs.

Plastic canvas: A plastic grid canvas that is used for stitching needlepoint.

Point protectors: Rubber tips used for capping knitting needles when knitting in progress is set aside.

Popcorn: A raised stitch pattern used in knitting and crochet that looks somewhat like a kernel of popped corn.

Pressing: Ironing lightly.

Pulled-thread embroidery: A method of embroidery that involves pulling the stitches tightly to create openwork patterns in the fabric.

Quilter's straight pins: Long, thin pins that are used to pin together thick quilt layers.

Quilting: The process of stitching the top, batting, and backing of a quilt together with small hand stitches or machine stitches.

Reverse appliqué: The technique of stacking fabric layers and cutting away portions to reveal layers underneath. The cut edges are turned under one layer at a time and appliquéd in place.

Ribbon embroidery: A technique that uses silk, rayon, or polyester ribbons in place of or in addition to threads to create embroidery stitches.

Ribbon thread: A narrow ribbon that is made specially for stitching cross-stitch and other needlecrafts.

Rotary cutter: A tool for cutting fabric that has a round razor blade attached to a plastic handle. It is used for precisely and quickly cutting fabric for patchwork.

San Blas appliqué: A reverse appliqué technique practiced by the Cuna Indians of South America that features colorful people, animals, and plants.

Sashing: Strips of fabric that are pieced between the blocks on a quilt.

Satin stitch appliqué: A method of machine appliqué in which the edges of the appliqué pieces are attached to the background fabric with close zigzag stitches in matching or contrasting thread.

Seam allowance: The distance between the cut edge of the fabric and the stitching line.

Seed beads: Small colored or clear beads used for embellishing needlecraft projects.

See-through ruler: A sturdy plastic ruler made for use with a rotary cutter.

Self-healing mat: A cutting mat made for use with a rotary cutter. Cuts made into the mat will not be permanent.

Shadow appliqué: The technique of sandwiching appliqué pieces between a sheer fabric and the background fabric.

Sharp: A hand-sewing needle that is used for appliqué and general sewing.

Six-strand floss: Cotton embroidery floss that is sold in skeins or on cards. Strands may be separated for stitching.

Slip knot: The loop used to begin knitting or crochet.

Slip stitch: The invisible stitch used for appliqué and for hand stitching binding in place.

Stitch count marker: A tool used in knitting to mark the location and count of knitting stitches.

Stitch holder: Large safety-pin-like tools for temporarily holding stitches in knitting.

Straight set: The arrangement of quilt blocks in a straight row with no sashing or other blocks between.

Strip piecing: The process of sewing precisely cut strips of fabric together that are cut across the seam to make pieces.

Tacking: A method of connecting the top, batting, and backing of a quilt with small, machine-stitched zigzags, patterns, or bows spaced evenly over the quilt.

Tapestry needle: A blunt-tipped needle that comes in many sizes and is used for a variety of needlework applications.

Tapestry wool: A 3-ply wool yarn used in embroidery or needlepoint.

Template plastic: This plastic is used for making durable appliqué and patchwork patterns that can be used repeatedly for marking patterns on fabric.

Transfer pencil: A pencil used to draw or trace a pattern that can be transferred to fabric when pressed with a hot iron.

Tying: The process of joining the top, batting, and backing in a quilt by stitching through the quilt with strong thread and tying individual knots spaced evenly across the quilt.

Waste canvas: A product used for stitching cross-stitch onto clothing or other fabric. After the cross-stitching is completed, the canvas is dampened, and its threads are removed one at a time with tweezers.

Waste knot: A knot that is left on the front of the fabric in cross-stitch and embroidery and is clipped off after stitching is begun.

Yarn bobbins: Small holders used for winding yarn for multi-colored knitting or crochet designs.